𝕮𝖊𝖓𝖙𝖊𝖓𝖆𝖗𝖞 𝕰𝖉𝖎𝖙𝖎𝖔𝖓

THE COMPLETE WORKS OF
RALPH WALDO EMERSON

WITH

A BIOGRAPHICAL

INTRODUCTION AND NOTES

BY EDWARD WALDO EMERSON AND

A GENERAL INDEX

VOLUME

VII

TWELVE CHAPTERS

BY

RALPH WALDO EMERSON

BOSTON AND NEW YORK
HOUGHTON MIFFLIN COMPANY
The Riverside Press Cambridge

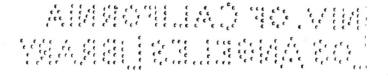

CONTENTS

I

SOCIETY AND SOLITUDE

SEYD melted the days like cups of pearl,
Served high and low, the lord and churl,
Loved harebells nodding on a rock,
A cabin hung with curling smoke,
Ring of axe or hum of wheel
Or gleam which use can paint on steel,
And huts and tents; nor loved he less
Stately lords in palaces,
Princely women hard to please,
Fenced by form and ceremony,
Decked by courtly rites and dress
And etiquette of gentilesse.
But when the mate of the snow and wind,
He left each civil scale behind:
Him wood-gods fed with honey wild
And of his memory beguiled.
In caves and hollow trees he crept
And near the wolf and panther slept.
He stood before the tumbling main
With joy too tense for sober brain;
He shared the life of the element,
The tie of blood and home was rent:
As if in him the welkin walked,
The winds took flesh, the mountains talked,
And he the bard, a crystal soul,
Sphered and concentric with the whole.

That each should in his house abide,
Therefore was the world so wide.

SOCIETY AND SOLITUDE

I FELL in with a humorist on my travels, who had in his chamber a cast of the Rondanini Medusa, and who assured me that the name which that fine work of art bore in the catalogues was a misnomer, as he was convinced that the sculptor who carved it intended it for Memory, the mother of the Muses.[1] In the conversation that followed, my new friend made some extraordinary confessions. "Do you not see," he said, "the penalty of learning, and that each of these scholars whom you have met at S——, though he were to be the last man, would, like the executioner in Hood's poem, guillotine the last but one?" He added many lively remarks, but his evident earnestness engaged my attention, and in the weeks that followed we became better acquainted. He had good abilities, a genial temper and no vices; but he had one defect, — he could not speak in the tone of the people. There was some paralysis on his will, such that when he met men on common terms he spoke weakly and from the point, like a flighty girl. His consciousness of the fault made it worse. He envied every drover and lumberman in the tavern their manly speech. He coveted Mirabeau's *don terrible de la familiarité*, believing that he whose sympathy goes lowest is the man from whom kings have the most to fear. For himself he declared that he could not get enough alone to write a letter to a friend. He left the city ; he hid himself in pastures. The solitary river was not solitary enough; the sun and moon put him out. When he bought a house, the first thing he did was to plant trees. He could not enough conceal himself. Set a hedge here ; set oaks there, — trees behind trees ; above all, set evergreens, for they will keep a secret all the year round. The most agreeable compliment you could pay him was to imply that you had not observed him in a house or a street where you had met him. Whilst he suffered at being seen where he was, he consoled himself with the delicious thought of the inconceivable number of places where he was not. All he wished of his tailor was to provide that sober mean of color and cut which would never detain the eye for a moment. He went to Vienna, to Smyrna, to London. In all the variety of costumes, a carnival, a kaleidoscope of clothes, to his horror he could never discover a man in the street who

wore anything like his own dress. He would
have given his soul for the ring of Gyges. His
dismay at his visibility had blunted the fears of
mortality. " Do you think," he said, " I am in
such great terror of being shot, — I, who am
only waiting to shuffle off my corporeal jacket
to slip away into the back stars, and put diame-
ters of the solar system and sidereal orbits between me and all souls, — there to wear out
ages in solitude, and forget memory itself, if it
be possible ? " He had a remorse running to
despair of his social *gaucheries*, and walked miles
and miles to get the twitchings out of his face,
the starts and shrugs out of his arms and shoulders. God may forgive sins, he said, but awkwardness has no forgiveness in heaven or earth.
He admired in Newton not so much his theory
of the moon as his letter to Collins, in which he
forbade him to insert his name with the solution
of the problem in the Philosophical Trans-
actions: " It would perhaps increase my acquaintance, the thing which I chiefly study to
decline." [1]

These conversations led me somewhat later
to the knowledge of similar cases, and to the
discovery that they are not of very infrequent
occurrence. Few substances are found pure in

nature. Those constitutions which can bear in open day the rough dealing of the world must be of that mean and average structure such as iron and salt, atmospheric air and water. But there are metals, like potassium and sodium, which, to be kept pure, must be kept under naphtha. Such are the talents determined on some specialty, which a culminating civilization fosters in the heart of great cities and in royal chambers. Nature protects her own work. To the culture of the world an Archimedes, a New-ton is indispensable; so she guards them by a certain aridity. If these had been good fellows, fond of dancing, port and clubs, we should have had no Theory of the Sphere and no Prin-cipia. They had that necessity of isolation which genius feels. Each must stand on his glass tripod if he would keep his electricity. Even Swedenborg, whose theory of the universe is based on affection, and who reprobates to weariness the danger and vice of pure intellect, is constrained to make an extraordinary excep-tion: " There are also angels who do not live consociated, but separate, house and house; these dwell in the midst of heaven, because they are the best of angels."

We have known many fine geniuses with that

imperfection that they cannot do anything useful, not so much as write one clean sentence. 'T is
worse, and tragic, that no man is fit for society
who has fine traits. At a distance he is admired,
but bring him hand to hand, he is a cripple.[r]
One protects himself by solitude, and one by
courtesy, and one by an acid, worldly manner,
— each concealing how he can the thinness of
his skin and his incapacity for strict association.
But there is no remedy that can reach the heart
of the disease but either habits of self-reliance
that should go in practice to making the man
independent of the human race, or else a religion of love. Now he hardly seems entitled to
marry; for how can he protect a woman, who
cannot protect himself?

We pray to be conventional. But the wary
Heaven takes care you shall not be, if there is
anything good in you. Dante was very bad company, and was never invited to dinner. Michel
Angelo had a sad, sour time of it. The ministers
of beauty are rarely beautiful in coaches and
saloons. Columbus discovered no isle or key so
lonely as himself. Yet each of these potentates
saw well the reason of his exclusion. Solitary
was he? Why, yes; but his society was limited
only by the amount of brain nature appropri-

ated in that age to carry on the government of the world. "If I stay," said Dante, when there was question of going to Rome, "who will go? and if I go, who will stay?"

But the necessity of solitude is deeper than we have said, and is organic.¹ I have seen many a philosopher whose world is large enough for only one person. He affects to be a good companion; but we are still surprising his secret, that he means and needs to impose his system on all the rest. The determination of each is *from* all the others, like that of each tree up into free space. 'T is no wonder, when each has his whole head, our societies should be so small. Like President Tyler, our party falls from us every day, and we must ride in a sulky at last. Dear heart! take it sadly home to thee, — there is no coöperation. We begin with friendships, and all our youth is a reconnoitring and recruiting of the holy fraternity they shall combine for the salvation of men. But so the remoter stars seem a nebula of united light, yet there is no group which a telescope will not resolve; and the dearest friends are separated by impassable gulfs. The coöperation is involuntary, and is put upon us by the Genius of Life, who reserves this as a part of his prerogative. 'T is fine for us to talk; we sit and muse and are serene and complete; but the moment we meet with any- body, each becomes a fraction.[1]

Though the stuff of tragedy and of romances is in a moral union of two superior persons whose confidence in each other for long years, out of sight and in sight, and against all appearances, is at last justified by victorious proof of probity to gods and men, causing joyful emotions, tears and glory, — though there be for heroes this *moral union*, yet they too are as far off as ever from an intellectual union, and the moral union is for comparatively low and external purposes, like the coöperation of a ship's company or of a fire-club. But how insular and pathetically solitary are all the people we know! Nor dare they tell what they think of each other when they meet in the street. We have a fine right, to be sure, to taunt men of the world with superficial and treacherous courtesies!

Such is the tragic necessity which strict science finds underneath our domestic and neighborly life, irresistibly driving each adult soul as with whips into the desert, and making our warm covenants sentimental and momentary.[2] We must infer that the ends of thought were peremptory, if they were to be secured at such ruinous cost.

They are deeper than can be told, and belong to the immensities and eternities. They reach down to that depth where society itself originates and disappears; where the question is, Which is first, man or men? where the individual is lost in his source.

But this banishment to the rocks and echoes no metaphysics can make right or tolerable. This result is so against nature, such a half-view, that it must be corrected by a common sense and experience. " A man is born by the side of his father, and there he remains." A man must be clothed with society, or we shall feel a certain bareness and poverty, as of a displaced and unfurnished member. He is to be dressed in arts and institutions, as well as in body garments.¹ Now and then a man exquisitely made can live alone, and must; but coop up most men and you undo them. " The king lived and ate in his hall with men, and understood men," said Selden. When a young barrister said to the late Mr. Mason, "I keep my chamber to read law," — "Read law!" replied the veteran, "'t is in the court-room you must read law." Nor is the rule otherwise for literature. If you would learn to write, 't is in the street you must learn it. Both for the vehicle and for the aims of fine arts you must frequent the public square. The people, and not the college, is the writer's home. A scholar is a candle which the love and desire of all men will light. Never his lands or his rents, but the power to charm the disguised soul that sits veiled under this bearded and that rosy visage is his rent and ration. His products are as needful as those of the baker or the weaver. Society cannot do without cultivated men. As soon as the first wants are satisfied, the higher wants become imperative.'

'T is hard to mesmerize ourselves, to whip our own top; but through sympathy we are capable of energy and endurance. Concert fires people to a certain fury of performance they can rarely reach alone. Here is the use of society: it is so easy with the great to be great; so easy to come up to an existing standard; — as easy as it is to the lover to swim to his maiden through waves so grim before. The benefits of affection are immense ; and the one event which never loses its romance is the encounter with superior persons on terms allowing the happiest intercourse.

It by no means follows that we are not fit for society, because *soirées* are tedious and because the *soirée* finds us tedious. A backwoodsman,

who had been sent to the university, told me
that when he heard the best-bred young men at
the law-school talk together, he reckoned himself a boor ; but whenever he caught them apart,
and had one to himself alone, then they were
the boors and he the better man.   And if we
recall the rare hours when we encountered the
best persons, we then found ourselves, and then
first society seemed to exist.   That was society,
though in the transom of a brig or on the Florida Keys.'

A cold sluggish blood thinks it has not facts
enough to the purpose, and must decline its turn
in the conversation.   But they who speak have
no more, — have less.   'T is not new facts that
avail, but the heat to dissolve everybody's facts.
Heat puts you in right relation with magazines
of facts.   The capital defect of cold, arid natures
is the want of animal spirits.   They seem a power
incredible, as if God should raise the dead.   The
recluse witnesses what others perform by their
aid, with a kind of fear.   It is as much out of
his possibility as the prowess of Cœur-de-Lion,
or an Irishman's day's work on the railroad.
'T is said the present and the future are always
rivals.   Animal spirits constitute the power of
the present, and their feats are like the structure

of a pyramid. Their result is a lord, a general, or a boon companion. Before these what a base mendicant is Memory with his leathern badge! But this genial heat is latent in all constitutions, and is disengaged only by the friction of society. As Bacon said of manners, "To obtain them, it only needs not to despise them," so we say of animal spirits that they are the spontaneous product of health and of a social habit. "For behavior, men learn it, as they take diseases, one of another."

But the people are to be taken in very small doses. If solitude is proud, so is society vulgar. In society, high advantages are set down to the individual as disqualifications. We sink as easily as we rise, through sympathy. So many men whom I know are degraded by their sympathies; their native aims being high enough, but their relation all too tender to the gross people about them. Men cannot afford to live together on their merits, and they adjust themselves by their demerits, — by their love of gossip, or by sheer tolerance and animal good nature. They untune and dissipate the brave aspirant.

The remedy is to reinforce each of these moods from the other. Conversation will not corrupt us if we come to the assembly in our own garb and speech and with the energy of health to select what is ours and reject what is not. Society we must have; but let it be society, and not exchanging news or eating from the same dish. Is it society to sit in one of your chairs? I cannot go to the houses of my nearest relatives, because I do not wish to be alone. Society exists by chemical affinity, and not otherwise.

Put any company of people together with freedom for conversation, and a rapid self-distribution takes place into sets and pairs. The best are accused of exclusiveness. It would be more true to say they separate as oil from water, as children from old people, without love or hatred in the matter, each seeking his like; and any interference with the affinities would produce constraint and suffocation. All conversation is a magnetic experiment. I know that my friend can talk eloquently; you know that he cannot articulate a sentence: we have seen him in different company. Assort your party, or invite none. Put Stubbs and Coleridge, Quintilian and Aunt Miriam, into pairs, and you make them all wretched. 'T is an extempore Sing-Sing built in a parlor. Leave them to seek their own mates, and they will be as merry as sparrows.[1]

A higher civility will reëstablish in our customs a certain reverence which we have lost.
What to do with these brisk young men who
break through all fences, and make themselves
at home in every house? I find out in an
instant if my companion does not want me,
and ropes cannot hold me when my welcome
is gone.   One would think that the affinities
would pronounce themselves with a surer reci-
procity.'

Here again, as so often, nature delights to
put us between extreme antagonisms, and our
safety is in the skill with which we keep the
diagonal line. Solitude is impracticable, and society fatal. We must keep our head in the one
and our hands in the other. The conditions are
met, if we keep our independence, yet do not
lose our sympathy. These wonderful horses
need to be driven by fine hands. We require
such a solitude as shall hold us to its revelations
when we are in the street and in palaces; for
most men are cowed in society, and say good
things to you in private, but will not stand to
them in public. But let us not be the victims
of words. Society and solitude are deceptive
names. It is not the circumstance of seeing
more or fewer people, but the readiness of

sympathy, that imports; and a sound mind will derive its principles from insight, with ever a purer ascent to the sufficient and absolute right, and will accept society as the natural element in which they are to be applied.[1]

II

CIVILIZATION

We flee away from cities, but we bring
The best of cities with us, these learned classifiers,
Men knowing what they seek, armed eyes of experts.
We praise the guide, we praise the forest life:
But will we sacrifice our dear-bought lore
Of books and arts and trained experiment,
Or count the Sioux a match for Agassiz?
O no, not we! . . .
 . . . Witness the mute all hail
The joyful traveller gives, when on the verge
Of craggy Indian wilderness he hears
From a log cabin stream Beethoven's notes
On the piano, played with master's hand.
' Well done!' he cries; ' the bear is kept at bay,
The lynx, the rattlesnake, the flood, the fire:
All the fierce enemies, ague, hunger, cold,
This thin spruce roof, this clayed log wall,
This wild plantation will suffice to chase.
Now speed the gay celerities of art,
What in the desert was impossible
Within four walls is possible again, —
Culture and libraries, mysteries of skill,
Traditioned fame of masters, eager strife
Of keen competing youths, joined or alone,
To outdo each other and extort applause.
Mind wakes a new-born giant from her sleep.
Twirl the old wheels! Time takes fresh start again,
On for a thousand years of genius more.'

CIVILIZATION

A CERTAIN degree of progress from the rudest state in which man is found, — a dweller in caves, or on trees, like an ape, — a cannibal, and eater of pounded snails, worms and offal, — a certain degree of progress from this extreme is called Civilization. It is a vague, complex name, of many degrees. Nobody has attempted a definition. Mr. Guizot, writing a book on the subject, does not. It implies the evolution of a highly organized man, brought to supreme delicacy of sentiment, as in practical power, religion, liberty, sense of honor and taste.[1] In the hesitation to define what it is, we usually suggest it by negations. A nation that has no clothing, no iron, no alphabet, no marriage, no arts of peace, no abstract thought, we call barbarous. And after many arts are invented or imported, as among the Turks and Moorish nations, it is often a little complaisant to call them civilized.

Each nation grows after its own genius, and has a civilization of its own. The Chinese and Japanese, though each complete in his way, is different from the man of Madrid or the man

of New York. The term imports a mysterious
progress. In the brutes is none ; and in mankind to-day the savage tribes are gradually extinguished rather than civilized. The Indians
of this country have not learned the white man's
work ; and in Africa the negro of to-day is the
negro of Herodotus. In other races the growth
is not arrested, but the like progress that is
made by a boy " when he cuts his eye-teeth,"
as we say, — childish illusions passing daily
away and he seeing things really and compre-
hensively, — is made by tribes. It is the learning the secret of cumulative power, of advancing
on one's self. It implies a facility of association, power to compare, the ceasing from fixed
ideas. The Indian is gloomy and distressed
when urged to depart from his habits and traditions. He is overpowered by the gaze of the
white, and his eye sinks. The occasion of one
of these starts of growth is always some novelty
that astounds the mind and provokes it to dare
to change. Thus there is a Cadmus, a Pytheas,
a Manco Capac at the beginning of each improvement, — some superior foreigner importing new and wonderful arts, and teaching them.[1]
Of course he must not know too much, but
must have the sympathy, language and gods of

those he would inform. But chiefly the sea-shore has been the point of departure, to knowledge, as to commerce. The most advanced nations are always those who navigate the most. The power which the sea requires in the sailor makes a man of him very fast, and the change of shores and population clears his head of much nonsense of his wigwam.[1]

Where shall we begin or end the list of those feats of liberty and wit, each of which feats made an epoch of history? Thus the effect of a framed or stone house is immense on the tranquillity, power and refinement of the builder. A man in a cave or in a camp, a nomad, will die with no more estate than the wolf or the horse leaves. But so simple a labor as a house being achieved, his chief enemies are kept at bay. He is safe from the teeth of wild animals, from frost, sunstroke and weather; and fine faculties begin to yield their fine harvest. Invention and art are born, manners and social beauty and delight. 'T is wonderful how soon a piano gets into a log hut on the frontier. You would think they found it under a pine stump. With it comes a Latin grammar,— and one of those tow-head boys has written a hymn on Sunday. Now let colleges, now let senates take heed! for here is one who opening these fine tastes on the basis of the pioneer's iron constitution, will gather all their laurels in his strong hands.'

When the Indian trail gets widened, graded and bridged to a good road, there is a benefactor, there is a missionary, a pacificator, a wealth-bringer, a maker of markets, a vent for industry. Another step in civility is the change from war, hunting and pasturage, to agriculture. Our Scandinavian forefathers have left us a significant legend to convey their sense of the importance of this step. "There was once a giantess who had a daughter, and the child saw a husbandman ploughing in the field. Then she ran and picked him up with her finger and thumb, and put him and his plough and his oxen into her apron, and carried them to her mother, and said, 'Mother, what sort of a beetle is this that I found wriggling in the sand?' But the mother said, 'Put it away, my child; we must be-gone out of this land, for these people will dwell in it.'" Another success is the post-office, with its educating energy augmented by cheapness and guarded by a certain religious sentiment in mankind; so that the power of a wafer or a drop of wax or gluten to guard a letter, as it flies over sea over land and comes to its address as if a battalion of artillery brought it, I look upon as a fine meter of civilization.[1]

The division of labor, the multiplication of the arts of peace, which is nothing but a large allowance to each man to choose his work according to his faculty, — to live by his better hand, — fills the State with useful and happy laborers; and they, creating demand by the very temptation of their productions, are rapidly and surely rewarded by good sale : and what a police and ten commandments their work thus becomes. So true is Dr. Johnson's remark that "men are seldom more innocently employed than when they are making money."

The skilful combinations of civil government, though they usually follow natural leadings, as the lines of race, language, religion and territory, yet require wisdom and conduct in the rulers, and in their result delight the imagination. "We see insurmountable multitudes obeying, in opposition to their strongest passions, the restraints of a power which they scarcely perceive, and the crimes of a single individual marked and punished at the distance of half the earth." [2]

Right position of woman in the State is another index. Poverty and industry with a healthy mind read very easily the laws of humanity, and love them: place the sexes in right relations of mutual respect, and a severe morality gives that essential charm to woman which educates all that is delicate, poetic and self-sacrificing; breeds courtesy and learning, conversation and wit, in her rough mate; so that I have thought a sufficient measure of civilization is the influence of good women.

Another measure of culture is the diffusion of knowledge, overrunning all the old barriers of caste, and, by the cheap press, bringing the university to every poor man's door in the newsboy's basket. Scraps of science, of thought, of poetry are in the coarsest sheet, so that in every house we hesitate to burn a newspaper until we have looked it through.

The ship, in its latest complete equipment, is an abridgment and compend of a nation's arts: the ship steered by compass and chart, longitude reckoned by lunar observation and by chronometer, driven by steam; and in wildest sea-mountains, at vast distances from home, —

> " The pulses of her iron heart
> Go beating through the storm." [1]

No use can lessen the wonder of this control by so weak a creature of forces so prodigious. I remember I watched, in crossing the sea, the beautiful skill whereby the engine in its constant working was made to produce two hundred gallons of fresh water out of salt water, every hour, — thereby supplying all the ship's want.

The skill that pervades complex details ; the man that maintains himself; the chimney taught to burn its own smoke ; the farm made to produce all that is consumed on it ; the very prison compelled to maintain itself and yield a revenue, and, better still, made a reform school and a manufactory of honest men out of rogues, as the steamer made fresh water out of salt, — all these are examples of that tendency to combine antagonisms and utilize evil which is the index of high civilization.

Civilization is the result of highly complex organization. In the snake, all the organs are sheathed ; no hands, no feet, no fins, no wings. In bird and beast the organs are released and begin to play. In man they are all unbound and full of joyful action. With this unswaddling he receives the absolute illumination we call Reason, and thereby true liberty.

Climate has much to do with this melioration. The highest civility has never loved the hot zones. Wherever snow falls there is usually civil freedom.¹ Where the banana grows the animal system is indolent and pampered at the cost of higher qualities: the man is sensual and cruel. But this scale is not invariable. High degrees of moral sentiment control the unfavorable influences of climate; and some of our grandest examples of men and of races come from the equatorial regions, — as the genius of Egypt, of India and of Arabia.

These feats are measures or traits of civility; and temperate climate is an important influence, though not quite indispensable, for there have been learning, philosophy and art in Iceland, and in the tropics. But one condition is essential to the social education of man, namely, morality. There can be no high civility without a deep morality, though it may not always call itself by that name, but sometimes the point of honor, as in the institution of chivalry; or patriotism, as in the Spartan and Roman republics; or the enthusiasm of some religious sect which imputes its virtue to its dogma; or the cabalism or *esprit de corps* of a masonic or other association of friends.

The evolution of a highly destined society must be moral; it must run in the grooves of the celestial wheels. It must be catholic in aims.

What is *moral?* It is the respecting in action
catholic or universal ends. Hear the definition
which Kant gives of moral conduct: "Act always so that the immediate motive of thy will
may become a universal rule for all intelligent
beings."

Civilization depends on morality. Everything
good in man leans on what is higher. This rule
holds in small as in great. Thus all our strength
and success in the work of our hands depend on
our borrowing the aid of the elements. You
have seen a carpenter on a ladder with a broad-
axe chopping upward chips from a beam. How
awkward! at what disadvantage he works! But
see him on the ground, dressing his timber
under him. Now, not his feeble muscles but the
force of gravity brings down the axe; that is to
say, the planet itself splits his stick. The farmer
had much ill temper, laziness and shirking to
endure from his hand-sawyers, until one day he
bethought him to put his saw-mill on the edge
of a waterfall; and the river never tires of turning his wheel; the river is good-natured, and
never hints an objection.

We had letters to send: couriers could not go
fast enough nor far enough; broke their wagons,
foundered their horses; bad roads in spring,

snowdrifts in winter, heats in summer; could not get the horses out of a walk. But we found out that the air and earth were full of Electricity, and always going our way, — just the way we wanted to send. *Would he take a message?* Just as lief as not; had nothing else to do; would carry it in no time. Only one doubt occurred, one staggering objection, — he had no carpet-bag, no visible pockets, no hands, not so much as a mouth, to carry a letter. But after much thought and many experiments we managed to meet the conditions, and to fold up the letter in such invisible compact form as he could carry in those invisible pockets of his, never wrought by needle and thread, — and it went like a charm.

I admire still more than the saw-mill the skill which, on the seashore, makes the tides drive the wheels and grind corn, and which thus engages the assistance of the moon, like a hired hand, to grind, and wind, and pump, and saw, and split stone, and roll iron.[1]

Now that is the wisdom of a man, in every instance of his labor, to hitch his wagon to a star,[2] and see his chore done by the gods themselves. That is the way we are strong, by borrowing the might of the elements. The forces of steam, gravity, galvanism, light, magnets, wind, fire, serve us day by day and cost us nothing.

Our astronomy is full of examples of calling in the aid of these magnificent helpers. Thus, on a planet so small as ours, the want of an adequate base for astronomical measurements is early felt, as, for example, in detecting the parallax of a star. But the astronomer, having by an observation fixed the place of a star, — by so simple an expedient as waiting six months and then repeating his observation, contrived to put the diameter of the earth's orbit, say two hundred millions of miles, between his first observation and his second, and this line afforded him a respectable base for his triangle.

All our arts aim to win this vantage. We cannot bring the heavenly powers to us, but if we will only choose our jobs in directions in which they travel, they will undertake them with the greatest pleasure. It is a peremptory rule with them that *they never go out of their road.* We are dapper little busybodies and run this way and that way superserviceably; but they swerve never from their foreordained paths, — neither the sun, nor the moon, nor a bubble of air, nor a mote of dust.

And as our handiworks borrow the elements,

so all our social and political action leans on
principles. To accomplish anything excellent
the will must work for catholic and universal
ends. A puny creature, walled in on every side,
as Daniel wrote, —

"Unless above himself he can
Erect himself, how poor a thing is man!" [1]

but when his will leans on a principle, when he
is the vehicle of ideas, he borrows their omni-
potence. Gibraltar may be strong, but ideas are
impregnable, and bestow on the hero their in-
vincibility. "It was a great instruction," said a
saint in Cromwell's war, "that the best courages
are but beams of the Almighty." [2] Hitch your
wagon to a star. Let us not fag in paltry works
which serve our pot and bag alone. Let us not
lie and steal. No god will help. We shall find
all their teams going the other way, — Charles's
Wain, Great Bear, Orion, Leo, Hercules: every
god will leave us. Work rather for those interests which the divinities honor and promote,
— justice, love, freedom, knowledge, utility.

If we can thus ride in Olympian chariots by
putting our works in the path of the celestial circuits, we can harness also evil agents,
the powers of darkness, and force them to serve
against their will the ends of wisdom and virtue.

Thus a wise government puts fines and penalties on pleasant vices. What a benefit would the American government, not yet relieved of its extreme need, render to itself and to every city, village and hamlet in the states, if it would tax whiskey and rum almost to the point of prohibition! Was it Bonaparte who said that he found vices very good patriots? — "he got five millions from the love of brandy, and he should be glad to know which of the virtues would pay him as much." Tobacco and opium have broad backs, and will cheerfully carry the load of armies, if you choose to make them pay high for such joy as they give and such harm as they do.

These are traits and measures and modes; and the true test of civilization is, not the census, nor the size of cities, nor the crops, — no, but the kind of man the country turns out.[1] I see the vast advantages of this country, spanning the breadth of the temperate zone. I see the immense material prosperity, — towns on towns, states on states, and wealth piled in the massive architecture of cities: California quartz-mountains dumped down in New York to be repiled architecturally alongshore from Canada to Cuba, and thence westward to California again. But it is not New York streets, built by the confluence of workmen and wealth of all nations, though stretching out towards Philadelphia until they touch it, and northward until they touch New Haven, Hartford, Springfield, Worcester and Boston, — not these that make the real estimation. But when I look over this constellation of cities which animate and illustrate the land, and see how little the government has to do with their daily life, how self-helped and self-directed all families are, — knots of men in purely natural societies, societies of trade, of kindred blood, of habitual hospitality, house and house, man acting on man by weight of opinion, of longer or better-directed industry ; the refining influence of women, the invitation which experience and permanent causes open to youth and labor : — when I see how much each virtuous and gifted person, whom all men consider, lives affectionately with scores of excellent people who are not known far from home, and perhaps with great reason reckons these people his superiors in virtue and in the symmetry and force of their qualities, — I see what cubic values America has, and in these a better certificate of civilization than great cities or enormous wealth.

In strictness, the vital refinements are the moral and intellectual steps. The appearance of the Hebrew Moses, of the Indian Buddh; in Greece, of the Seven Wise Masters, of the acute and upright Socrates, and of the stoic Zeno; in Judæa, the advent of Jesus, and, in modern Christendom, of the realists Huss, Savonarola and Luther, — are casual facts which carry forward races to new convictions and elevate the rule of life. In the presence of these agencies it is frivolous to insist on the invention of printing or gunpowder, of steam-power or gas-light, percussion-caps and rubber-shoes, which are toys thrown off from that security, freedom and exhilaration which a healthy morality creates in society. These arts add a comfort and smoothness to house and street life;[1] but a purer morality, which kindles genius, civilizes civilization, casts backward all that we held sacred into the profane, as the flame of oil throws a shadow when shined upon by the flame of the Bude-light.[2] Not the less the popular measures of progress will ever be the arts and the laws.

But if there be a country which cannot stand any one of these tests, — a country where knowledge cannot be diffused without perils of mob law and statute law; where speech is not free; where the post-office is violated, mail-bags

VII

opened and letters tampered with; where public debts and private debts outside of the State are repudiated; where liberty is attacked in the primary institution of social life; where the position of the white woman is injuriously affected by the outlawry of the black woman; where the arts, such as they have, are all imported, having no indigenous life; where the laborer is not secured in the earnings of his own hands; where suffrage is not free or equal; — that country is, in all these respects, not civil, but barbarous; and no advantages of soil, climate or coast can resist these suicidal mischiefs.[1]

Morality and all the incidents of morality are essential; as, justice to the citizen, and personal liberty. Montesquieu says: "Countries are well cultivated, not as they are fertile, but as they are free;" and the remark holds not less but more true of the culture of men than of the tillage of land. And the highest proof of civility is that the whole public action of the State is directed on securing the greatest good of the greatest number.[2]

III

ART

I FRAMED his tongue to music,
  I armed his hand with skill,
I moulded his face to beauty
  And his heart the throne of Will.

ART

ALL departments of life at the present day
— Trade, Politics, Letters, Science, or
Religion — seem to feel, and to labor to express, the identity of their law. They are rays
of one sun; they translate each into a new language the sense of the other. They are sublime when seen as emanations of a Necessity
contradistinguished from the vulgar Fate by
being instant and alive, and dissolving man as
well as his works in its flowing beneficence.
This influence is conspicuously visible in the
principles and history of Art.[1]

On one side in primary communication with
absolute truth through thought and instinct,
the human mind on the other side tends, by an
equal necessity, to the publication and embodi-
ment of its thought, modified and dwarfed by
the impurity and untruth which in all our experience injure the individuality through which
it passes. The child not only suffers, but cries;
not only hungers, but eats. The man not only
thinks, but speaks and acts. Every thought
that arises in the mind, in its rising aims to pass
out of the mind into act; just as every plant,

in the moment of germination, struggles up to light. Thought is the seed of action; but action is as much its second form as thought is its first. It rises in thought, to the end that it may be uttered and acted. The more profound the thought, the more burdensome. Always in proportion to the depth of its sense does it knock importunately at the gates of the soul, to be spoken, to be done. What is in, will out. It struggles to the birth. Speech is a great pleasure, and action a great pleasure; they cannot be foreborne.

The utterance of thought and emotion in speech and action may be conscious or unconscious. The sucking child is an unconscious actor. The man in an ecstasy of fear or anger is an unconscious actor. A large part of our habitual actions are unconsciously done, and most of our necessary words are unconsciously said.

The conscious utterance of thought, by speech or action, to any end, is Art.[1] From the first imitative babble of a child to the despotism of eloquence; from his first pile of toys or chip bridge to the masonry of Minot Rock Lighthouse or the Pacific Railroad; from the tattooing of the Owhyhees to the Vatican Gal-

lery; from the simplest expedient of private
prudence to the American Constitution; from
its first to its last works, Art is the spirit's voluntary use and combination of things to serve
its end. The Will distinguishes it as spiritual
action. Relatively to themselves, the bee, the
bird, the beaver, have no art; for what they do
they do instinctively; but relatively to the Supreme Being, they have. And the same is true of
all unconscious action: relatively to the doer,
it is instinct; relatively to the First Cause, it is
Art. In this sense, recognizing the Spirit which
informs Nature, Plato rightly said, "Those
things which are said to be done by Nature
are indeed done by Divine Art." Art, univer-
sally, is the spirit creative. It was defined by
Aristotle, "The reason of the thing, without
the matter."

If we follow the popular distinction of works
according to their aim, we should say, the Spirit,
in its creation, aims at use or at beauty, and
hence Art divides itself into the Useful and the
Fine Arts.

The useful arts comprehend not only those
that lie next to instinct, as agriculture, building,
weaving, etc., but also navigation, practical chemistry and the construction of all the grand and

delicate tools and instruments by which ·man
serves himself; as language, the watch, the ship,
the decimal cipher ; and also the sciences, so far
as they are made serviceable to political economy.

When we reflect on the pleasure we receive
from a ship, a railroad, a dry-dock ; or from a
picture, a dramatic representation, a statue,
a poem, — we find that these have not a quite
simple, but a blended origin. We find that the
question, What is Art? leads us directly to
another, — Who is the Artist ? And the solution of this is the key to the history of Art.

I hasten to state the principle which prescribes,
through different means, its firm law to the useful
and the beautiful arts. The law is this. The universal soul is the alone creator of the useful and
the beautiful ; therefore to make anything useful
or beautiful, the individual must be submitted to
the universal mind.[1]

In the first place let us consider this in reference to the useful arts. Here the omnipotent
agent is Nature ; all human acts are satellites to
her orb. Nature is the representative of the universal mind, and the law becomes this, — that
Art must be a complement to Nature, strictly
subsidiary. It was said, in allusion to the great
structures of the ancient Romans, the aqueducts

and bridges, that " their Art was a Nature work
ing to municipal ends." That is a true account
of all just works of useful art. Smeaton built
Eddystone Lighthouse on the model of an oak
tree, as being the form in Nature best designed to
resist a constant assailing force. Dollond formed
his achromatic telescope on the model of the human eye. Duhamel built a bridge by letting in
a piece of stronger timber for the middle of the
under-surface, getting his hint from the structure
of the shin-bone.

The first and last lesson of the useful arts is
that Nature tyrannizes over our works. They
must be conformed to her law, or they will be
ground to powder by her omnipresent activity.
Nothing droll, nothing whimsical will endure.
Nature is ever interfering with Art. You cannot build your house or pagoda as you will, but
as you must. There is a quick bound set to your
caprice.[1] The leaning tower can only lean so far.
The veranda or pagoda roof can curve upward
only to a certain point. The slope of your roof
is determined by the weight of snow. It is only
within narrow limits that the discretion of the
architect may range : gravity, wind, sun, rain, the
size of men and animals, and such like, have
more to say than he. It is the law of fluids that

prescribes the shape of the boat, — keel, rudder
and bows, — and, in the finer fluid above, the
form and tackle of the sails. Man seems to have
no option about his tools, but merely the necessity to learn from Nature what will fit best, as
if he were fitting a screw or a door. Beneath a
necessity thus almighty, what is artificial in man's
life seems insignificant. He seems to take his
task so minutely from intimations of Nature that
his works become as it were hers, and he is no
longer free.

But if we work within this limit, she yields us
all her strength. All powerful action is performed
by bringing the forces of Nature to bear upon our
objects.[1] We do not grind corn or lift the loom
by our own strength, but we build a mill in such
position as to set the north wind to play upon
our instrument, or the elastic force of steam, or
the ebb and flow of the sea. So in our handi-
work, we do few things by muscular force, but
we place ourselves in such attitudes as to bring
the force of gravity, that is, the weight of the
planet, to bear upon the spade or the axe we
wield. In short, in all our operations we seek
not to use our own, but to bring a quite infinite
force to bear.

Let us now consider this law as it affects the

works that have beauty for their end, that is, the productions of the Fine Arts. Here again the prominent fact is subordination of man. His art is the least part of his work of art. A great deduction is to be made before we can know his proper contribution to it.[1]

Music, Eloquence, Poetry, Painting, Sculpture, Architecture. This is a rough enumeration of the Fine Arts. I omit Rhetoric, which only respects the form of eloquence and poetry. Architecture and eloquence are mixed arts, whose end is sometimes beauty and sometimes use.

It will be seen that in each of these arts there is much which is not spiritual. Each has a material basis, and in each the creating intellect is crippled in some degree by the stuff on which it works. The basis of poetry is language, which is material only on one side. It is a demi-god. But being applied primarily to the common necessities of man, it is not new-created by the poet for his own ends.

The basis of music is the qualities of the air and the vibrations of sonorous bodies. The pulsation of a stretched string or wire gives the ear the pleasure of sweet sound, before yet the musician has enhanced this pleasure by concords and combinations.

Eloquence, as far as it is a fine art, is modified how much by the material organization of the orator, the tone of the voice, the physical strength, the play of the eye and countenance. All this is so much deduction from the purely spiritual pleasure, as so much deduction from the merit of Art, and is the attribute of Nature.

In painting, bright colors stimulate the eye before yet they are harmonized into a landscape. In sculpture and in architecture the material, as marble or granite, and in architecture the mass, are sources of great pleasure quite independent of the artificial arrangement. The art resides in the model, in the plan; for it is on that the genius of the artist is expended, not on the statue or the temple. Just as much better as is the polished statue of dazzling marble than the clay model, or as much more impressive as is the granite cathedral or pyramid than the ground-plan or profile of them on paper, so much more beauty owe they to Nature than to Art.

There is a still larger deduction to be made from the genius of the artist in favor of Nature than I have yet specified.

A jumble of musical sounds on a viol or a flute, in which the rhythm of the tune is played without one of the notes being right, gives plea-

sure to the unskilful ear. A very coarse imitation of the human form on canvas, or in wax-
work; a coarse sketch in colors of a landscape,
in which imitation is all that is attempted, — these
things give to unpractised eyes, to the uncultured,
who do not ask a fine spiritual delight, almost
as much pleasure as a statue of Canova or a
picture of Titian. And in the statue of Canova
or the picture of Titian, these give the great part
of the pleasure; they are the basis on which the
fine spirit rears a higher delight, but to which
these are indispensable.

Another deduction from the genius of the
artist is what is conventional in his art, of which
there is much in every work of art. Thus how
much is there that is not original in every particular building, in every statue, in every tune,
painting, poem or harangue! — whatever is
national or usual; as the usage of building all
Roman churches in the form of a cross, the
prescribed distribution of parts of a theatre, the
custom of draping a statue in classical costume.
Yet who will deny that the merely conventional
part of the performance contributes much to its
effect?

One consideration more exhausts I believe all
the deductions from the genius of the artist in

any given work. This is the adventitious. Thus the pleasure that a noble temple gives us is only in part owing to the temple. It is exalted by the beauty of sunlight, the play of the clouds, the landscape around it, its grouping with the houses, trees and towers in its vicinity.[1] The pleasure of eloquence is in greatest part owing often to the stimulus of the occasion which produces it, — to the magic of sympathy, which exalts the feeling of each by radiating on him the feeling of all.

The effect of music belongs how much to the place, as the church, or the moonlight walk ; or to the company ; or, if on the stage, to what went before in the play, or to the expectation of what shall come after.

In poetry, " It is tradition more than invention that helps the poet to a good fable."[2] The adventitious beauty of poetry may be felt in the greater delight which a verse gives in happy quotation than in the poem.

It is a curious proof of our conviction that the artist does not feel himself to be the parent of his work, and is as much surprised at the effect as we, that we are so unwilling to impute our best sense of any work of art to the author. The highest praise we can attribute to any writer, painter, sculptor, builder, is, that he actually pos-

sessed the thought or feeling with which he has
inspired us. We hesitate at doing Spenser so
great an honor as to think that he intended by
his allegory the sense we affix to it. We grudge
to Homer the wide human circumspection his
commentators ascribe to him.

Even Shakspeare, of whom we can believe
everything, we think indebted to Goethe and
to Coleridge for the wisdom they detect in his
Hamlet and Antony. Especially have we this
infirmity of faith in contemporary genius. We
fear that Allston and Greenough did not foresee
and design all the effect they produce on us.
Our arts are happy hits. We are like the musician on the lake, whose melody is sweeter than
he knows, or like a traveller surprised by a mountain echo, whose trivial word returns to him in
romantic thunders.

In view of these facts, I say that the power
of Nature predominates over the human will in
all works of even the fine arts, in all that respects
their material and external circumstances. Nature paints the best part of the picture, carves
the best part of the statue, builds the best part
of the house, and speaks the best part of the
oration. For all the advantages to which I have
adverted are such as the artist did not consciously

produce. He relied on their aid, he put himself
in the way to receive aid from some of them;
but he saw that his planting and his watering
waited for the sunlight of Nature, or were vain.[1]

Let us proceed to the consideration of the
law stated in the beginning of this essay, as it affects the purely spiritual part of a work of art.

As, in useful art, so far as it is useful, the
work must be strictly subordinated to the laws
of Nature, so as to become a sort of continua-
tion and in no wise a contradiction of Nature;
so in art that aims at beauty must the parts be
subordinated to Ideal Nature, and everything
individual abstracted, so that it shall be the production of the universal soul. The artist who
is to produce a work which is to be admired,
not by his friends or his towns-people or his
contemporaries, but by all men, and which is
to be more beautiful to the eye in proportion to
its culture, must disindividualize himself, and
be a man of no party and no manner and no
age, but one through whom the soul of all men
circulates as the common air through his lungs.[2]
He must work in the spirit in which we conceive a prophet to speak, or an angel of the
Lord to act; that is, he is not to speak his own
words, or do his own works, or think his own

thoughts, but he is to be an organ through which the universal mind acts.

In speaking of the useful arts, I pointed to the fact that we do not dig, or grind, or hew, by our muscular strength, but by bringing the weight of the planet to bear on the spade, axe or bar. Precisely analogous to this, in the fine arts, is the manner of our intellectual work. We aim to hinder our individuality from acting. So much as we can shove aside our egotism, our prejudice and will, and bring the omniscience of reason upon the subject before us, so perfect is the work. The wonders of Shakspeare are things which he saw whilst he stood aside, and then returned to record them. The poet aims at getting observations without aim; to subject to thought things seen without (voluntary) thought.[1]

In eloquence, the great triumphs of the art are when the orator is lifted above himself; when consciously he makes himself the mere tongue of the occasion and the hour, and says what cannot but be said. Hence the term *abandonment*, to describe the self-surrender of the orator. Not his will, but the principle on which he is horsed, the great connection and crisis of events, thunder in the ear of the crowd.

VII

In poetry, where every word is free, every word is necessary. Good poetry could not have been otherwise written than it is. The first time you hear it, it sounds rather as if copied out of some invisible tablet in the Eternal mind than as if arbitrarily composed by the poet. The feeling of all great poets has accorded with this. They found the verse, not made it. The muse brought it to them.

In sculpture, did ever anybody call the Apollo a fancy piece? Or say of the Laocoön how it might be made different? A master-piece of art has in the mind a fixed place in the chain of being, as much as a plant or a crystal.[1]

The whole language of men, especially of artists, in reference to this subject, points at the belief that every work of art, in proportion to its excellence, partakes of the precision of fate : no room was there for choice, no play for fancy ; for in the moment or in the successive moments when that form was seen, the iron lids of Reason were unclosed, which ordinarily are heavy with slumber. The individual mind became for the moment the vent of the mind of humanity.

There is but one Reason. The mind that made the world is not one mind, but *the* mind.

And every work of art is a more or less pure manifestation of the same. Therefore we arrive at this conclusion, which I offer as a confirmation of the whole view, that the delight which a work of art affords, seems to arise from our recognizing in it the mind that formed Nature, again in active operation. It differs from the works of Nature in this, that they are organically reproductive. This is not, but spiritually it is prolific by its powerful action on the intellects of men.

Hence it follows that a study of admirable works of art sharpens our perceptions of the beauty of Nature ; that a certain analogy reigns throughout the wonders of both ; that the contemplation of a work of great art draws us into a state of mind which may be called religious. It conspires with all exalted sentiments.

Proceeding from absolute mind, whose nature is goodness as much as truth, the great works are always attuned to moral nature. If the earth and sea conspire with virtue more than vice, — so do the masterpieces of art. The galleries of ancient sculpture in Naples and Rome strike no deeper conviction into the mind than the contrast of the purity, the severity expressed in these fine old heads, with the frivolity and grossness of the mob that exhibits and the mob that gazes at them. These are the countenances of the first-born, — the face of man in the morning of the world. No mark is on these lofty features of sloth or luxury or meanness, and they surprise you with a moral admonition, as they speak of nothing around you, but remind you of the fragrant thoughts and the purest resolutions of your youth.'

Herein is the explanation of the analogies, which exist in all the arts. They are the re-appearance of one mind, working in many materials to many temporary ends. Raphael paints wisdom, Handel sings it, Phidias carves it, Shakspeare writes it, Wren builds it, Columbus sails it, Luther preaches it, Washington arms it, Watt mechanizes it. Painting was called " silent poetry," and poetry "speaking painting." The laws of each art are convertible into the laws of every other.

Herein we have an explanation of the necessity that reigns in all the kingdom of Art. Arising out of eternal Reason, one and perfect, whatever is beautiful rests on the foundation of the necessary. Nothing is arbitrary, nothing is insulated in beauty. It depends forever on the necessary and the useful. The plumage of the

bird, the mimic plumage of the insect, has a reason for its rich colors in the constitution of the
animal. Fitness is so inseparable an accompani-
ment of beauty that it has been taken for it.
The most perfect form to answer an end is so
far beautiful. We feel, in seeing a noble building, which rhymes well, as we do in hearing a
perfect song, that it is spiritually organic; that
is, had a necessity, in Nature, for being; was one
of the possible forms in the Divine mind, and is
now only discovered and executed by the artist,
not arbitrarily composed by him.

And so every genuine work of art has as
much reason for being as the earth and the sun.
The gayest charm of beauty has a root in the
constitution of things. The Iliad of Homer, the
songs of David, the odes of Pindar, the tragedies of Æschylus, the Doric temples, the Gothic
cathedrals, the plays of Shakspeare, all and each
were made not for sport but in grave earnest, in
tears and smiles of suffering and loving men.[1]

Viewed from this point the history of Art
becomes intelligible, and moreover one of the
most agreeable studies. We see how each work
of art sprang irresistibly from necessity, and,
moreover, took its form from the broad hint of
Nature.[2] Beautiful in this wise is the obvious

origin of all the known orders of architecture;
namely, that they were the idealizing of the
primitive abodes of each people.[1] There was no
wilfulness in the savages in this perpetuating of
their first rude abodes. The first form in which
they built a house would be the first form of
their public and religious edifice also. This
form becomes immediately sacred in the eyes
of their children, and as more traditions cluster
round it, is imitated with more splendor in each
succeeding generation.

In like manner it has been remarked by
Goethe that the granite breaks into parallelo-
pipeds, which broken in two, one part would
be an obelisk; that in Upper Egypt the inhab-
itants would naturally mark a memorable spot
by setting up so conspicuous a stone. Again,
he suggested, we may see in any stone wall, on
a fragment of rock, the projecting veins of
harder stone which have resisted the action of
frost and water which has decomposed the rest.
This appearance certainly gave the hint of the
hieroglyphics inscribed on their obelisk. The
amphitheatre of the old Romans, — any one
may see its origin who looks at the crowd running together to see any fight, sickness, or odd
appearance in the street. The first comers gather

round in a circle, those behind stand on tiptoe,
and farther back they climb on fences or win-
dow-sills, and so make a cup of which the object of attention occupies the hollow area. The
architect put benches in this, and enclosed the
cup with a wall, — and behold a Coliseum!

It would be easy to show of many fine things
in the world — in the customs of nations, the
etiquette of courts, the constitution of governments — the origin in quite simple local necessities. Heraldry, for example, and the ceremonies of a coronation, are a dignified repetition of
the occurrences that might befall a dragoon and
his footboy. The College of Cardinals were
originally the parish priests of Rome. The leaning towers originated from the civil discords
which induced every lord to build a tower. Then
it became a point of family pride, — and for
more pride the novelty of a leaning tower was
built.

This strict dependence of Art upon material
and ideal Nature, this adamantine necessity
which underlies it, has made all its past and
may foreshow its future history. It never was
in the power of any man or any community to
call the arts into being. They come to serve his
actual wants, never to please his fancy. These

arts have their origin always in some enthusiasm, as love, patriotism or religion. Who carved
marble? The believing man, who wished to
symbolize their gods to the waiting Greeks.

The Gothic cathedrals were built when the
builder and the priest and the people were overpowered by their faith. Love and fear laid every
stone.¹ The Madonnas of Raphael and Titian
were made to be worshipped. Tragedy was instituted for the like purpose, and the miracles
of music: all sprang out of some genuine enthusiasm, and never out of dilettanteism and
holidays. Now they languish, because their
purpose is merely exhibition.² Who cares, who
knows what works of art our government have
ordered to be made for the Capitol? They are
a mere flourish to please the eye of persons who
have associations with books and galleries. But
in Greece, the Demos of Athens divided into
political factions upon the merits of Phidias.

In this country, at this time, other interests
than religion and patriotism are predominant,
and the arts, the daughters of enthusiasm, do not
flourish. The genuine offspring of our ruling
passions we behold. Popular institutions, the
school, the reading-room, the telegraph, the
post-office, the exchange, the insurance com-

pany, and the immense harvest of economical inventions, are the fruit of the equality and the boundless liberty of lucrative callings. These are superficial wants; and their fruits are these superficial institutions. But, as far as they accelerate the end of political freedom and national education, they are preparing the soil of man for fairer flowers and fruits in another age. For beauty, truth and goodness are not obsolete; they spring eternal in the breast of man; they are as indigenous in Massachusetts as in Tuscany or the Isles of Greece. And that Eternal Spirit whose triple face they are, moulds from them forever, for his mortal child, images to remind him of the Infinite and Fair.[1]

IV

ELOQUENCE

FOR whom the Muses smile upon,
And touch with soft persuasion,
His words, like a storm-wind, can bring
Terror and beauty on their wing;
In his every syllable
Lurketh nature veritable;
And though he speak in midnight dark, —
In heaven no star, on earth no spark, —
Yet before the listener's eye
Swims the world in ecstasy,
The forest waves, the morning breaks,
The pastures sleep, ripple the lakes,
Leaves twinkle, flowers like persons be
And life pulsates in rock or tree.

ELOQUENCE

IT is the doctrine of the popular music-masters that whoever can speak can sing. So probably every man is eloquent once in his life. Our temperaments differ in capacity of heat, or, we boil at different degrees. One man is brought to the boiling-point by the excitement of conversation in the parlor. The waters, of course, are not very deep. He has a two-inch enthusiasm, a patty-pan ebullition. Another requires the additional caloric of a multitude and a public debate; a third needs an antagonist, or a hot indignation; a fourth needs a revolution; and a fifth, nothing less than the grandeur of absolute ideas, the splendors and shades of Heaven and Hell.

But, because every man is an orator, how long soever he may have been a mute, an assembly of men is so much more susceptible. The eloquence of one stimulates all the rest, some up to the speaking-point, and all others to a degree that makes them good receivers and conductors, and they avenge themselves for their enforced silence by increased loquacity on their return to the fireside.

The plight of these phlegmatic brains is better than that of those who prematurely boil, and who impatiently break silence before their time. Our county conventions often exhibit a small-pot-soon-hot style of eloquence. We are too much reminded of a medical experiment where a series of patients are taking nitrous-oxide gas. Each patient in turn exhibits similar symptoms, —redness in the face, volubility, violent gesticulation, delirious attitudes, occasional stamping, an alarming loss of perception of the passage of time, a selfish enjoyment of his sensations, and loss of perception of the sufferings of the audience.

Plato says that the punishment which the wise suffer who refuse to take part in the government, is, to live under the government of worse men ; and the like regret is suggested to all the auditors, as the penalty of abstaining to speak, — that they shall hear worse orators than themselves.[1]

But this lust to speak marks the universal feeling of the energy of the engine, and the curiosity men feel to touch the springs. Of all the musical instruments on which men play, a popular assembly is that which has the largest compass and variety, and out of which, by genius and study, the most wonderful effects can be drawn. An audience is not a simple addition of the individuals that compose it. Their sympathy gives them a certain social organism, which fills each member, in his own degree, and most of all the orator, as a jar in a battery is charged with the whole electricity of the battery. No one can survey the face of an excited assembly, without being apprised of new opportunity for painting in fire human thought, and being agitated to agitate. How many orators sit mute there below! They come to get justice done to that ear and intuition which no Chatham and no Demosthenes has begun to satisfy.

The Welsh Triads say, "Many are the friends of the golden tongue."[1] Who can wonder at the attractiveness of Parliament, or of Congress, or the bar, for our ambitious young men, when the highest bribes of society are at the feet of the successful orator? He has his audience at his devotion. All other fames must hush before his. He is the true potentate; for they are not kings who sit on thrones, but they who know how to govern. The definitions of eloquence describe its attraction for young men. Antiphon the Rhamnusian, one of Plutarch's ten orators, advertised in Athens "that he would cure distempers of the mind with words."[2] No man has

a prosperity so high or firm but two or three
words can dishearten it. There is no calamity
which right words will not begin to redress.
Isocrates described his art as "the power of
magnifying what was small and diminishing what
was great,"—an acute but partial definition.
Among the Spartans, the art assumed a Spartan
shape, namely, of the sharpest weapon. Socrates says: "If any one wishes to converse with
the meanest of the Lacedæmonians, he will at
first find him despicable in conversation, but
when a proper opportunity offers, this same person, like a skilful jaculator, will hurl a sentence
worthy of attention, short and contorted, so that
he who converses with him will appear to be in
no respect superior to a boy." Plato's definition of rhetoric is, "the art of ruling the minds
of men." The Koran says, "A mountain may
change its place, but a man will not change his
disposition;" yet the end of eloquence is — is
it not?— to alter in a pair of hours, perhaps
in a half hour's discourse, the convictions and
habits of years. Young men, too, are eager to
enjoy this sense of added power and enlarged
sympathetic existence. The orator sees himself
the organ of a multitude, and concentrating their
valors and powers : —

" But now the blood of twenty thousand men
    Blushed in my face." [1]

That which he wishes, that which eloquence
ought to reach, is not a particular skill in telling a story, or neatly summing up evidence, or
arguing logically, or dexterously addressing the
prejudice of the company,— no, but a taking
sovereign possession of the audience. Him we
call an artist who shall play on an assembly of
men as a master on the keys of the piano,—
who, seeing the people furious, shall soften and
compose them, shall draw them, when he will,
to laughter and to tears. Bring him to his audience, and, be they who they may,— coarse or
refined, pleased or displeased, sulky or savage,
with their opinions in the keeping of a con-
fessor, or with their opinions in their bank-
safes,— he will have them pleased and humored
as he chooses; and they shall carry and execute
that which he bids them.

This is that despotism which poets have celebrated in the Pied Piper of Hamelin, whose
music drew like the power of gravitation,— drew
soldiers and priests, traders and feasters, women
and boys, rats and mice; or that of the minstrel
of Meudon, who made the pall-bearers dance
around the bier.[2] This is a power of many

VII

degrees and requiring in the orator a great range of faculty and experience, requiring a large composite man, such as Nature rarely organizes; so that in our experience we are forced to gather up the figure in fragments, here one talent and there another.

The audience is a constant meter of the orator. There are many audiences in every public assembly, each one of which rules in turn. If anything comic and coarse is spoken, you shall see the emergence of the boys and rowdies, so loud and vivacious that you might think the house was filled with them. If new topics are started, graver and higher, these roisters recede; a more chaste and wise attention takes place. You would think the boys slept, and that the men have any degree of profoundness. If the speaker utter a noble sentiment, the attention deepens, a new and highest audience now listens, and the audiences of the fun and of facts and of the understanding are all silenced and awed. There is also something excellent in every audience, — the capacity of virtue. They are ready to be beatified. They know so much more than the orator, — and are so just! There is a tablet there for every line he can inscribe, though he should mount to the highest levels. Humble persons are con-

scious of new illumination; narrow brows expand with enlarged affections; — delicate spirits,
long unknown to themselves, masked and muffled in coarsest fortunes, who now hear their own
native language for the first time, and leap to
hear it.[1] But all these several audiences, each
above each, which successively appear to greet
the variety of style and topic, are really composed out of the same persons; nay, sometimes
the same individual will take active part in them
all, in turn.

This range of many powers in the consum-
mate speaker, and of many audiences in one assembly, leads us to consider the successive stages
of oratory.

Perhaps it is the lowest of the qualities of an
orator, but it is, on so many occasions, of chief
importance, — a certain robust and radiant physical health; or, — shall I say? — great volumes of animal heat. When each auditor feels
himself to make too large a part of the assembly, and shudders with cold at the thinness of
the morning audience, and with fear lest all will
heavily fail through one bad speech, mere energy
and mellowness are then inestimable. Wisdom
and learning would be harsh and unwelcome,
compared with a substantial cordial man, made

of milk as we say, who is a house-warmer, with his obvious honesty and good meaning, and a hue-and-cry style of harangue, which inundates the assembly with a flood of animal spirits, and makes all safe and secure, so that any and every sort of good speaking becomes at once practicable. I do not rate this animal eloquence very highly; and yet, as we must be fed and warmed before we can do any work well, — even the best, — so is this semi-animal exuberance, like a good stove, of the first necessity in a cold house.

Climate has much to do with it, — climate and race. Set a New Englander to describe any accident which happened in his presence. What hesitation and reserve in his narrative! He tells with difficulty some particulars, and gets as fast as he can to the result, and, though he cannot describe, hopes to suggest the whole scene. Now listen to a poor Irishwoman recounting some experience of hers. Her speech flows like a river, — so unconsidered, so humorous, so pathetic, such justice done to all the parts! [1] It is a true transubstantiation, — the fact converted into speech, all warm and colored and alive, as it fell out. Our Southern people are almost all speakers, and have every advantage over the New

England people, whose climate is so cold that 't is said we do not like to open our mouths very wide.¹ But neither can the Southerner in the United States, nor the Irish, compare with the lively inhabitant of the south of Europe. The traveller in Sicily needs no gayer melo-dramatic exhibition than the *table d'hôte* of his inn will afford him in the conversation of the joyous guests. They mimic the voice and man-ner of the person they describe; they crow, squeal, hiss, cackle, bark, and scream like mad, and, were it only by the physical strength exerted in telling the story, keep the table in unbounded excitement. But in every constitution some large degree of animal vigor is necessary as material foundation for the higher qualities of the art.

But eloquence must be attractive, or it is none. The virtue of books is to be readable, and of orators to be interesting; and this is a gift of Nature; as Demosthenes, the most laborious student in that kind, signified his sense of this necessity when he wrote, "Good Fortune," as his motto on his shield. As we know, the power of discourse of certain individuals amounts to fascination, though it may have no lasting effect. Some portion of this sugar must intermingle. The right eloquence needs no bell to call the people together, and no constable to keep them. It draws the children from their play, the old from their arm-chairs, the invalid from his warm chamber: it holds the hearer fast; steals away his feet, that he shall not depart; his memory, that he shall not remember the most pressing affairs; his belief, that he shall not admit any opposing considerations. The pictures we have of it in semi-barbarous ages, when it has some advantages in the simpler habit of the people, show what it aims at. It is said that the Khans or story-tellers in Ispahan and other cities of the East, attain a controlling power over their audience, keeping them for many hours attentive to the most fanciful and extravagant adventures. The whole world knows pretty well the style of these improvisators, and how fascinating they are, in our translations of the Arabian Nights. Scheherezade tells these stories to save her life, and the delight of young Europe and young America in them proves that she fairly earned it. And who does not remember in childhood some white or black or yellow Scheherezade, who, by that talent of telling endless feats of fairies and magicians and kings and queens, was more dear and wonderful to a circle of children than any orator in England or America is now?[1]

The more indolent and imaginative complexion of the Eastern nations makes them much more impressible by these appeals to the fancy.

These legends are only exaggerations of real occurrences, and every literature contains these high compliments to the art of the orator and the bard, from the Hebrew and the Greek down to the Scottish Glenkindie, who

> "harpit a fish out o' saut-water,
> Or water out of a stone,
> Or milk out of a maiden's breast
> Who bairn had never none." [1]

Homer specially delighted in drawing the same figure. For what is the Odyssey but a history of the orator, in the largest style, carried through a series of adventures furnishing brilliant opportunities to his talent? See with what care and pleasure the poet brings him on the stage. Helen is pointing out to Priam, from a tower, the different Grecian chiefs. "The old man asked: 'Tell me, dear child, who is that man, shorter by a head than Agamemnon, yet he looks broader in his shoulders and breast. His arms lie on the ground, but he, like a leader, walks about the bands of the men. He seems to me like a stately ram, who goes as a master of the flock.' Him answered Helen, daughter of Jove, 'This is the

wise Ulysses, son of Laertes, who was reared in
the state of craggy Ithaca, knowing all wiles and
wise counsels.' To her the prudent Antenor replied again : ' O woman, you have spoken truly.
For once the wise Ulysses came hither on an
embassy, with Menelaus, beloved by Mars. I
received them and entertained them at my house.
I became acquainted with the genius and the prudent judgments of both. When they mixed with
the assembled Trojans, and stood, the broad
shoulders of Menelaus rose above the other;
but, both sitting, Ulysses was more majestic.
When they conversed, and interweaved stories
and opinions with all, Menelaus spoke suc-
cinctly, — few but very sweet words, since he
was not talkative nor superfluous in speech, and
was the younger. But when the wise Ulysses
arose and stood and looked down, fixing his eyes
on the ground, and neither moved his sceptre
backward nor forward, but held it still, like an
awkward person, you would say it was some
angry or foolish man ; but when he sent his
great voice forth out of his breast, and his words
fell like the winter snows, not then would any
mortal contend with Ulysses ; and we, beholding, wondered not afterwards so much at his aspect.' " [1] Thus he does not fail to arm Ulysses

at first with this power of overcoming all opposition by the blandishments of speech. Plutarch
tells us that Thucydides, when Archidamus, king
of Sparta, asked him which was the best wrest-
ler, Pericles or he, replied, "When I throw him,
he says he was never down, and he persuades
the very spectators to believe him." Philip of
Macedon said of Demosthenes, on hearing the
report of one of his orations, "Had I been there,
he would have persuaded me to take up arms
against myself;" and Warren Hastings said of
Burke's speech on his impeachment, "As I listened to the orator, I felt for more than half an
hour as if I were the most culpable being on
earth."

In these examples, higher qualities have already entered, but the power of detaining the
ear by pleasing speech, and addressing the fancy
and imagination, often exists without higher
merits. Thus separated, as this fascination of
discourse aims only at amusement, though it be
decisive in its momentary effect, it is yet a juggle, and of no lasting power. It is heard like a
band of music passing through the streets, which
converts all the passengers into poets, but is
forgotten as soon as it has turned the next
corner; and unless this oiled tongue could, in

Oriental phrase, lick the sun and moon away, it must take its place with opium and brandy. I know no remedy against it but cotton-wool, or the wax which Ulysses stuffed into the ears of his sailors to pass the Sirens safely.[1]

There are all degrees of power, and the least are interesting, but they must not be confounded. There is the glib tongue and cool self-possession of the salesman in a large shop, which, as is well known, overpower the prudence and resolution of housekeepers of both sexes. There is a petty lawyer's fluency, which is sufficiently impressive to him who is devoid of that talent, though it be, in so many cases, nothing more than a facility of expressing with accuracy and speed what everybody thinks and says more slowly; without new information, or precision of thought, but the same thing, neither less nor more. It requires no special insight to edit one of our country newspapers. Yet whoever can say off currently, sentence by sentence, matter neither better nor worse than what is there printed, will be very impressive to our easily pleased population. These talkers are of that class who prosper, like the celebrated schoolmaster, by being only one lesson ahead of the pupil. Add a little sarcasm and prompt allusion

to passing occurrences, and you have the mis-
chievous member of Congress. A spice of malice, a ruffian touch in his rhetoric, will do him
no harm with his audience. These accomplishments are of the same kind, and only a degree
higher than the coaxing of the auctioneer, or
the vituperative style well described in the street-
word "jawing." These kinds of public and private speaking have their use and convenience
to the practitioners; but we may say of such
collectively that the habit of oratory is apt to
disqualify them for eloquence.

One of our statesmen [1] said, " The curse of
this country is eloquent men." And one cannot
wonder at the uneasiness sometimes manifested
by trained statesmen, with large experience of
public affairs, when they observe the dispropor-
tionate advantage suddenly given to oratory
over the most solid and accumulated public service. In a Senate or other business committee,
the solid result depends on a few men with
working talent. They know how to deal with
the facts before them, to put things into a practical shape, and they value men only as they can
forward the work. But a new man comes there
who has no capacity for helping them at all, is
insignificant, and nobody in the committee, but

has a talent for speaking. In the debate with open doors, this precious person makes a speech which is printed and read all over the Union, and he at once becomes famous, and takes the lead in the public mind over all these executive men, who, of course, are full of indignation to find one who has no tact or skill and knows he has none, put over them by means of this talking-power which they despise.

Leaving behind us these pretensions, better or worse, to come a little nearer to the verity, — eloquence is attractive as an example of the magic of personal ascendency, — a total and resultant power, rare, because it requires a rich coincidence of powers, intellect, will, sympathy, organs and, over all, good fortune in the cause. We have a half belief that the person is possible who can counterpoise all other persons. We believe that there may be a man who is a match for events, one who never found his match, against whom other men being dashed are broken, — one of inexhaustible personal resources, who can give you any odds and beat you. What we really wish for is a mind equal to any exigency. You are safe in your rural district, or in the city, in broad daylight, amidst the police, and under the eyes of a hundred thousand people. But how is

it on the Atlantic, in a storm, — do you understand how to infuse your reason into men dis-
abled by terror, and to bring yourself off safe
then? — how among thieves, or among an in-
furiated populace, or among cannibals? Face
to face with a highwayman who has every
temptation and opportunity for violence and
plunder, can you bring yourself off safe by your
wit exercised through speech? — a problem easy
enough to Cæsar or Napoleon. Whenever a
man of that stamp arrives, the highwayman
has found a master. What a difference between
men in power of face! A man succeeds because he has more power of eye than another,
and so coaxes or confounds him. The newspapers, every week, report the adventures of
some impudent swindler, who, by steadiness of
carriage, duped those who should have known
better. Yet any swindlers we have known are
novices and bunglers, as is attested by their ill
name. A greater power of face would accomplish anything, and, with the rest of their takings,
take away the bad name. A greater power of
carrying the thing loftily and with perfect assurance, would confound merchant, banker, judge,
men of influence and power, poet and president,
and might head any party, unseat any sovereign,

and abrogate any constitution in Europe and
America. It was said that a man has at one step
attained vast power, who has renounced his moral
sentiment, and settled it with himself that he will
no longer stick at anything. It was said of Sir
William Pepperell, one of the worthies of New
England, that, "put him where you might, he
commanded, and saw what he willed come to
pass." Julius Cæsar said to Metellus, when that
tribune interfered to hinder him from entering
the Roman treasury, "Young man, it is easier
for me to put you to death than to say that I
will;" and the youth yielded. In earlier days,
he was taken by pirates. What then? He threw
himself into their ship, established the most
extraordinary intimacies, told them stories, de-
claimed to them; if they did not applaud his
speeches, he threatened them with hanging,—
which he performed afterwards,—and, in a short
time, was master of all on board. A man this is
who cannot be disconcerted, and so can never
play his last card, but has a reserve of power when
he has hit his mark. With a serene face, he sub-
verts a kingdom. What is told of him is miraculous; it affects men so. The confidence of men
in him is lavish, and he changes the face of the
world, and histories, poems and new philoso-

phies arise to account for him. A supreme commander over all his passions and affections; but
the secret of his ruling is higher than that. It is
the power of Nature running without impediment from the brain and will into the hands.[1]
Men and women are his game. Where they are,
he cannot be without resource. "Whoso can
speak well," said Luther, "is a man." It was
men of this stamp that the Grecian States used
to ask of Sparta for generals. They did not send
to Lacedæmon for troops, but they said, "Send
us a commander;" and Pausanias, or Gylippus,
or Brasidas, or Agis, was despatched by the
Ephors.

It is easy to illustrate this overpowering personality by these examples of soldiers and kings;
but there are men of the most peaceful way of
life and peaceful principle, who are felt wherever
they go, as sensibly as a July sun or a December frost, — men who, if they speak, are heard,
though they speak in a whisper, — who, when
they act, act effectually, and what they do is
imitated; and these examples may be found on
very humble platforms as well as on high ones.

In old countries a high money value is set on
the services of men who have achieved a personal distinction. He who has points to carry

must hire, not a skilful attorney, but a commanding person. A barrister in England is reputed to have made thirty or forty thousand pounds per annum in representing the claims of railroad companies before committees of the House of Commons. His clients pay not so much for legal as for manly accomplishments,— for courage, conduct and a commanding social position, which enable him to make their claims heard and respected.[1]

I know very well that among our cool and calculating people, where every man mounts guard over himself, where heats and panics and abandonments are quite out of the system, there is a good deal of skepticism as to extraordinary influence. To talk of an overpowering mind rouses the same jealousy and defiance which one may observe round a table where anybody is recounting the marvellous anecdotes of mesmerism. Each auditor puts a final stroke to the discourse by exclaiming, " Can he mesmerize *me?* " So each man inquires if any orator can change *his* convictions.

But does any one suppose himself to be quite impregnable? Does he think that not possibly a man may come to him who shall persuade him out of his most settled determination?— for

example, good sedate citizen as he is, to make
a fanatic of him, — or, if he is penurious, to
squander money for some purpose he now least
thinks of, — or, if he is a prudent, industrious
person, to forsake his work, and give days and
weeks to a new interest? No, he defies any one,
every one. Ah! he is thinking of resistance, and
of a different turn from his own. But what if
one should come of the same turn of mind as
his own, and who sees much farther on his own
way than he? A man who has tastes like mine,
but in greater power, will rule me any day, and
make me love my ruler.

Thus it is not powers of speech that we primarily consider under this word *eloquence*, but the
power that being present, gives them their perfection, and being absent, leaves them a merely
superficial value. Eloquence is the appropriate
organ of the highest personal energy. Personal
ascendency may exist with or without adequate
talent for its expression. It is as surely felt as
a mountain or a planet; but when it is weaponed
with a power of speech, it seems first to become
truly human, works actively in all directions,
and supplies the imagination with fine materials.

This circumstance enters into every consideration of the power of orators, and is the key

VII

to all their effects. In the assembly, you shall
find the orator and the audience in perpetual
balance ; and the predominance of either is in-
dicated by the choice of topic. If the talents for
speaking exist, but not the strong personality,
then there are good speakers who perfectly receive and express the will of the audience, and
the commonest populace is flattered by hearing its low mind returned to it with every
ornament which happy talent can add. But if
there be personality in the orator, the face of
things changes. The audience is thrown into
the attitude of pupil, follows like a child its
preceptor, and hears what he has to say. It
is as if, amidst the king's council at Madrid,
Ximenes urged that an advantage might be
gained of France, and Mendoza that Flanders
might be kept down, and Columbus, being introduced, was interrogated whether his geographical
knowledge could aid the cabinet; and he can
say nothing to one party or to the other, but
he can show how all Europe can be dimin-
ished and reduced under the king, by annexing
to Spain a continent as large as six or seven
Europes.

This balance between the orator and the audience is expressed in what is called the perti-

nence of the speaker.[1] There is always a rivalry
between the orator and the occasion, between
the demands of the hour and the prepossession
of the individual. The emergency which has
convened the meeting is usually of more importance than anything the debaters have in their
minds, and therefore becomes imperative to
them. But if one of them have anything of
commanding necessity in his heart, how speedily
he will find vent for it, and with the applause
of the assembly! This balance is observed in
the privatest intercourse. Poor Tom never
knew the time when the present occurrence was
so trivial that he could tell what was passing in
his mind without being checked for unseason-
able speech; but let Bacon speak and wise men
would rather listen though the revolution of
kingdoms was on foot. I have heard it reported
of an eloquent preacher, whose voice is not
yet forgotten in this city,[2] that, on occasions
of death or tragic disaster which overspread
the congregation with gloom, he ascended the
pulpit with more than his usual alacrity,
and turning to his favorite lessons of devout
and jubilant thankfulness, — "Let us praise
the Lord," — carried audience, mourners and
mourning along with him, and swept away all the

impertinence of private sorrow with his hosan-
nas and songs of praise. Pepys says of Lord
Clarendon (with whom " he is mad in love ") on
his return from a conference, " I did never observe how much easier a man do speak when he
knows all the company to be below him, than
in him ; for, though he spoke indeed excellent
well, yet his manner and freedom of doing it,
as if he played with it, and was informing only
all the rest of the company, was mighty pretty."

This rivalry between the orator and the
occasion is inevitable, and the occasion always
yields to the eminence of the speaker; for a
great man is the greatest of occasions. Of course
the interest of the audience and of the orator
conspire. It is well with them only when his
influence is complete ; then only they are well
pleased. Especially he consults his power by
making instead of taking his theme. If he
should attempt to instruct the people in that
which they already know, he would fail; but
by making them wise in that which he knows,
he has the advantage of the assembly every
moment. Napoleon's tactics of marching on
the angle of an army, and always presenting a
superiority of numbers, is the orator's secret
also.

The several talents which the orator employs, the splendid weapons which went to the equipment of Demosthenes, of Æschines, of Demades the natural orator, of Fox, of Pitt, of Patrick Henry, of Adams, of Mirabeau, deserve a special enumeration. We must not quite omit to name the principal pieces.

The orator, as we have seen, must be a substantial personality. Then, first, he must have power of statement, — must have the fact, and know how to tell it.[1] In any knot of men conversing on any subject, the person who knows most about it will have the ear of the company if he wishes it, and lead the conversation, no matter what genius or distinction other men there present may have; and in any public assembly, him who has the facts and can and will state them, people will listen to, though he is otherwise ignorant, though he is hoarse and ungraceful, though he stutters and screams.

In a court of justice the audience are impartial; they really wish to sift the statements and know what the truth is. And in the examination of witnesses there usually leap out, quite unexpectedly, three or four stubborn words or phrases which are the pith and fate of the business, which sink into the ear of all parties, and stick there, and determine the cause. All the rest is repetition and qualifying; and the court and the county have really come together to arrive at these three or four memorable expressions which betrayed the mind and meaning of somebody.

In every company the man with the fact is like the guide you hire to lead your party up a mountain, or through a difficult country. He may not compare with any of the party in mind or breeding or courage or possessions, but he is much more important to the present need than any of them.[1] That is what we go to the court-house for, — the statement of the fact, and of a general fact, the real relation of all the parties; and it is the certainty with which, indifferently in any affair that is well handled, the truth stares us in the face through all the disguises that are put upon it, — a piece of the well-known human life, — that makes the interest of a court-room to the intelligent spectator.

I remember long ago being attracted, by the distinction of the counsel and the local importance of the cause, into the court-room. The prisoner's counsel were the strongest and cunningest lawyers in the commonwealth. They drove the attorney for the state from corner to corner, taking his reasons from under him, and reducing him to silence, but not to submission. When hard pressed, he revenged himself, in his turn, on the judge, by requiring the court to define what *salvage* was. The court, thus pushed, tried words, and said everything it could think of to fill the time, supposing cases, and describing duties of insurers, captains, pilots and miscellaneous sea-officers that are or might be, — like a schoolmaster puzzled by a hard sum, who reads the context with emphasis. But all this flood not serving the cuttle-fish to get away in, the horrible shark of the district attorney being still there, grimly awaiting with his " The court must define,"— the poor court pleaded its inferiority. The superior court must establish the law for this, and it read away piteously the decisions of the Supreme Court, but read to those who had no pity. The judge was forced at last to rule something, and the lawyers saved their rogue under the fog of a definition. The parts were so well cast and discriminated that it was an interesting game to watch. The government was well enough represented. It was stupid, but it had a strong will and possession, and stood on that to the last. The judge had a task beyond his preparation, yet his position remained real : he was there to represent a great reality, — the justice of states, which we could well enough see beetling over his head, and which his trifling talk nowise affected, and did not impede, since he was entirely well meaning.

The statement of the fact, however, sinks before the statement of the law, which requires immeasurably higher powers, and is a rarest gift, being in all great masters one and the same thing,—in lawyers nothing technical, but always some piece of common sense, alike interesting to laymen as to clerks. Lord Mansfield's merit is the merit of common sense.' It is the same quality we admire in Aristotle, Montaigne, Cervantes, or in Samuel Johnson or Franklin. Its application to law seems quite accidental. Each of Mansfield's famous decisions contains a level sentence or two which hit the mark. His sentences are not always finished to the eye, but are finished to the mind. The sentences are involved, but a solid proposition is set forth, a true distinction is drawn. They come from and they go to the sound human understanding; and I read without surprise that the black-letter lawyers of the day sneered at his " equitable decisions," as if they were not also learned. This, indeed, is what speech is for, — to make the statement; and all that is called eloquence seems to me of little use for the most part to those who have it, but inestimable to such as have something to say.

Next to the knowledge of the fact and its law is method, which constitutes the genius and efficiency of all remarkable men. A crowd of men go up to Faneuil Hall; they are all pretty well acquainted with the object of the meeting; they have all read the facts in the same newspapers. The orator possesses no information which his hearers have not, yet he teaches them to see the thing with his eyes. By the new placing, the circumstances acquire new solidity and worth. Every fact gains consequence by his naming it, and trifles become important. His expressions fix themselves in men's memories, and fly from mouth to mouth. His mind has some new principle of order. Where he looks, all things fly into their places. What will he say next? Let this man speak, and this man only. By applying the habits of a higher style of thought to the common affairs of this world, he introduces beauty and magnificence wherever he goes. Such a power was Burke's, and of this genius we have had some brilliant examples in our own political and legal men.

Imagery. The orator must be, to a certain extent, a poet. We are such imaginative creatures that nothing so works on the human mind, barbarous or civil, as a trope. Condense some daily experience into a glowing symbol, and an audience is electrified. They feel as if they already possessed some new right and power over a fact which they can detach, and so completely master in thought. It is a wonderful aid to the memory, which carries away the image and never loses it. A popular assembly, like the House of Commons, or the French Chamber, or the American Congress, is commanded by these two powers, — first by a fact, then by skill of statement. Put the argument into a concrete shape, into an image, — some hard phrase, round and solid as a ball, which they can see and handle and carry home with them, — and the cause is half won.

Statement, method, imagery, selection, tenacity of memory, power of dealing with facts, of illuminating them, of sinking them by ridicule or by diversion of the mind, rapid generalization, humor, pathos, are keys which the orator holds ; and yet these fine gifts are not eloquence, and do often hinder a man's attainment of it. And if we come to the heart of the mystery, perhaps we should say that the truly eloquent man is a sane man with power to communicate his sanity.[1] If you arm the man with the extraordinary weapons of this art, give him a grasp of facts, learning, quick fancy, sarcasm, splendid allusion, interminable illustration, — all these talents, so potent and charming, have an equal power to ensnare and mislead the audience and the orator. His talents are too much for him, his horses run away with him; and people always perceive whether you drive or whether the horses take the bits in their teeth and run.[2] But these talents are quite something else when they are subordinated and serve him; and we go to Washington, or to Westminster Hall, or might well go round the world, to see a man who drives, and is not run away with, — a man who, in prosecuting great designs, has an absolute command of the means of representing his ideas, and uses them only to express these; placing facts, placing men; amid the inconceivable levity of human beings, never for an instant warped from his erectness. There is for every man a statement possible of that truth which he is most unwilling to receive, — a statement possible, so broad and so pungent that he cannot get away from it, but must either bend to it or die of it. Else there would be no such word as eloquence, which means this. The listener cannot hide from himself that something has been shown him and the whole world which he did not wish to see; and as he cannot dispose of it, it disposes of him. The history of public men and affairs in America will readily furnish tragic examples of this fatal force.[1]

For the triumphs of the art somewhat more must still be required, namely a reinforcing of man from events, so as to give the double force of reason and destiny. In transcendent eloquence, there was ever some crisis in affairs, such as could deeply engage the man to the cause he pleads, and draw all this wide power to a point. For the explosions and eruptions, there must be accumulations of heat somewhere, beds of ignited anthracite at the centre. And in cases where profound conviction has been wrought, the eloquent man is he who is no beautiful speaker, but who is inwardly drunk with a certain belief. It agitates and tears him, and perhaps almost bereaves him of the power of articulation.[2] Then it rushes from him as in short, abrupt screams, in torrents of meaning. The possession the subject has of his mind is so entire that it insures an order of expression which

is the order of Nature itself, and so the order
of greatest force, and inimitable by any art.
And the main distinction between him and other
well-graced actors [1] is the conviction, communicated by every word, that his mind is contem-
plating a whole, and inflamed by the contemplation of the whole, and that the words and
sentences uttered by him, however admirable,
fall from him as unregarded parts of that terrible whole which he sees and which he means
that you shall see. Add to this concentration
a certain regnant calmness, which, in all the tu-
mult, never utters a premature syllable, but
keeps the secret of its means and method; and
the orator stands before the people as a demoni-
acal power to whose miracles they have no key.
This terrible earnestness makes good the ancient
superstition of the hunter, that the bullet will
hit its mark, which is first dipped in the marks-
man's blood.

Eloquence must be grounded on the plainest
narrative. Afterwards, it may warm itself until
it exhales symbols of every kind and color,
speaks only through the most poetic forms;
but, first and last, it must still be at bottom a
biblical statement of fact. The orator is thereby
an orator, that he keeps his feet ever on a fact.

Thus only is he invincible. No gifts, no graces, no power of wit or learning or illustration will make any amends for want of this. All audiences are just to this point. Fame of voice or of rhetoric will carry people a few times to hear a speaker; but they soon begin to ask, "What is he driving at?" and if this man does not stand for anything, he will be deserted. A good upholder of anything which they believe, a fact-speaker of any kind, they will long follow; but a pause in the speaker's own character is very properly a loss of attraction. The preacher enumerates his classes of men and I do not find my place therein; I suspect then that no man does. Everything is my cousin; and whilst he speaks things, I feel that he is touching some of my relations, and I am uneasy; but whilst he deals in words we are released from attention.[1] If you would lift me you must be on higher ground. If you would liberate me you must be free. If you would correct my false view of facts,— hold up to me the same facts in the true order of thought, and I cannot go back from the new conviction.

The power of Chatham, of Pericles, of Luther, rested on this strength of character, which, because it did not and could not fear anybody, made nothing of their antagonists, and became sometimes exquisitely provoking and sometimes terrific to these.

We are slenderly furnished with anecdotes of these men, nor can we help ourselves by those heavy books in which their discourses are reported. Some of them were writers, like Burke; but most of them were not, and no record at all adequate to their fame remains. Besides, what is best is lost, — the fiery life of the moment. But the conditions for eloquence always exist. It is always dying out of famous places and appearing in corners. Wherever the polarities meet, wherever the fresh moral sentiment, the instinct of freedom and duty, come in direct opposition to fossil conservatism and the thirst of gain, the spark will pass. The resistance to slavery in this country has been a fruitful nursery of orators.[1] The natural connection by which it drew to itself a train of moral reforms, and the slight yet sufficient party organization it offered, reinforced the city with new blood from the woods and mountains. Wild men, John Baptists, Hermit Peters, John Knoxes, utter the savage sentiment of Nature in the heart of commercial capitals. They send us every year some piece of aboriginal strength, some

tough oak-stick of a man who is not to be
silenced or insulted or intimidated by a mob,
because he is more mob than they, — one who
mobs the mob, — some sturdy countryman, on
whom neither money, nor politeness, nor hard
words, nor eggs, nor blows, nor brickbats make
any impression. He is fit to meet the barroom
wits and bullies ; he is a wit and a bully himself,
and something more : he is a graduate of the
plough, and the stub-hoe, and the bushwhacker ;
knows all the secrets of swamp and snow-bank,
and has nothing to learn of labor or poverty or
the rough of farming. His hard head went
through, in childhood, the drill of Calvinism,
with text and mortification, so that he stands
in the New England assembly a purer bit of
New England than any, and flings his sarcasms
right and left. He has not only the documents
in his pocket to answer all cavils and to prove
all his positions, but he has the eternal reason
in his head.[1] This man scornfully renounces
your civil organizations, — county, or city, or
governor, or army ; — is his own navy and
artillery, judge and jury, legislature and executive. He has learned his lessons in a bitter
school. Yet, if the pupil be of a texture to
bear it, the best university that can be recom-

mended to a man of ideas is the gauntlet of
the mobs.

He who will train himself to mastery in this
science of persuasion must lay the emphasis of
education, not on popular arts, but on character
and insight. Let him see that his speech is not
differenced from action; that when he has spoken
he has not done nothing, nor done wrong, but
has cleared his own skirts, has engaged himself
to wholesome exertion. Let him look on opposition as opportunity. He cannot be defeated
or put down. There is a principle of resurrection in him, an immortality of purpose. Men
are averse and hostile, to give value to their
suffrages. It is not the people that are in fault
for not being convinced, but he that cannot con-
vince them. He should mould them, armed as
he is with the reason and love which are also
the core of their nature. He is not to neutralize
their opposition, but he is to convert them into
· fiery apostles and publishers of the same wisdom.

The highest platform of eloquence is the
moral sentiment. It is what is called affirmative truth, and has the property of invigorating
the hearer ; and it conveys a hint of our eternity, when he feels himself addressed on grounds
which will remain when everything else is taken,

VII

and which have no trace of time or place or party. Everything hostile is stricken down in the presence of the sentiments; their majesty is felt by the most obdurate.[1] It is observable that as soon as one acts for large masses, the moral element will and must be allowed for, will and must work; and the men least accustomed to appeal to these sentiments invariably recall them when they address nations. Napoleon, even, must accept and use it as he can.

It is only to these simple strokes that the highest power belongs, — when a weak human hand touches, point by point, the eternal beams and rafters on which the whole structure of Nature and society is laid.[2] In this tossing sea of delusion we feel with our feet the adamant; in this dominion of chance we find a principle of permanence. For I do not accept that definition of Isocrates, that the office of his art is to make the great small and the small great; but I esteem this to be its perfection, — when the orator sees through all masks to the eternal scale of truth, in such sort that he can hold up before the eyes of men the fact of to-day steadily to that standard, thereby making the great great, and the small small, which is the true way to astonish and to reform mankind.[3]

All the chief orators of the world have been grave men, relying on this reality. One thought the philosophers of Demosthenes's own time found running through all his orations, — this namely, that "virtue secures its own success." "To stand on one's own feet" Heeren[1] finds the key-note to the discourses of Demosthenes, as of Chatham.

Eloquence, like every other art, rests on laws the most exact and determinate. It is the best speech of the best soul. It may well stand as the exponent of all that is grand and immortal in the mind. If it do not so become an instrument, but aspires to be somewhat of itself, and to glitter for show, it is false and weak. In its right exercise, it is an elastic, unexhausted power, — who has sounded, who has estimated it? — expanding with the expansion of our interests and affections. Its great masters, whilst they valued every help to its attainment, and thought no pains too great which contributed in any manner to further it, — resembling the Arabian warrior of fame, who wore seventeen weapons in his belt, and in personal combat used them all occasionally,[2] — yet subordinated all means; never permitted any talent — neither voice, rhythm, poetic power, anecdote, sarcasm

— to appear for show; but were grave men, who preferred their integrity to their talent, and esteemed that object for which they toiled, whether the prosperity of their country, or the laws, or a reformation, or liberty of speech or of the press, or letters, or morals, as above the whole world, and themselves also.[1]

V

DOMESTIC LIFE

I REACHED the middle of the mount
 Up which the incarnate soul must climb,
And paused for them, and looked around,
 With me who walked through space and time.

Five rosy boys with morning light
 Had leaped from one fair mother's arms,
Fronted the sun with hope as bright,
 And greeted God with childhood's psalms.

THOU shalt make thy house
The temple of a nation's vows.
Spirits of a higher strain
Who sought thee once shall seek again.
I detected many a god
Forth already on the road,
Ancestors of beauty come
In thy breast to make a home.

DOMESTIC LIFE

THE perfection of the providence for child-hood is easily acknowledged. The care which covers the seed of the tree under tough husks and stony cases provides for the human plant the mother's breast and the father's house. The size of the nestler is comic, and its tiny beseeching weakness is compensated perfectly by the happy patronizing look of the mother, who is a sort of high reposing Providence toward it. Welcome to the parents the puny struggler, strong in his weakness, his little arms more irresistible than the soldier's, his lips touched with persuasion which Chatham and Pericles in manhood had not. His unaffected lamentations when he lifts up his voice on high, or, more beautiful, the sobbing child, — the face all liquid .grief, as he tries to swallow his vexation, — soften all hearts to pity, and to mirthful and clamorous compassion. The small despot asks so little that all reason and all nature are on his side.[1] His ignorance is more charming than all knowledge, and his little sins more bewitching than any virtue. His flesh is angels' flesh, all alive. "Infancy," said Coleridge, "presents body and spirit in unity: the body is all animated." All day, between his three or four sleeps, he coos like a pigeon-house, sputters and spurs and puts on his faces of importance ; and when he fasts, the little Pharisee fails not to sound his trumpet before him. By lamplight he delights in shadows on the wall ; by daylight, in yellow and scarlet. Carry him out of doors, — he is overpowered by the light and by the extent of natural objects, and is silent.[1] Then presently begins his use of his fingers, and he studies power, the lesson of his race. First it appears in no great harm, in architectural tastes. Out of blocks, thread-spools, cards and checkers, he will build his pyramid with the gravity of Palladio. With an acoustic apparatus of whistle and rattle he explores the laws of sound. But chiefly, like his senior countrymen, the young American studies new and speedier modes of transportation. Mistrusting the cunning of his small legs, he wishes to ride on the necks and shoulders of all flesh. The small enchanter nothing can withstand, — no seniority of age, no gravity of character; uncles, aunts, grandsires, grandams, fall an easy prey : he conforms to nobody, all conform to him ; all caper and make mouths and babble and chirrup to him.

On the strongest shoulders he rides, and pulls
the hair of laurelled heads.[1]

"The childhood," said Milton, "shows the
man, as morning shows the day." The child
realizes to every man his own earliest remembrance, and so supplies a defect in our education, or enables us to live over the unconscious
history with a sympathy so tender as to be almost personal experience.[2]

Fast — almost too fast for the wistful curiosity of the parents, studious of the witchcraft of
curls and dimples and broken words — the little talker grows to a boy. He walks daily among
wonders: fire, light, darkness, the moon, the
stars, the furniture of the house, the red tin
horse, the domestics, who like rude foster-mo-
thers befriend and feed him, the faces that claim
his kisses, are all in turn absorbing; yet warm,
cheerful and with good appetite the little sovereign subdues them without knowing it; the
new knowledge is taken up into the life of to-
day and becomes the means of more. The blowing rose is a new event; the garden full of
flowers is Eden over again to the small Adam;
the rain, the ice, the frost, make epochs in his
life. What a holiday is the first snow in which
Twoshoes can be trusted abroad![3]

What art can paint or gild any object in after-
life with the glow which Nature gives to the
first baubles of childhood! St. Peter's cannot
have the magical power over us that the red and
gold covers of our first picture-book possessed.
How the imagination cleaves to the warm glo-
ries of that tinsel even now! What entertainments make every day bright and short for the
fine freshman! The street is old as Nature; the
persons all have their sacredness. His imaginative life dresses all things in their best. His
fears adorn the dark parts with poetry. He has
heard of wild horses and of bad boys, and with
a pleasing terror he watches at his gate for the
passing of those varieties of each species. The
first ride into the country, the first bath in running water, the first time the skates are put
on, the first game out of doors in moonlight,
the books of the nursery, are new chapters
of joy. The Arabian Nights' Entertainments,
the Seven Champions of Christendom, Robin-
son Crusoe and the Pilgrim's Progress, — what
mines of thought and emotion, what a ward-
robe to dress the whole world withal, are in this
encyclopædia of young thinking![1] And so by
beautiful traits, which without art yet seem the
masterpiece of wisdom, provoking the love that

watches and educates him, the little pilgrim prosecutes the journey through Nature which he has thus gayly begun. He grows up the ornament and joy of the house, which rings to his glee, to rosy boyhood.[1]

The household is the home of the *man*, as well as of the child.[2] The events that occur therein are more near and affecting to us than those which are sought in senates and academies. Domestic events are certainly our affair. What are called public events may or may not be ours. If a man wishes to acquaint himself with the real history of the world, with the spirit of the age, he must not go first to the state-house or the court-room. The subtle spirit of life must be sought in facts nearer. It is what is done and suffered in the house, in the constitution, in the temperament, in the personal history, that has the profoundest interest for us. Fact is better than fiction, if only we could get pure fact. Do you think any rhetoric or any romance would get your ear from the wise gypsy who could tell straight on the real fortunes of the man; who could reconcile your moral character and your natural history; who could explain your misfortunes, your fevers, your debts, your temperament, your habits of thought, your tastes, and, in every explanation, not sever you from the whole, but unite you to it? Is it not plain that not in senates, or courts, or chambers of commerce, but in the dwelling-house must the true character and hope of the time be consulted? These facts are, to be sure, harder to read. It is easier to count the census, or compute the square extent of a territory, to criticise its polity, books, art, than to come to the persons and dwellings of men and read their character and hope in their way of life. Yet we are always hovering round this better divination. In one form or another we are always returning to it. The physiognomy and phrenology of to-day are rash and mechanical systems enough, but they rest on everlasting foundations. We are sure that the sacred form of man is not seen in these whimsical, pitiful and sinister masks (masks which we wear and which we meet), these bloated and shrivelled bodies, bald heads, bead eyes, short winds, puny and precarious healths and early deaths.[1] We live ruins amidst ruins. The great facts are the near ones. The account of the body is to be sought in the mind. The history of your fortunes is written first in your life.

Let us come then out of the public square and enter the domestic precinct. Let us go to the

sitting-room, the table-talk and the expenditure
of our contemporaries. An increased consciousness of the soul, you say, characterizes the period.
Let us see if it has not only arranged the atoms
at the circumference, but the atoms at the core.
Does the household obey an idea? Do you see
the man, — his form, genius and aspiration, —
in his economy? Is that translucent, thorough-
lighted? There should be nothing confounding
and conventional in economy, but the genius
and love of the man so conspicuously marked
in all his estate that the eye that knew him should
read his character in his property, in his grounds,
in his ornaments, in every expense. A man's
money should not follow the direction of his
neighbor's money, but should represent to him
the things he would willingliest do with it. I
am not one thing and my expenditure another.
My expenditure is me. That our expenditure
and our character are twain, is the vice of society.

We ask the price of many things in shops and
stalls, but some things each man buys without
hesitation; if it were only letters at the post-
office, conveyance in carriages and boats, tools
for his work, books that are written to his condition, etc. Let him never buy anything else

than what he wants, never subscribe at others'
instance, never give unwillingly. Thus, a scholar
is a literary foundation. All his expense is for
Aristotle, Fabricius, Erasmus and Petrarch. Do
not ask him to help with his savings young
drapers or grocers to stock their shops, or eager
agents to lobby in legislatures, or join a company
to build a factory or a fishing-craft. These things
are also to be done, but not by such as he. How
could such a book as Plato's Dialogues have
come down, but for the sacred savings of scholars
and their fantastic appropriation of them? [1]

Another man is a mechanical genius, an inventor of looms, a builder of ships, — a ship-
building foundation, and could achieve nothing
if he should dissipate himself on books or on
horses. Another is a farmer, an agricultural
foundation; another is a chemist, and the same
rule holds for all. We must not make believe
with our money, but spend heartily, and buy *up*
and not *down*.

I am afraid that, so considered, our houses
will not be found to have unity and to express
the best thought. The household, the calling,
the friendships, of the citizen are not homo-
geneous. His house ought to show us his honest
opinion of what makes his well-being when he

rests among his kindred, and forgets all affectation, compliance, and even exertion of will. He
brings home whatever commodities and ornaments have for years allured his pursuit, and his
character must be seen in them. But what idea
predominates in our houses? Thrift first, then
convenience and pleasure. Take off all the roofs,
from street to street, and we shall seldom find
the temple of any higher god than Prudence.
The progress of domestic living has been in
cleanliness, in ventilation, in health, in decorum,
in countless means and arts of comfort, in the
concentration of all the utilities of every clime in
each house. They are arranged for low benefits.
The houses of the rich are confectioners' shops,
where we get sweetmeats and wine ; the houses
of the poor are imitations of these to the extent
of their ability. With these ends housekeeping
is not beautiful ; it cheers and raises neither the
husband, the wife, nor the child ; neither the
host nor the guest ; it oppresses women. A
house kept to the end of prudence is laborious
without joy ; a house kept to the end of display
is impossible to all but a few women, and their
success is dearly bought.[1]

If we look at this matter curiously, it becomes
dangerous. We need all the force of an idea to

lift this load, for the wealth and multiplication of conveniences embarrass us, especially in northern climates. The shortest enumeration of our wants in this rugged climate appalls us by the multitude of things not easy to be done. And if you look at the multitude of particulars, one would say : Good housekeeping is impossible; order is too precious a thing to dwell with men and women. See, in families where there is both substance and taste, at what expense any favorite punctuality is maintained. If the children, for example, are considered, dressed, dieted, attended, kept in proper company, schooled and at home fostered by the parents, — then does the hospitality of the house suffer ; friends are less carefully bestowed, the daily table less catered. If the hours of meals are punctual, the apartments are slovenly. If the linens and hangings are clean and fine and the furniture good, the yard, the garden, the fences are neglected. If all are well attended, then must the master and mistress be studious of particulars at the cost of their own accomplishments and growth; or persons are treated as things.[1]

The difficulties to be overcome must be freely admitted ; they are many and great. Nor are they to be disposed of by any criticism or amendment of particulars taken one at a time, but only by the arrangement of the household to a higher end than those to which our dwellings are usually built and furnished. And is there any calamity more grave, or that more invokes the best good will to remove it, than this? — to go from chamber to chamber and see no beauty; to find in the housemates no aim; to hear an endless chatter and blast; to be compelled to criticise; to hear only to dissent and to be disgusted; to find no invitation to what is good in us, and no receptacle for what is wise : — this is a great price to pay for sweet bread and warm lodging, — being defrauded of affinity, of repose, of genial culture and the inmost presence of beauty.[1]

It is a sufficient accusation of our ways of living, and certainly ought to open our ear to every good-minded reformer, that our idea of domestic well-being now needs wealth to execute it. Give me the means, says the wife, and your house shall not annoy your taste nor waste your time. On hearing this we understand how these Means have come to be so omnipotent on earth. And indeed the love of wealth seems to grow chiefly out of the root of the love of the Beautiful. The desire of gold

VII

is not for gold. It is not the love of much wheat and wool and household stuff. It is the means of freedom and benefit. We scorn shifts; we desire the elegance of munificence; we desire at least to put no stint or limit on our parents, relatives, guests or dependents; we desire to play the benefactor and the prince with our townsmen, with the stranger at the gate, with the bard or the beauty, with the man or woman of worth who alights at our door. How can we do this, if the wants of each day imprison us in lucrative labors, and constrain us to a continual vigilance lest we be betrayed into expense?

Give us wealth, and the home shall exist. But that is a very imperfect and inglorious solution of the problem, and therefore no solution. "*Give us wealth.*" You ask too much. Few have wealth, but all must have a home. Men are not born rich; and in getting wealth the man is generally sacrificed, and often is sacrificed without acquiring wealth at last. Besides, that cannot be the right answer;—there are objections to wealth. Wealth is a shift. The wise man angles with himself only, and with no meaner bait. Our whole use of wealth needs revision and reform. Generosity does not consist in giving money or money's worth. These

so-called *goods* are only the shadow of good.
To give money to a sufferer is only a come-off.
It is only a postponement of the real payment,
a bribe paid for silence, a credit system in which
a paper promise to pay answers for the time
instead of liquidation. We owe to man higher
succors than food and fire. We owe to man
man.[1] If he is sick, is unable, is mean-spirited
and odious, it is because there is so much of
his nature which is unlawfully withholden from
him. He should be visited in this his prison
with rebuke to the evil demons, with manly
encouragement, with no mean-spirited offer
of condolence because you have not money, or
mean offer of money as the utmost benefit, but
by your heroism, your purity and your faith.
You are to bring with you that spirit which is
understanding, health and self-help. To offer
him money in lieu of these is to do him the
same wrong as when the bridegroom offers his
betrothed virgin a sum of money to release him
from his engagements. The great depend on
their heart, not on their purse. Genius and virtue, like diamonds, are best plain-set, — set in
lead, set in poverty. The greatest man in history
was the poorest. How was it with the captains
and sages of Greece and Rome, with Socrates,

with Epaminondas? Aristides was made general receiver of Greece, to collect the tribute which each state was to furnish against the barbarian. "Poor," says Plutarch, "when he set about it, poorer when he had finished it." How was it with Æmilius and Cato? What kind of a house was kept by Paul and John, by Milton and Marvell, by Samuel Johnson, by Samuel Adams in Boston and Jean Paul Richter at Baireuth?

I think it plain that this voice of communities and ages, 'Give us wealth, and the good household shall exist,' is vicious, and leaves the whole difficulty untouched. It is better, certainly, in this form, 'Give us your labor, and the household begins.' I see not how serious labor, the labor of all and every day, is to be avoided; and many things betoken a revolution of opinion and practice in regard to manual labor that may go far to aid our practical inquiry. Another age may divide the manual labor of the world more equally on all the members of society, and so make the labors of a few hours avail to the wants and add to the vigor of the man. But the reform that applies itself to the household must not be partial. It must correct the whole system of our social living. It must come with plain living and high thinking; it must break up caste, and put domestic service on another foundation. It must come in connection with a true acceptance by each man of his vocation, — not chosen by his parents or friends, but by his genius, with earnestness and love.

Nor is this redress so hopeless as it seems. Certainly, if we begin by reforming particulars of our present system, correcting a few evils and letting the rest stand, we shall soon give up in despair. For our social forms are very far from truth and equity. But the way to set the axe at the root of the tree is to raise our aim. Let us understand then that a house should bear witness in all its economy that human culture is the end to which it is built and garnished. It stands there under the sun and moon to ends analogous, and not less noble than theirs. It is not for festivity, it is not for sleep: but the pine and the oak shall gladly descend from the mountains to uphold the roof of men as faithful and necessary as themselves; to be the shelter always open to good and true persons; — a hall which shines with sincerity, brows ever tranquil, and a demeanor impossible to disconcert; whose inmates know what they want; who do not ask your house how theirs should be kept. They have aims; they cannot pause for trifles.[1] The diet of the house does not create its order, but knowledge, character, action, absorb so much life and yield so much entertainment that the refectory has ceased to be so curiously studied. With a change of aim has followed a change of the whole scale by which men and things were wont to be measured. Wealth and poverty are seen for what they are. It begins to be seen that the poor are only they who feel poor, and poverty consists in feeling poor. The rich, as we reckon them, and among them the very rich, —in a true scale would be found very indigent and ragged. The great make us feel, first of all, the indifference of circumstances. They call into activity the higher perceptions and subdue the low habits of comfort and luxury; but the higher perceptions find their objects everywhere; only the low habits need palaces and banquets.

Let a man, then, say, My house is here in the county, for the culture of the county; — an eating-house and sleeping-house for travellers it shall be, but it shall be much more. I pray you, O excellent wife, not to cumber yourself and me to get a rich dinner for this man or this woman who has alighted at our gate, nor a bed-chamber made ready at too great a cost. These things, if they are curious in them, they can get for a dollar at any village. But let this stranger, if he will, in your looks, in your accent and behavior, read your heart and earnestness, your thought and will, which he cannot buy at any price, in any village or city; and which he may well travel fifty miles, and dine sparely and sleep hard in order to behold. Certainly, let the board be spread and let the bed be dressed for the traveller; but let not the emphasis of hospitality lie in these things. Honor to the house where they are simple to the verge of hardship, so that there the intellect is awake and reads the laws of the universe, the soul worships truth and love, honor and courtesy flow into all deeds.[1]

There was never a country in the world which could so easily exhibit this heroism as ours; never any where the state has made such efficient provision for popular education, where intellectual entertainment is so within reach of youthful ambition.[2] The poor man's son is educated. There is many a humble house in every city, in every town, where talent and taste and sometimes genius dwell with poverty and labor. Who has not seen, and who can see unmoved, under a low roof, the eager, blushing boys discharging as they can their household chores,

and hastening into the sitting-room to the study
of to-morrow's merciless lesson, yet stealing
time to read one chapter more of the novel
hardly smuggled into the tolerance of father and
mother, — atoning for the same by some pages
of Plutarch or Goldsmith ; the warm sympathy
with which they kindle each other in school-
yard or in barn or wood-shed with scraps of
poetry or song, with phrases of the last oration,
or mimicry of the orator ; the youthful criticism,
on Sunday, of the sermons ; the school declamation faithfully rehearsed at home, sometimes to
the fatigue, sometimes to the admiration of
sisters ; the first solitary joys of literary vanity,
when the translation or the theme has been completed, sitting alone near the top of the house ;
the cautious comparison of the attractive advertisement of the arrival of Macready, Booth or
Kemble, or of the discourse of a well-known
speaker, with the expense of the entertainment ;
the affectionate delight with which they greet
the return of each one after the early separations
which school or business require ; the foresight
with which, during such absences, they hive the
honey which opportunity offers, for the ear and
imagination of the others ; and the unrestrained
glee with which they disburden themselves of

their early mental treasures when the holidays
bring them again together? What is the hoop
that holds them stanch? It is the iron band of
poverty, of necessity, of austerity, which, exclud-
ing them from the sensual enjoyments which
make other boys too early old, has directed their
activity in safe and right channels, and made
them, despite themselves, reverers of the grand,
the beautiful and the good. Ah! short-sighted
students of books, of Nature and of man! too
happy, could they know their advantages.[1] They
pine for freedom from that mild parental yoke;
they sigh for fine clothes, for rides, for the
theatre and premature freedom and dissipation,
which others possess. Woe to them if their
wishes were crowned! The angels that dwell
with them and are weaving laurels of life for
their youthful brows, are Toil and Want, and
Truth, and Mutual Faith.[2]

In many parts of true economy a cheering
lesson may be learned from the mode of life and
manners of the later Romans, as described to
us in the letters of the younger Pliny. Nor can
I resist the temptation of quoting so trite an
instance as the noble housekeeping of Lord Falk-
land in Clarendon: "His house being within
little more than ten miles from Oxford, he con-

tracted familiarity and friendship with the most polite and accurate men of that University, who found such an immenseness of wit and such a solidity of judgment in him, so infinite a fancy, bound in by a most logical ratiocination, such a vast knowledge that he was not ignorant in anything, yet such an excessive humility, as if he had known nothing, that they frequently resorted and dwelt with him, as in a college situated in a purer air; so that his house was a university in a less volume, whither they came, not so much for repose as study, and to examine and refine those grosser propositions which laziness and consent made current in vulgar conversation."

I honor that man whose ambition it is, not to win laurels in the state or the army, not to be a jurist or a naturalist, not to be a poet or a commander, but to be a master of living well, and to administer the offices of master or servant, of husband, father and friend. But it requires as much breadth of power for this as for those other functions, — as much, or more, — and the reason for the failure is the same. I think the vice of our housekeeping is that it does not hold man sacred. The vice of government, the vice of education, the vice of religion, is one with that of private life.

In the old fables we used to read of a cloak
brought from fairy-land as a gift for the fairest
and purest in Prince Arthur's court. It was to
be her prize whom it would fit. Every one was
eager to try it on, but it would fit nobody : for
one it was a world too wide, for the next it
dragged on the ground, and for the third it
shrunk to a scarf. They, of course, said that
the devil was in the mantle, for really the truth
was in the mantle, and was exposing the ugliness which each would fain conceal. All drew
back with terror from the garment. The innocent Venelas alone could wear it.[1] In like manner, every man is provided in his thought with
a measure of man which he applies to every
passenger. Unhappily, not one in many thousands comes up to the stature and proportions
of the model. Neither does the measurer himself; neither do the people in the street; neither
do the select individuals whom he admires, —
the heroes of the race. When he inspects them
critically, he discovers that their aims are low,
that they are too quickly satisfied. He observes
the swiftness with which life culminates, and the
humility of the expectations of the greatest part
of men. To each occurs, soon after the age of
puberty, some event or society or way of living,

which becomes the crisis of life and the chief
fact in their history.   In woman, it is love and
marriage (which is more reasonable); and yet it
is pitiful to date and measure all the facts and
sequel of an unfolding life from such a youthful
and generally inconsiderate period as the age of
courtship and marriage. In men, it is their place
of education, choice of an employment, settlement in a town, or removal to the East or to
the West, or some other magnified trifle which
makes the meridian moment, and all the after
years and actions only derive interest from their
relation to that. Hence it comes that we soon
catch the trick of each man's conversation, and
knowing his two or three main facts, anticipate
what he thinks of each new topic that rises. It
is scarcely less perceivable in educated men, so
called, than in the uneducated. I have seen
finely endowed men at college festivals, ten,
twenty years after they had left the halls, returning, as it seemed, the same boys who went away.
The same jokes pleased, the same straws tickled;
the manhood and offices they brought thither
at this return seemed mere ornamental masks;
underneath they were boys yet. We never come
to be citizens of the world, but are still villagers,
who think that every thing in their petty town

is a little superior to the same thing anywhere else. In each the circumstance signalized differs, but in each it is made the coals of an ever-burning egotism. In one, it was his going to sea; in a second, the difficulties he combated in going to college; in a third, his journey to the West, or his voyage to Canton; in a fourth, his coming out of the Quaker Society; in a fifth, his new diet and regimen; in a sixth, his coming forth from the abolition organizations; and in a seventh, his going into them. It is a life of toys and trinkets. We are too easily pleased.

I think this sad result appears in the manners. The men we see in each other do not give us the image and likeness of man. The men we see are whipped through the world; they are harried, wrinkled, anxious; they all seem the hacks of some invisible riders. How seldom do we behold tranquillity! We have never yet seen a man. We do not know the majestic manners that belong to him, which appease and exalt the beholder. There are no divine persons with us, and the multitude do not hasten to be divine. And yet we hold fast, all our lives long, a faith in a better life, in better men, in clean and noble relations, notwithstanding our total inexperience of a true

society.[1] Certainly this was not the intention
of Nature, to produce, with all this immense
expenditure of means and power, so cheap and
humble a result. The aspirations in the heart
after the good and true teach us better, — nay,
the men themselves suggest a better life.

Every individual nature has its own beauty.
One is struck in every company, at every fireside, with the riches of Nature, when he hears so
many new tones, all musical, sees in each person
original manners, which have a proper and peculiar charm, and reads new expressions of face.
He perceives that Nature has laid for each the
foundations of a divine building, if the soul will
build thereon. There is no face, no form, which
one cannot in fancy associate with great power
of intellect or with generosity of soul. In our
experience, to be sure, beauty is not, as it ought
to be, the dower of man and of woman as
invariably as sensation. Beauty is, even in
the beautiful, occasional, — or, as one has said,
culminating and perfect only a single moment,
before which it is unripe, and after which it is
on the wane. But beauty is never quite absent
from our eyes. Every face, every figure, suggests its own right and sound estate. Our
friends are not their own highest form. But

let the hearts they have agitated witness what
power has lurked in the traits of these structures
of clay that pass and repass us!¹ The secret
power of form over the imagination and affections transcends all our philosophy. The first
glance we meet may satisfy us that matter is
the vehicle of higher powers than its own, and
that no laws of line or surface can ever account
for the inexhaustible expressiveness of form.
We see heads that turn on the pivot of the
spine, — no more ; and we see heads that seem
to turn on a pivot as deep as the axle of the
world, — so slow, and lazily, and great, they
move. We see on the lip of our companion
the presence or absence of the great masters of
thought and poetry to his mind. We read in
his brow, on meeting him after many years,
that he is where we left him, or that he has
made great strides.

Whilst thus Nature and the hints we draw
from man suggest a true and lofty life, a household equal to the beauty and grandeur of this
world, especially we learn the same lesson from
those best relations to individual men which
the heart is always prompting us to form.
Happy will that house be in which the relations are formed from character ; after the high-

est, and not after the lowest order; the house in which character marries, and not confusion and a miscellany of unavowable motives. Then shall marriage be a covenant to secure to either party the sweetness and honor of being a calm, continuing, inevitable benefactor to the other. Yes, and the sufficient reply to the skeptic who doubts the competence of man to elevate and to be elevated is in that desire and power to stand in joyful and ennobling intercourse with individuals, which makes the faith and the practice of all reasonable men.

The ornament of a house is the friends who frequent it. There is no event greater in life than the appearance of new persons about our hearth, except it be the progress of the character which draws them. It has been finely added by Landor to his definition of the *great man*, " It is he who can call together the most select company when it pleases him." A verse of the old Greek Menander remains, which runs in translation : —

" Not on the store of sprightly wine,
 Nor plenty of delicious meats,
 Though generous Nature did design
 To court us with perpetual treats, —
'T is not on these we for content depend,
So much as on the shadow of a Friend." [1]

It is the happiness which, where it is truly known, postpones all other satisfactions, and makes politics and commerce and churches cheap. For we figure to ourselves, — do we not? — that when men shall meet as they should, as states meet, — each a benefactor, a shower of falling stars, so rich with deeds, with thoughts, with so much accomplishment, — it shall be the festival of Nature, which all things symbolize; and perhaps Love is only the highest symbol of Friendship, as all other things seem symbols of love. In the progress of each man's character, his relations to the best men, which at first seem only the romances of youth, acquire a graver importance; and he will have learned the lesson of life who is skilful in the ethics of friendship.

Beyond its primary ends of the conjugal, parental and amicable relations, the household should cherish the beautiful arts and the sentiment of veneration.

1. Whatever brings the dweller into a finer life, what educates his eye, or ear, or hand, whatever purifies and enlarges him, may well find place there. And yet let him not think that a property in beautiful objects is necessary to

vII

his apprehension of them, and seek to turn his
house into a museum. Rather let the noble
practice of the Greeks find place in our society,
and let the creations of the plastic arts be collected with care in galleries by the piety and
taste of the people, and yielded as freely as the
sunlight to all. Meantime, be it remembered, we
are artists ourselves, and competitors, each one,
with Phidias and Raphael in the production of
what is graceful or grand. The fountain of
beauty is the heart, and every generous thought
illustrates the walls of your chamber.' Why
should we owe our power of attracting our
friends to pictures and vases, to cameos and
architecture? Why should we convert ourselves
into showmen and appendages to our fine houses
and our works of art? If by love and nobleness
we take up into ourselves the beauty we admire,
we shall spend it again on all around us. The
man, the woman, needs not the embellishment
of canvas and marble, whose every act is a subject for the sculptor, and to whose eye the gods
and nymphs never appear ancient, for they know
by heart the whole instinct of majesty.

I do not undervalue the fine instruction which
statues and pictures give. But I think the public museum in each town will one day relieve

the private house of this charge of owning and exhibiting them. I go to Rome and see on the walls of the Vatican the Transfiguration, painted by Raphael, reckoned the first picture in the world ; or in the Sistine Chapel I see the grand sibyls and prophets, painted in fresco by Michel Angelo, — which have every day now for three hundred years inflamed the imagination and exalted the piety of what vast multitudes of men of all nations ! I wish to bring home to my children and my friends copies of these admirable forms, which I can find in the shops of the engravers ; but I do not wish the vexation of owning them. I wish to find in my own town a library and museum which is the property of the town, where I can deposit this precious treasure, where I and my children can see it from time to time, and where it has its proper place among hundreds of such donations from other citizens who have brought thither whatever articles they have judged to be in their nature rather a public than a private property.

A collection of this kind, the property of each town, would dignify the town, and we should love and respect our neighbors more. Obviously, it would be easy for every town to discharge this truly municipal duty. Every one of us would gladly contribute his share ; and the more gladly, the more considerable the institution had become.[1]

2. Certainly, not aloof from this homage to beauty, but in strict connection therewith, the house will come to be esteemed a Sanctuary. The language of a ruder age has given to common law the maxim that every man's house is his castle : the progress of truth will make every house a shrine.[2] Will not man one day open his eyes and see how dear he is to the soul of Nature, — how near it is to him ? Will he not see, through all he miscalls accident, that Law prevails for ever and ever ; that his private being is a part of it ; that its home is in his own unsounded heart ; that his economy, his labor, his good and bad fortune, his health and manners are all a curious and exact demonstration in miniature of the Genius of the Eternal Providence ? When he perceives the Law, he ceases to despond. Whilst he sees it, every thought and act is raised, and becomes an act of religion. Does the consecration of Sunday confess the desecration of the entire week ? Does the consecration of the church confess the profanation of the house ? Let us read the incantation back-

ward. Let the man stand on his feet. Let religion cease to be occasional; and the pulses of thought that go to the borders of the universe, let them proceed from the bosom of the Household.

These are the consolations, — these are the ends to which the household is instituted and the roof-tree stands. If these are sought and in any good degree attained, can the state, can commerce, can climate, can the labor of many for one, yield anything better, or half as good? Beside these aims, Society is weak and the State an intrusion. I think that the heroism which at this day would make on us the impression of Epaminondas and Phocion must be that of a domestic conqueror. He who shall bravely and gracefully subdue this Gorgon of Convention and Fashion, and show men how to lead a clean, handsome and heroic life amid the beggarly elements of our cities and villages; whoso shall teach me how to eat my meat and take my repose and deal with men, without any shame following, will restore the life of man to splendor, and make his own name dear to all history.[1]

VI

FARMING

To these men
The landscape is an armory of powers,
Which, one by one, they know to draw and use.
They harness beast, bird, insect, to their work;
They prove the virtues of each bed of rock,
And, like the chemist mid his loaded jars,
Draw from each stratum its adapted use
To drug their crops or weapon their arts withal.
They turn the frost upon their chemic heap,
They set the wind to winnow pulse and grain,
They thank the spring-flood for its fertile slime,
And on cheap summit-levels of the snow
Slide with the sledge to inaccessible woods
O'er meadows bottomless. So, year by year,
They fight the elements with elements,
And by the order in the field disclose
The order regnant in the yeoman's brain.
What these strong masters wrote at large in miles,
I followed in small copy in my acre;
For there's no rood has not a star above it;
The cordial quality of pear or plum
Ascends as gladly in a single tree
As in broad orchards resonant with bees;
And every atom poises for itself,
And for the whole.

He planted where the deluge ploughed,
His hired hands were wind and cloud;
His eyes detect the Gods concealed
In the hummock of the field.

FARMING

THE glory of the farmer is that, in the division of labors, it is his part to create. All trade rests at last on his primitive activity. He stands close to Nature; he obtains from the earth the bread and the meat. The food which was not, he causes to be. The first farmer was the first man, and all historic nobility rests on possession and use of land. Men do not like hard work, but every man has an exceptional respect for tillage, and a feeling that this is the original calling of his race, that he himself is only excused from it by some circumstance which made him delegate it for a time to other hands. If he have not some skill which recommends him to the farmer, some product for which the farmer will give him corn, he must himself return into his due place among the planters.[1] And the profession has in all eyes its ancient charm, as standing nearest to God, the first cause.

Then the beauty of Nature, the tranquillity and innocence of the countryman, his independence and his pleasing arts, — the care of bees, of poultry, of sheep, of cows, the dairy, the care of hay, of fruits, of orchards and forests, and the reaction of these on the workman, in giving him a strength and plain dignity like the face and manners of Nature, — all men acknowledge. All men keep the farm in reserve as an asylum where, in case of mischance, to hide their poverty, — or a solitude, if they do not succeed in society. And who knows how many glances of remorse are turned this way from the bankrupts of trade, from mortified pleaders in courts and senates, or from the victims of idleness and pleasure? Poisoned by town life and town vices, the sufferer resolves: ' Well, my children, whom I have injured, shall go back to the land, to be recruited and cured by that which should have been my nursery, and now shall be their hospital.'

The farmer's office is precise and important, but you must not try to paint him in rose-color; you cannot make pretty compliments to fate and gravitation, whose minister he is. He represents the necessities. It is the beauty of the great economy of the world that makes his comeliness. He bends to the order of the seasons, the weather, the soils and crops, as the sails of a ship bend to the wind. He represents continuous hard labor, year in, year out, and small gains. He is a slow person, timed to Nature, and not to city watches. He takes the pace of seasons, plants and chemistry. Nature never hurries: atom by atom, little by little, she achieves her work. The lesson one learns in fishing, yachting, hunting or planting is the manners of Nature; patience with the delays of wind and sun, delays of the seasons, bad weather, excess or lack of water, — patience with the slowness of our feet, with the parsimony of our strength, with the largeness of sea and land we must traverse, etc. The farmer times himself to Nature, and acquires that livelong patience which belongs to her. Slow, narrow man, his rule is that the earth shall feed and clothe him; and he must wait for his crop to grow.¹ His entertainments, his liberties and his spending must be on a farmer's scale, and not on a merchant's. It were as false for farmers to use a wholesale and massy expense, as for states to use a minute economy. But if thus pinched on one side, he has compensatory advantages. He is permanent, clings to his land as the rocks do. In the town where I live, farms remain in the same families for seven and eight generations; and most of the first settlers (in 1635), should they reappear on the farms today, would find their own blood and names still in possession. And the like fact holds in the surrounding towns.

This hard work will always be done by one
kind of man; not by scheming speculators, nor
by soldiers, nor professors, nor readers of Tennyson; but by men of endurance — deep-chested,
long-winded, tough, slow and sure, and timely.[1]
The farmer has a great health, and the appetite
of health, and means to his end; he has broad
lands for his home, wood to burn great fires,
plenty of plain food; his milk at least is un-
watered; and for sleep, he has cheaper and better and more of it than citizens.

He has grave trusts confided to him. In the
great household of Nature, the farmer stands at
the door of the bread-room, and weighs to each
his loaf. It is for him to say whether men shall
marry or not. Early marriages and the number
of births are indissolubly connected with abundance of food; or, as Burke said, " Man breeds
at the mouth." Then he is the Board of Quar-
antine. The farmer is a hoarded capital of
health, as the farm is the capital of wealth; and
it is from him that the health and power, moral
and intellectual, of the cities came. The city is
always recruited from the country. The men in
cities who are the centres of energy, the driving-
wheels of trade, politics or practical arts, and the
women of beauty and genius, are the children or

grandchildren of farmers, and are spending the energies which their fathers' hardy, silent life accumulated in frosty furrows, in poverty, necessity and darkness.[1]

He is the continuous benefactor. He who digs a well, constructs a stone fountain, plants a grove of trees by the roadside, plants an orchard, builds a durable house, reclaims a swamp, or so much as puts a stone seat by the wayside, makes the land so far lovely and desirable, makes a fortune which he cannot carry away with him, but which is useful to his country long afterwards. The man that works at home helps society at large with somewhat more of certainty than he who devotes himself to charities. If it be true that, not by votes of political parties but by the eternal laws of political economy, slaves are driven out of a slave state as fast as it is surrounded by free states, then the true abolitionist is the farmer, who, heedless of laws and constitutions, stands all day in the field, investing his labor in the land, and making a product with which no forced labor can compete.

We commonly say that the rich man can speak the truth, can afford honesty, can afford independence of opinion and action; — and that is the theory of nobility. But it is the rich man in a true sense, that is to say, not the man of large income and large expenditure, but solely the man whose outlay is less than his income and is steadily kept so.[1]

In English factories, the boy that watches the loom, to tie the thread when the wheel stops to indicate that a thread is broken, is called a *minder*. And in this great factory of our Copernican globe, shifting its slides, rotating its constellations, times and tides, bringing now the day of planting, then of watering, then of weeding, then of reaping, then of curing and storing, — the farmer is the *minder*. His machine is of colossal proportions; the diameter of the waterwheel, the arms of the levers, the power of the battery, are out of all mechanic measure; and it takes him long to understand its parts and its working. This pump never "sucks;" these screws are never loose; this machine is never out of gear; the vat and piston, wheels and tires, never wear out, but are self-repairing.

Who are the farmer's servants? Not the Irish, nor the coolies, but Geology and Chemistry, the quarry of the air, the water of the brook, the lightning of the cloud, the castings of the worm, the plough of the frost.[2] Long before he was born, the sun of ages decomposed the rocks, mellowed his land, soaked it with light and heat, covered it with vegetable film, then with forests, and accumulated the sphagnum whose decays made the peat of his meadow.

Science has shown the great circles in which Nature works; the manner in which marine plants balance the marine animals, as the land plants supply the oxygen which the animals consume, and the animals the carbon which the plants absorb. These activities are incessant. Nature works on a method of *all for each and each for all.* The strain that is made on one point bears on every arch and foundation of the structure. There is a perfect solidarity. You cannot detach an atom from its holdings, or strip off from it the electricity, gravitation, chemic affinity or the relation to light and heat and leave the atom bare. No, it brings with it its universal ties.

Nature, like a cautious testator, ties up her estate so as not to bestow it all on one generation, but has a forelooking tenderness and equal regard to the next and the next, and the fourth and the fortieth age. There lie the inexhaustible magazines. The eternal rocks, as we call them, have held their oxygen or lime undiminished, entire, as it was. No particle of oxygen can rust or wear, but has the same energy as on the first morning.' The good rocks, those patient waiters, say to him: 'We have the sacred power as we received it. We have not failed of our trust, and now — when in our immense day the hour is at last struck — take the gas we have hoarded, mingle it with water, and let it be free to grow in plants and animals and obey the thought of man.'

The earth works for him; the earth is a machine which yields almost gratuitous service to every application of intellect. Every plant is a manufacturer of soil. In the stomach of the plant development begins. The tree can draw on the whole air, the whole earth, on all the rolling main. The plant is all suction-pipe, — imbibing from the ground by its root, from the air by its leaves, with all its might.

The air works for him. The atmosphere, a sharp solvent, drinks the essence and spirit of every solid on the globe, — a menstruum which melts the mountains into it. Air is matter subdued by heat. As the sea is the grand receptacle of all rivers, so the air is the receptacle from which all things spring, and into which they all return. The invisible and creeping air takes form and solid mass. Our senses are skeptics, and believe only the impression of the moment,

and do not believe the chemical fact that these
huge mountain chains are made up of gases and
rolling wind.[1] But Nature is as subtle as she is
strong. She turns her capital day by day; deals
never with dead, but ever with quick subjects.
All things are flowing, even those that seem im-
movable. The adamant is always passing into
smoke. The plants imbibe the materials which
they want from the air and the ground. They
burn, that is, exhale and decompose their own
bodies into the air and earth again. The animal
burns, or undergoes the like perpetual consumption. The earth burns, the mountains burn and
decompose, slower, but incessantly. It is almost
inevitable to push the generalization up into
higher parts of Nature, rank over rank into sen-
tient beings. Nations burn with internal fire
of thought and affection, which wastes while
it works. We shall find finer combustion and
finer fuel. Intellect is a fire: rash and pitiless it
melts this wonderful bone-house which is called
man.[2] Genius even, as it is the greatest good,
is the greatest harm. Whilst all thus burns,—
the universe in a blaze kindled from the torch
of the sun,— it needs a perpetual tempering, a
phlegm, a sleep, atmospheres of azote, deluges
of water, to check the fury of the conflagration;

VII

a hoarding to check the spending, a centrip-
etence equal to the centrifugence; and this is
invariably supplied.

The railroad dirt-cars are good excavators,
but there is no porter like Gravitation, who will
bring down any weights which man cannot carry,
and if he wants aid, knows where to find his fellow laborers. Water works in masses, and sets
its irresistible shoulder to your mills or your
ships, or transports vast boulders of rock in its
iceberg a thousand miles. But its far greater
power depends on its talent of becoming little,
and entering the smallest holes and pores. By
this agency, carrying in solution elements needful to every plant, the vegetable world exists.[1]

But as I said, we must not paint the farmer
in rose-color. Whilst these grand energies have
wrought for him and made his task possible,
he is habitually engaged in small economies, and
is taught the power that lurks in petty things.
Great is the force of a few simple arrangements;
for instance, the powers of a fence. On the
prairie you wander a hundred miles and hardly
find a stick or a stone. At rare intervals a thin
oak-opening has been spared, and every such
section has been long occupied. But the farmer
manages to procure wood from far, puts up a

rail-fence, and at once the seeds sprout and the oaks rise. It was only browsing and fire which had kept them down. Plant fruit-trees by the roadside, and their fruit will never be allowed to ripen. Draw a pine fence about them, and for fifty years they mature for the owner their delicate fruit. There is a great deal of enchantment in a chestnut rail or picketed pine boards.[1]

Nature suggests every economical expedient somewhere on a great scale. Set out a pine-tree, and it dies in the first year, or lives a poor spindle. But Nature drops a pine-cone in Mariposa, and it lives fifteen centuries, grows three or four hundred feet high, and thirty in diameter, — grows in a grove of giants, like a colonnade of Thebes. Ask the tree how it was done. It did not grow on a ridge, but in a basin, where it found deep soil, cold enough and dry enough for the pine; defended itself from the sun by growing in groves, and from the wind by the walls of the mountain. The roots that shot deepest, and the stems of happiest exposure, drew the nourishment from the rest, until the less thrifty perished and manured the soil for the stronger, and the mammoth Sequoias rose to their enormous proportions. The traveller who saw them remembered his orchard at home,

where every year, in the destroying wind, his
forlorn trees pined like suffering virtue. In
September, when the pears hang heaviest and
are taking from the sun their gay colors, comes
usually a gusty day which shakes the whole garden and throws down the heaviest fruit in bruised
heaps. The planter took the hint of the Sequoias, built a high wall, or — better — surrounded the orchard with a nursery of birches
and evergreens. Thus he had the mountain
basin in miniature; and his pears grew to the
size of melons, and the vines beneath them ran
an eighth of a mile. But this shelter creates a
new climate. The wall that keeps off the strong
wind keeps off the cold wind. The high wall
reflecting the heat back on the soil gives that
acre a quadruple share of sunshine, —

> "Enclosing in the garden square
> A dead and standing pool of air," [1]

and makes a little Cuba within it, whilst all without is Labrador.

The chemist comes to his aid every year by
following out some new hint drawn from Nature,
and now affirms that this dreary space occupied
by the farmer is needless; he will concentrate
his kitchen-garden into a box of one or two rods
square, will take the roots into his laboratory;

the vines and stalks and stems may go sprawling about in the fields outside, he will attend to the roots in his tub, gorge them with food that is good for them. The smaller his garden, the better he can feed it, and the larger the crop. As he nursed his Thanksgiving turkeys on bread and milk, so he will pamper his peaches and grapes on the viands they like best. If they have an appetite for potash, or salt, or iron, or ground bones, or even now and then for a dead hog, he will indulge them. They keep the secret well, and never tell on your table whence they drew their sunset complexion or their delicate flavors.

See what the farmer accomplishes by a cartload of tiles : he alters the climate by letting off water which kept the land cold through constant evaporation, and allows the warm rain to bring down into the roots the temperature of the air and of the surface soil ; and he deepens the soil, since the discharge of this standing water allows the roots of his plants to penetrate below the surface to the subsoil, and accelerates the ripening of the crop. The town of Concord is one of the oldest towns in this country, far on now in its third century. The selectmen have once in every five years perambulated the boundaries,

and yet, in this very year, a large quantity of
land has been discovered and added to the town
without a murmur of complaint from any quarter.
By drainage we went down to a subsoil we did
not know, and have found there is a Concord
under old Concord, which we are now getting
the best crops from; a Middlesex under Middlesex; and, in fine, that Massachusetts has a
basement story more valuable and that promises
to pay a better rent than all the superstructure.
But these tiles have acquired by association a new
interest.   These tiles are political economists,
confuters of Malthus and Ricardo; they are so
many Young Americans announcing a better era,
— more bread. They drain the land, make it
sweet and friable; have made English Chat Moss
a garden, and will now do as much for the Dismal Swamp. But beyond this benefit they are
the text of better opinions and better auguries
for mankind.

There has been a nightmare bred in England
of indigestion and spleen among landlords and
loom-lords, namely, the dogma that men breed
too fast for the powers of the soil; that men
multiply in a geometrical ratio, whilst corn mul-
tiplies only in an arithmetical; and hence that,
the more prosperous we are, the faster we

approach these frightful limits : nay, the plight
of every new generation is worse than of the
foregoing, because the first comers take up
the best lands ; the next, the second best ; and
each succeeding wave of population is driven
to poorer, so that the land is ever yielding less
returns to enlarging hosts of eaters. Henry
Carey of Philadelphia[1] replied : "Not so,
Mr. Malthus, but just the opposite of so is
the fact."

The first planter, the savage, without helpers,
without tools, looking chiefly to safety from his
enemy, — man or beast, — takes poor land. The
better lands are loaded with timber, which he cannot clear ; they need drainage, which he cannot
attempt. He cannot plough, or fell trees, or
drain the rich swamp. He is a poor creature ;
he scratches with a sharp stick, lives in a cave or
a hutch, has no road but the trail of the moose
or bear ; he lives on their flesh when he can kill
one, on roots and fruits when he cannot. He
falls, and is lame ; he coughs, he has a stitch in
his side, he has a fever and chills ; when he is
hungry, he cannot always kill and eat a bear, —
chances of war, — sometimes the bear eats him.
'T is long before he digs or plants at all, and
then only a patch. Later he learns that his

planting is better than hunting; that the earth works faster for him than he can work for himself, — works for him when he is asleep, when it rains, when heat overcomes him. The sunstroke which knocks him down brings his corn up.[1] As his family thrive, and other planters come up around him, he begins to fell trees and clear good land; and when, by and by, there is more skill, and tools and roads, the new generations are strong enough to open the lowlands, where the wash of mountains has accumulated the best soil, which yield a hundred-fold the former crops. The last lands are the best lands. It needs science and great numbers to cultivate the best lands, and in the best manner. Thus true political economy is not mean, but liberal, and on the pattern of the sun and sky. Population increases in the ratio of morality; credit exists in the ratio of morality.

Meantime we cannot enumerate the incidents and agents of the farm without reverting to their influence on the farmer. He carries out this cumulative preparation of means to their last effect. This crust of soil which ages have refined he refines again for the feeding of a civil and instructed people. The great elements with which he deals cannot leave him unaffected, or unconscious of his ministry; but their influence somewhat resembles that which the same Nature has on the child, — of subduing and silencing him.[1] We see the farmer with pleasure and respect when we think what powers and utilities are so meekly worn. He knows every secret of labor; he changes the face of the landscape. Put him on a new planet and he would know where to begin; yet there is no arrogance in his bearing, but a perfect gentleness. The farmer stands well on the world. Plain in manners as in dress, he would not shine in palaces; he is absolutely unknown and inadmissible therein; living or dying, he never shall be heard of in them; yet the drawing-room heroes put down beside him would shrivel in his presence; he solid and unexpressive, they expressed to gold-leaf. But he stands well on the world, — as Adam did, as an Indian does, as Homer's heroes, Agamemnon or Achilles, do. He is a person whom a poet of any clime — Milton, Firdusi, or Cervantes — would appreciate as being really a piece of the old Nature, comparable to sun and moon, rainbow and flood; because he is, as all natural persons are, representative of Nature as much as these.[2]

That uncorrupted behavior which we admire

in animals and in young children belongs to him, to the hunter, the sailor, — the man who lives in the presence of Nature. Cities force growth and make men talkative and entertaining, but they make them artificial. What possesses interest for us is the *naturel* of each, his constitutional excellence. This is forever a surprise, engaging and lovely ; we cannot be satiated with knowing it, and about it ; and it is this which the conversation with Nature cherishes and guards.

VII

WORKS AND DAYS

DAUGHTERS of Time, the hypocritic Days,
Muffled and dumb like barefoot dervishes,
And marching single in an endless file,
Bring diadems and fagots in their hands.
To each they offer gifts after his will,
Bread, kingdoms, stars and sky that holds them all
I, in my pleached garden, watched the pomp,
Forgot my morning wishes, hastily
Took a few herbs and apples, and the Day
Turned and departed silent. I, too late,
Under her solemn fillet saw the scorn.

THIS passing moment is an edifice
Which the Omnipotent cannot rebuild.

WORKS AND DAYS

OUR nineteenth century is the age of tools.
They grew out of our structure. "Man
is the meter of all things," said Aristotle; "the
hand is the instrument of instruments, and the
mind is the form of forms." [1] The human body
is the magazine of inventions, the patent office,
where are the models from which every hint was
taken. All the tools and engines on earth are
only extensions of its limbs and senses. One
definition of man is "an intelligence served by
organs." Machines can only second, not supply,
his unaided senses. The body is a meter. The
eye appreciates finer differences than art can
expose. The apprentice clings to his foot-rule;
a practised mechanic will measure by his thumb
and his arm with equal precision; and a good
surveyor will pace sixteen rods more accurately
than another man can measure them by tape. [2]
The sympathy of eye and hand by which an
Indian or a practised slinger hits his mark with
a stone, or a wood-chopper or a carpenter swings
his axe to a hair-line on his log, are examples;
and there is no sense or organ which is not
capable of exquisite performance.

Men love to wonder, and that is the seed of our science; and such is the mechanical determination of our age, and so recent are our best contrivances, that use has not dulled our joy and pride in them; and we pity our fathers for dying before steam and galvanism, sulphuric ether and ocean telegraphs, photograph and spectroscope arrived, as cheated out of half their human estate. These arts open great gates of a future, promising to make the world plastic and to lift human life out of its beggary to a god-like ease and power.

Our century to be sure had inherited a tolerable apparatus. We had the compass, the printing-press, watches, the spiral spring, the barometer, the telescope. Yet so many inventions have been added that life seems almost made over new; and as Leibnitz said of Newton, that " if he reckoned all that had been done by mathematicians from the beginning of the world down to Newton, and what had been done by him, his would be the better half," so one might say that the inventions of the last fifty years counterpoise those of the fifty centuries before them. For the vast production and manifold application of iron is new; and our common and indispensable utensils of house and farm are new; the sewing-machine, the power-loom, the McCormick reaper, the mowing-machines, gaslight, lucifer matches, and the immense productions of the laboratory, are new in this century, and one franc's worth of coal does the work of a laborer for twenty days.

Why need I speak of steam, the enemy of space and time, with its enormous strength and delicate applicability, which is made in hospitals to bring a bowl of gruel to a sick man's bed, and can twist beams of iron like candy-braids, and vies with the forces which upheaved and doubled over the geologic strata? Steam is an apt scholar and a strong-shouldered fellow, but it has not yet done all its work. It already walks about the field like a man, and will do anything required of it. It irrigates crops, and drags away a mountain. It must sew our shirts, it must drive our gigs; taught by Mr. Babbage, it must calculate interest and logarithms. Lord Chancellor Thurlow thought it might be made to draw bills and answers in chancery. If that were satire, it is yet coming to render many higher services of a mechanico-intellectual kind, and will leave the satire short of the fact.

How excellent are the mechanical aids we have applied to the human body, as in dentistry, in vaccination, in the rhinoplastic treatment; in the beautiful aid of ether, like a finer sleep; and in the boldest promiser of all, — the transfusion of the blood, — which, in Paris, it was claimed, enables a man to change his blood as often as his linen!

What of this dapper caoutchouc and gutta-percha, which make water-pipes and stomach-pumps, belting for mill-wheels, and diving-bells, and rain-proof coats for all climates, which teach us to defy the wet, and put every man on a footing with the beaver and the crocodile? What of the grand tools with which we engineer, like kobolds and enchanters, tunnelling Alps, canalling the American Isthmus, piercing the Arabian desert? In Massachusetts we fight the sea successfully with beach-grass and broom, and the blowing sand-barrens with pine plantations. The soil of Holland, once the most populous in Europe, is below the level of the sea. Egypt, where no rain fell for three thousand years, now, it is said, thanks Mehemet Ali's irrigations and planted forests for late-returning showers. The old Hebrew king said, "He makes the wrath of man to praise him." And there is no argument of theism better than the grandeur of ends brought about by paltry means. The chain of Western railroads from Chicago to the Pacific has planted cities and civilization in less time than it costs to bring an orchard into bearing.

What shall we say of the ocean telegraph, that extension of the eye and ear, whose sudden performance astonished mankind as if the intellect were taking the brute earth itself into training, and shooting the first thrills of life and thought through the unwilling brain? [1]

There does not seem any limit to these new informations of the same Spirit that made the elements at first, and now, through man, works them. Art and power will go on as they have done, — will make day out of night, time out of space, and space out of time.

Invention breeds invention. No sooner is the electric telegraph devised than gutta-percha, the very material it requires, is found. The aëronaut is provided with gun-cotton, the very fuel he wants for his balloon. When commerce is vastly enlarged, California and Australia expose the gold it needs. When Europe is over-populated, America and Australia crave to be peopled; and so throughout, every chance is timed, as if Nature, who made the lock, knew where to find the key.

VII

Another result of our arts is the new inter-course which is surprising us with new solutions of the embarrassing political problems. The intercourse is not new, but the scale is new. Our selfishness would have held slaves, or would have excluded from a quarter of the planet all that are not born on the soil of that quarter. Our politics are disgusting; but what can they help or hinder when from time to time the primal instincts are impressed on masses of mankind, when the nations are in exodus and flux? Nature loves to cross her stocks, — and German, Chinese, Turk, Russ and Kanaka were putting out to sea,¹ and intermarrying race with race; and commerce took the hint, and ships were built capacious enough to carry the people of a county.²

This thousand-handed art has introduced a new element into the state. The science of power is forced to remember the power of science. Civilization mounts and climbs. Malthus, when he stated that the mouths went on multiplying geometrically and the food only arithmetically, forgot to say that the human mind was also a factor in political economy, and that the aug-menting wants of society would be met by an augmenting power of invention.

Yes, we have a pretty artillery of tools now in our social arrangements : we ride four times as fast as our fathers did ; travel, grind, weave, forge, plant, till and excavate better. We have new shoes, gloves, glasses and gimlets ; we have the calculus ; we have the newspaper, which does its best to make every square acre of land and sea give an account of itself at your breakfast-table ; we have money, and paper money ; we have language, — the finest tool of all, and nearest to the mind. Much will have more. Man flatters himself that his command over Nature must increase. Things begin to obey him. We are to have the balloon yet, and the next war will be fought in the air. We may yet find a rose-water that will wash the negro white. He sees the skull of the English race changing from its Saxon type under the exigencies of American life.

Tantalus, who in old times was seen vainly trying to quench his thirst with a flowing stream which ebbed whenever he approached it, has been seen again lately. He is in Paris, in New York, in Boston. He is now in great spirits ; thinks he shall reach it yet ; thinks he shall bottle the wave. It is however getting a little doubtful. Things have an ugly look still. No matter how many centuries of culture have preceded, the new man always finds himself standing on the brink of chaos, always in a crisis. Can anybody remember when the times were not hard, and money not scarce ? Can anybody remember when sensible men, and the right sort of men, and the right sort of women, were plentiful? Tantalus begins to think steam a delusion, and galvanism no better than it should be.

Many facts concur to show that we must look deeper for our salvation than to steam, photographs, balloons or astronomy.[1] These tools have some questionable properties. They are reagents. Machinery is aggressive. The weaver becomes a web, the machinist a machine. If you do not use the tools, they use you. All tools are in one sense edge-tools, and dangerous. A man builds a fine house; and now he has a master, and a task for life : he is to furnish, watch, show it, and keep it in repair, the rest of his days.[2] A man has a reputation, and is no longer free, but must respect that. A man makes a picture or a book, and, if it succeeds, 't is often the worse for him. I saw a brave man the other day, hitherto as free as the hawk or the fox of the wilderness, constructing his cabinet of drawers for shells, eggs, minerals and mounted birds.

It was easy to see that he was amusing himself with making pretty links for his own limbs.

Then the political economist thinks "'t is doubtful if all the mechanical inventions that ever existed have lightened the day's toil of one human being." The machine unmakes the man. Now that the machine is so perfect, the engineer is nobody. Every new step in improving the engine restricts one more act of the engineer, — unteaches him. Once it took Archimedes; now it only needs a fireman, and a boy to know the coppers, to pull up the handles or mind the water-tank. But when the engine breaks, they can do nothing.

What sickening details in the daily journals! I believe they have ceased to publish the New-gate Calendar and the Pirate's Own Book since the family newspapers, namely the New York Tribune and the London Times, have quite superseded them in the freshness as well as the horror of their records of crime. Politics were never more corrupt and brutal; and Trade, that pride and darling of our ocean, that educator of nations, that benefactor in spite of itself, ends in shameful defaulting, bubble and bankruptcy, all over the world.[1]

Of course we resort to the enumeration of his

arts and inventions as a measure of the worth of man. But if, with all his arts, he is a felon, we cannot assume the mechanical skill or chemical resources as the measure of worth. Let us try another gauge.

What have these arts done for the character, for the worth of mankind? Are men better? 'T is sometimes questioned whether morals have not declined as the arts have ascended. Here are great arts and little men. Here is greatness begotten of paltriness. We cannot trace the triumphs of civilization to such benefactors as we wish. The greatest meliorator of the world is selfish, huckstering Trade. Every victory over matter ought to recommend to man the worth of his nature. But now one wonders who did all this good. Look up the inventors. Each has his own knack; his genius is in veins and spots. But the great, equal, symmetrical brain, fed from a great heart, you shall not find. Every one has more to hide than he has to show, or is lamed by his excellence. 'T is too plain that with the material power the moral progress has not kept pace. It appears that we have not made a judicious investment. Works and days were offered us, and we took works.

The new study of the Sanskrit has shown us

the origin of the old names of God,—Dyaus, Deus, Zeus, Zeu pater, Jupiter,—names of the sun, still recognizable through the modifications of our vernacular words, importing that the Day is the Divine Power and Manifestation, and indicating that those ancient men, in their attempts to express the Supreme Power of the universe, called him the Day, and that this name was accepted by all the tribes.[1]

Hesiod wrote a poem which he called Works and Days, in which he marked the changes of the Greek year, instructing the husbandman at the rising of what constellation he might safely sow, when to reap, when to gather wood, when the sailor might launch his boat in security from storms, and what admonitions of the planets he must heed. It is full of economies for Grecian life, noting the proper age for marriage, the rules of household thrift and of hospitality. The poem is full of piety as well as prudence, and is adapted to all meridians by adding the ethics of works and of days. But he has not pushed his study of days into such inquiry and analysis as they invite.

A farmer said " he should like to have all the land that joined his own." Bonaparte, who had the same appetite, endeavored to make the

Mediterranean a French lake. Czar Alexander was more expansive, and wished to call the Pacific *my ocean;* and the Americans were obliged to resist his attempts to make it a close sea. But if he had the earth for his pasture and the sea for his pond, he would be a pauper still. He only is rich who owns the day. There is no king, rich man, fairy or demon who possesses such power as that. The days are ever divine as to the first Aryans. They are of the least pretension and of the greatest capacity of anything that exists. They come and go like muffled and veiled figures, sent from a distant friendly party; but they say nothing, and if we do not use the gifts they bring, they carry them as silently away.[1]

How the day fits itself to the mind, winds itself round it like a fine drapery, clothing all its fancies! Any holiday communicates to us its color. We wear its cockade and favors in our humor. Remember what boys think in the ·morning of " Election day," of the Fourth of July, of Thanksgiving or Christmas. The very stars in their courses wink to them of nuts and cakes, bonbons, presents and fire-works. Cannot memory still descry the old school-house and its porch, somewhat hacked by jack-knives, where you spun tops and snapped marbles; and do you not recall that life was then calendared by moments, threw itself into nervous knots of glittering hours, even as now, and not spread itself abroad an equable felicity? In college terms, and in years that followed, the young graduate, when the Commencement anniversary returned, though he were in a swamp, would see a festive light and find the air faintly echoing with plausive academic thunders. In solitude and in the country, what dignity distinguishes the holy time! The old Sabbath, or Seventh Day, white with the religions of unknown thousands of years, when this hallowed hour dawns out of the deep, — a clean page, which the wise may inscribe with truth, whilst the savage scrawls it with fetishes, — the cathedral music of history breathes through it a psalm to our solitude.

So, in the common experience of the scholar, the weathers fit his moods. A thousand tunes the variable wind plays, a thousand spectacles it brings, and each is the frame or dwelling of a new spirit. I used formerly to choose my time with some nicety for each favorite book. One author is good for winter, and one for the dogdays. The scholar must look long for the right hour for Plato's Timæus. At last the elect

morning arrives, the early dawn, — a few lights
conspicuous in the heaven, as of a world just
created and still becoming, — and in its wide
leisures we dare open that book.'

There are days when the great are near us,
when there is no frown on their brow, no con-
descension even; when they take us by the hand,
and we share their thought. There are days
which are the carnival of the year. The angels
assume flesh, and repeatedly become visible.
The imagination of the gods is excited and rushes
on every side into forms. Yesterday not a bird
peeped; the world was barren, peaked and pin-
ing: to-day 't is inconceivably populous; creation swarms and meliorates.

The days are made on a loom whereof the
warp and woof are past and future time. They
are majestically dressed, as if every god brought
a thread to the skyey web. 'T is pitiful the
things by which we are rich or poor, — a matter
of coins, coats and carpets, a little more or less
stone, or wood, or paint, the fashion of a cloak
or hat; like the luck of naked Indians, of whom
one is proud in the possession of a glass bead or
a red feather, and the rest miserable in the want
of it. But the treasures which Nature spent itself to amass, — the secular, refined, composite

anatomy of man, which all strata go to form,
which the prior races, from infusory and saurian,
existed to ripen ; the surrounding plastic natures ; the earth with its foods ; the intellectual,
temperamenting air ; the sea with its invitations ;
the heaven deep with worlds ; and the answering
brain and nervous structure replying to these ;
the eye that looketh into the deeps, which again
look back to the eye, abyss to abyss ; — these,
not like a glass bead, or the coins or carpets, are
given immeasurably to all.[1]

This miracle is hurled into every beggar's
hands. The blue sky is a covering for a market
and for the cherubim and seraphim. The sky
is the varnish or glory with which the Artist has
washed the whole work, — the verge or confines
of matter and spirit. Nature could no farther go.
Could our happiest dream come to pass in solid
fact, — could a power open our eyes to behold
"millions of spiritual creatures walk the earth,"[2]
— I believe I should find that mid-plain on which
they moved floored beneath and arched above
with the same web of blue depth which weaves
itself over me now, as I trudge the streets on
my affairs.

It is singular that our rich English language
should have no word to denote the face of the

world. *Kinde* was the old English term, which, however, filled only half the range of our fine Latin word, with its delicate future tense, — *natura, about to be born,* or what German philosophy denotes as a *becoming.* But nothing expresses that power which seems to work for beauty alone. The Greek *Kosmos* did; and therefore, with great propriety, Humboldt entitles his book, which recounts the last results of science, *Cosmos.*

Such are the days, — the earth is the cup, the sky is the cover, of the immense bounty of Nature which is offered us for our daily aliment; but what a force of *illusion* begins life with us and attends us to the end![1] We are coaxed, flattered and duped from morn to eve, from birth to death; and where is the old eye that ever saw through the deception? The Hindoos represent Maia, the illusory energy of Vishnu, as one of his principal attributes. As if, in this gale of warring elements which life is, it was necessary to bind souls to human life as mariners in a tempest lash themselves to the mast and bulwarks of a ship, and Nature employed certain illusions as her ties and straps, — a rattle, a doll, an apple, for a child; skates, a river, a boat, a horse, a gun, for the growing boy; and

I will not begin to name those of the youth and adult, for they are numberless. Seldom and slowly the mask falls and the pupil is permitted to see that all is one stuff, cooked and painted under many counterfeit appearances.[1] Hume's doctrine was that the circumstances vary, the amount of happiness does not; that the beggar cracking fleas in the sunshine under a hedge, and the duke rolling by in his chariot; the girl equipped for her first ball, and the orator returning triumphant from the debate, had different means, but the same quantity of pleasant excitement.

This element of illusion lends all its force to hide the values of present time. Who is he that does not always find himself doing something less than his best task? "What are you doing?" "O, nothing; I have been doing thus, or I shall do so or so, but now I am only—" Ah! poor dupe, will you never slip out of the web of the master juggler,—never learn that as soon as the irrecoverable years have woven their blue glory between to-day and us these passing hours shall glitter and draw us as the wildest romance and the homes of beauty and poetry? How difficult to deal erect with them! The events they bring, their trade, entertainments and

gossip, their urgent work, all throw dust in the
eyes and distract attention. He is a strong man
who can look them in the eye, see through this
juggle, feel their identity, and keep his own ; who
can know surely that one will be like another to
the end of the world, nor permit love, or death,
or politics, or money, war or pleasure to draw
him from his task.[1]

The world is always equal to itself, and every
man in moments of deeper thought is apprised
that he is repeating the experiences of the people
in the streets of Thebes or Byzantium. An
everlasting Now reigns in Nature, which hangs
the same roses on our bushes which charmed
the Roman and the Chaldæan in their hanging-
gardens. 'To what end, then,' he asks, 'should
I study languages, and traverse countries, to learn
so simple truths ? '

History of ancient art, excavated cities, re-
covery of books and inscriptions, — yes, the
works were beautiful, and the history worth
knowing ; and academies convene to settle the
claims of the old schools. What journeys and
measurements, — Niebuhr and Müller and Lay-
ard, — to identify the plain of Troy and Nim-
roud town ! And your homage to Dante costs
you so much sailing ; and to ascertain the dis-

coverers of America needs as much voyaging as
the discovery cost. Poor child! that flexile clay
of which these old brothers moulded their admirable symbols was not Persian, nor Mem-
phian, nor Teutonic, nor local at all, but was
common lime and silex and water and sunlight,
the heat of the blood and the heaving of the
lungs; it was that clay which thou heldest but
now in thy foolish hands, and threwest away to
go and seek in vain in sepulchres, mummy-pits
and old book-shops of Asia Minor, Egypt and
England. It was the deep to-day which all men
scorn; the rich poverty which men hate; the
populous, all-loving solitude which men quit
for the tattle of towns. HE lurks, *he* hides, —
he who is success, reality, joy and power.[1] One
of the illusions is that the present hour is not
the critical, decisive hour. Write it on your
heart that every day is the best day in the year.
No man has learned anything rightly until he
knows that every day is Doomsday.[2] 'T is the
old secret of the gods that they come in low disguises. 'T is the vulgar great who come dizened
with gold and jewels. Real kings hide away
their crowns in their wardrobes, and affect a
plain and poor exterior. In the Norse legend
of our ancestors, Odin dwells in a fisher's hut

and patches a boat. In the Hindoo legends, Hari dwells a peasant among peasants. In the Greek legend, Apollo lodges with the shepherds of Admetus, and Jove liked to rusticate among the poor Ethiopians. So, in our history, Jesus is born in a barn, and his twelve peers are fishermen. 'T is the very principle of science that Nature shows herself best in leasts; it was the maxim of Aristotle and Lucretius; and, in modern times, of Swedenborg and of Hahnemann. The order of changes in the egg determines the age of fossil strata. So it was the rule of our poets, in the legends of fairy lore, that the fairies largest in power were the least in size. In the Christian graces, humility stands highest of all, in the form of the Madonna; and in life, this is the secret of the wise. We owe to genius always the same debt, of lifting the curtain from the common, and showing us that divinities are sitting disguised in the seeming gang of gypsies and pedlers. In daily life, what distinguishes the master is the using those materials he has, instead of looking about for what are more renowned, or what others have used well. " A general," said Bonaparte,[1] " always has troops enough, if he only knows how to employ those he has, and bivouacs with them." Do not refuse the employment which the hour brings you, for one more ambitious.[1] The highest heaven of wisdom is alike near from every point, and thou must find it, if at all, by methods native to thyself alone.

That work is ever the more pleasant to the imagination which is not now required. How wistfully, when we have promised to attend the working committee, we look at the distant hills and their seductions!

The use of history is to give value to the present hour and its duty. That is good which commends to me my country, my climate, my means and materials, my associates. I knew a man in a certain religious exaltation who " thought it an honor to wash his own face." He seemed to me more sane than those who hold themselves cheap.

Zoölogists may deny that horse-hairs in the water change to worms, but I find that whatever is old corrupts, and the past turns to snakes.[2] The reverence for the deeds of our ancestors is a treacherous sentiment. Their merit was not to reverence the old, but to honor the present moment; and we falsely make them excuses of the very habit which they hated and defied.

Another illusion is that there is not time

VII

enough for our work. Yet we might reflect that though many creatures eat from one dish, each, according to its constitution, assimilates from the elements what belongs to it, whether time, or space, or light, or water, or food. A snake converts whatever prey the meadow yields him into snake; a fox, into fox; and Peter and John are working up all existence into Peter and John. A poor Indian chief of the Six Nations of New York made a wiser reply than any philosopher, to some one complaining that he had not enough time. "Well," said Red Jacket, "I suppose you have all there is."

A third illusion haunts us, that a long duration, as a year, a decade, a century, is valuable. But an old French sentence says, "God works in moments," — "*En peu d'heure Dieu labeure.*" We ask for long life, but 't is deep life, or grand moments, that signify. Let the measure of time be spiritual, not mechanical. Life is unnecessarily long. Moments of insight, of fine personal relation, a smile, a glance, — what ample borrowers of eternity they are![1] Life culminates and concentrates; and Homer said, "The gods ever give to mortals their apportioned share of reason only on one day."[2]

I am of the opinion of the poet Wordsworth,

that "there is no real happiness in this life but in intellect and virtue." I am of the opinion of Pliny that "whilst we are musing on these things, we are adding to the length of our lives." I am of the opinion of Glauco, who said, " The measure of life, O Socrates, is, with the wise, the speaking and hearing such discourses as yours."

He only can enrich me who can recommend to me the space between sun and sun. 'T is the measure of a man, — his apprehension of a day. For we do not listen with the best regard to the verses of a man who is only a poet, nor to his problems if he is only an algebraist ; but if a man is at once acquainted with the geometric foundations of things and with their festal splendor, his poetry is exact and his arithmetic musical. And him I reckon the most learned scholar, not who can unearth for me the buried dynasties of Sesostris and Ptolemy, the Sothiac era, the Olympiads and consulships, but who can unfold the theory of this particular Wednesday. Can he uncover the ligaments concealed from all but piety, which attach the dull men and things we know to the First Cause ? These passing fifteen minutes, men think, are time, not eternity ; are low and subaltern, are but hope or memory ; that is, the way *to* or the way *from* welfare, but not welfare. Can he show their tie? That interpreter shall guide us from a menial and eleemosynary existence into riches and stability. He dignifies the place where he is.¹ This mendicant America, this curious, peering, itinerant, imitative America, studious of Greece and Rome, of England and Germany, will take off its dusty shoes, will take off its glazed traveller's-cap and sit at home with repose and deep joy on its face. The world has no such landscape, the æons of history no such hour, the future no equal second opportunity. Now let poets sing! now let arts unfold!

One more view remains. But life is good only when it is magical and musical, a perfect timing and consent, and when we do not anatomize it. You must treat the days respectfully, you must be a day yourself, and not interrogate it like a college professor. The world is enigmatical, — . everything said, and everything known or done, — and must not be taken literally, but genially. We must be at the top of our condition to understand anything rightly. You must hear the bird's song without attempting to render it into nouns and verbs. Cannot we be a little abstemious and obedient? Cannot we let the morning be?

Everything in the universe goes by indirec-
tion. There are no straight lines. I remember
well the foreign scholar who made a week of my
youth happy by his visit. "The savages in the
islands," he said, "delight to play with the surf,
coming in on the top of the rollers, then swimming out again, and repeat the delicious man-
œuvre for hours. Well, human life is made up
of such transits. There can be no greatness without abandonment. But here your very astronomy is an espionage. I dare not go out of doors
and see the moon and stars, but they seem to
measure my tasks, to ask how many lines or
pages are finished since I saw them last. Not
so, as I told you, was it in Belleisle. The days
at Belleisle were all different, and only joined
by a perfect love of the same object. Just to fill
the hour, — that is happiness. Fill my hour, ye
gods, so that I shall not say, whilst I have done
this, ' Behold, also, an hour of my life is gone,'
— but rather, ' I have lived an hour.' " [1]

We do not want factitious men, who can do
any literary or professional feat, as, to write
poems, or advocate a cause, or carry a measure,
for money; or turn their ability indifferently in
any particular direction by the strong effort of
will. No, what has been best done in the world,

— the works of genius, — cost nothing. There is no painful effort, but it is the spontaneous flowing of the thought. Shakspeare made his Hamlet as a bird weaves its nest. Poems have been written between sleeping and waking, irresponsibly. Fancy defines herself: —

> " Forms that men spy
> With the half-shut eye
> In the beams of the setting sun, am I." [1]

The masters painted for joy, and knew not that virtue had gone out of them. They could not paint the like in cold blood. The masters of English lyric wrote their songs so. It was a fine efflorescence of fine powers; as was said of the letters of the Frenchwoman, — " the charming accident of their more charming existence." Then the poet is never the poorer for his song. A song is no song unless the circumstance is free and fine. If the singer sing from a sense of duty or from seeing no way of escape, I had rather have none. Those only can sleep who do not care to sleep; and those only write or speak best who do not too much respect the writing or the speaking.

The same rule holds in science. The savant is often an amateur. His performance is a memoir to the Academy on fish-worms, tadpoles,

or spiders' legs; he observes as other academi-
cians observe; he is on stilts at a microscope,
and his memoir finished and read and printed,
he retreats into his routinary existence, which is
quite separate from his scientific. But in Newton, science was as easy as breathing; he used
the same wit to weigh the moon that he used to
buckle his shoes; and all his life was simple,
wise and majestic. So was it in Archimedes,—
always self-same, like the sky. In Linnæus, in
Franklin, the like sweetness and equality,—no
stilts, no tiptoe; and their results are wholesome
and memorable to all men.

In stripping time of its illusions, in seeking
to find what is the heart of the day, we come to
the quality of the moment, and drop the duration altogether. It is the depth at which we live
and not at all the surface extension that imports.
We pierce to the eternity, of which time is the
flitting surface; and, really, the least acceleration
of thought and the least increase of power of
thought, make life to seem and to be of vast
duration. We call it time; but when that
acceleration and that deepening take effect, it
acquires another and a higher name.

There are people who do not need much
experimenting; who, after years of activity, say,

We knew all this before; who love at first sight
and hate at first sight; discern the affinities and
repulsions; who do not care so much for conditions as others, for they are always in one condition and enjoy themselves; who dictate to
others and are not dictated to; who in their
consciousness of deserving success constantly
slight the ordinary means of attaining it;[1] who
have self-existence and self-help; who are suffered to be themselves in society; who are great
in the present; who have no talents, or care not
to have them,— being that which was before
talent, and shall be after it, and of which talent
seems only a tool : this is character, the highest
name at which philosophy has arrived.

'T is not important how the hero does this or
this, but what he is. What he is will appear in
every gesture and syllable. In this way the moment and the character are one.

It is a fine fable for the advantage of character over talent, the Greek legend of the strife
of Jove and Phœbus. Phœbus challenged the
gods, and said, "Who will outshoot the far-
darting Apollo?" Zeus said, "I will." Mars
shook the lots in his helmet, and that of Apollo
leaped out first. Apollo stretched his bow and
shot his arrow into the extreme west. Then

Zeus rose, and with one stride cleared the whole distance, and said, "Where shall I shoot? there is no space left." So the bowman's prize was adjudged to him who drew no bow.

And this is the progress of every earnest mind; from the works of man and the activity of the hands to a delight in the faculties which rule them; from a respect to the works to a wise wonder at this mystic element of time in which he is conditioned; from local skills and the economy which reckons the amount of production *per* hour to the finer economy which respects the quality of what is done, and the right we have to the work, or the fidelity with which it flows from ourselves; then to the depth of thought it betrays, looking to its universality, or that its roots are in eternity, not in time. Then it flows from character, that sublime health which values one moment as another, and makes us great in all conditions, and as the only definition we have of freedom and power.[1]

VIII

BOOKS

O DAY of days when we can read! The reader and the book, — either without the other is naught.

THAT book is good
Which puts me in a working mood.
Unless to Thought be added Will
Apollo is an imbecile.

BOOKS

IT is easy to accuse books, and bad ones are
easily found ; and the best are but records,
and not the things recorded; and certainly
there is dilettanteism enough, and books that
are merely neutral and do nothing for us. In
Plato's Gorgias, Socrates says : " The ship-
master walks in a modest garb near the sea,
after bringing his passengers from Ægina or
from Pontus ; not thinking he has done anything extraordinary, and certainly knowing that
his passengers are the same and in no respect
better than when he took them on board." So
is it with books, for the most part : they work
no redemption in us. The bookseller might
certainly know that his customers are in no respect better for the purchase and consumption
of his wares. The volume is dear at a dollar,
and after reading to weariness the lettered backs,
we leave the shop with a sigh, and learn, as I did
without surprise of a surly bank director, that
in bank parlors they estimate all stocks of this
kind as rubbish.[1]

But it is not less true that there are books
which are of that importance in a man's private

experience as to verify for him the fables of
Cornelius Agrippa, of Michael Scott,[1] or of the
old Orpheus of Thrace, — books which take
rank in our life with parents and lovers and
passionate experiences, so medicinal, so strin-
gent, so revolutionary, so authoritative,[2] —
books which are the work and the proof of
faculties so comprehensive, so nearly equal to
the world which they paint, that though one
shuts them with meaner ones, he feels his exclusion from them to accuse his way of living.

Consider what you have in the smallest
chosen library. A company of the wisest and
wittiest men that could be picked out of all
civil countries in a thousand years have set in
best order the results of their learning and wisdom. The men themselves were hid and inaccessible, solitary, impatient of interruption,
fenced by etiquette ; but the thought which they
did not uncover to their bosom friend is here
written out in transparent words to us, the
strangers of another age.

We owe to books those general benefits which
come from high intellectual action. Thus, I
think, we often owe to them the perception of
immortality. They impart sympathetic activity
to the moral power. Go with mean people and

you think life is mean. Then read Plutarch, and the world is a proud place, peopled with men of positive quality, with heroes and demigods standing around us, who will not let us sleep.¹ Then, they address the imagination: only poetry inspires poetry. They become the organic culture of the time. College education is the reading of certain books which the common sense of all scholars agrees will represent the science already accumulated. If you know that, — for instance in geometry, if you have read Euclid and Laplace, — your opinion has some value ; if you do not know these, you are not entitled to give any opinion on the subject. Whenever any skeptic or bigot claims to be heard on the questions of intellect and morals, we ask if he is familiar with the books of Plato, where all his pert objections have once for all been disposed of. If not, he has no right to our time. Let him go and find himself answered there.

Meantime the colleges, whilst they provide us with libraries, furnish no professor of books ; and I think no chair is so much wanted. In a library we are surrounded by many hundreds of dear friends, but they are imprisoned by an enchanter in these paper and leathern boxes ;

and though they know us, and have been waiting two, ten, or twenty centuries for us, — some
of them, — and are eager to give us a sign and
unbosom themselves, it is the law of their limbo
that they must not speak until spoken to ; and
as the enchanter has dressed them, like bat-
talions of infantry, in coat and jacket of one cut,
by the thousand and ten thousand, your chance
of hitting on the right one is to be computed by
the arithmetical rule of Permutation and Combination, — not a choice out of three caskets,
but out of half a million caskets, all alike. But
it happens in our experience that in this lottery
there are at least fifty or a hundred blanks to a
prize. It seems then as if some charitable soul,
after losing a great deal of time among the false
books and alighting upon a few true ones which
made him happy and wise, would do a right act
in naming those which have been bridges or
ships to carry him safely over dark morasses and
barren oceans, into the heart of sacred cities,
into palaces and temples.[1] This would be best
done by those great masters of books who from
time to time appear, — the Fabricii, the Seldens,
Magliabecchis, Scaligers, Mirandolas, Bayles,
Johnsons, whose eyes sweep the whole horizon
of learning.[2] But private readers, reading purely

for love of the book, would serve us by leaving each the shortest note of what he found.

There are books; and it is practicable to read them, because they are so few. We look over with a sigh the monumental libraries of Paris, of the Vatican and the British Museum. In 1858, the number of printed books in the Imperial Library at Paris was estimated at eight hundred thousand volumes, with an annual increase of twelve thousand volumes; so that the number of printed books extant to-day may easily exceed a million. It is easy to count the number of pages which a diligent man can read in a day, and the number of years which human life in favorable circumstances allows to reading; and to demonstrate that though he should read from dawn till dark, for sixty years, he must die in the first alcoves. But nothing can be more deceptive than this arithmetic, where none but a natural method is really pertinent. I visit occasionally the Cambridge Library, and I can seldom go there without renewing the conviction that the best of it all is already within the four walls of my study at home. The inspection of the catalogue brings me continually back to the few standard writers who are on every private shelf; and to these it can afford only the

most slight and casual additions. The crowds
and centuries of books are only commentary
and elucidation, echoes and weakeners of these
few great voices of time.

The best rule of reading will be a method
from Nature, and not a mechanical one of hours
and pages. It holds each student to a pursuit
of his native aim, instead of a desultory miscellany. Let him read what is proper to him, and
not waste his memory on a crowd of mediocrities. As whole nations have derived their
culture from a single book,—as the Bible has
been the literature as well as the religion of large
portions of Europe; as Hafiz was the eminent
genius of the Persians, Confucius of the Chinese,
Cervantes of the Spaniards; so, perhaps, the
human mind would be a gainer if all the second-
ary writers were lost,— say, in England, all but
Shakspeare, Milton and Bacon,—through the
profounder study so drawn to those wonderful
minds. With this pilot of his own genius, let
the student read one, or let him read many, he
will read advantageously. Dr. Johnson said:
" Whilst you stand deliberating which book
your son shall read first, another boy has read
both : read anything five hours a day, and you
will soon be learned."

Nature is much our friend in this matter. Nature is always clarifying her water and her wine. No filtration can be so perfect. She does the same thing by books as by her gases and plants. There is always a selection in writers, and then a selection from the selection. In the first place, all books that get fairly into the vital air of the world were written by the successful class, by the affirming and advancing class, who utter what tens of thousands feel though they cannot say.[1] There has already been a scrutiny and choice from many hundreds of young pens before the pamphlet or political chapter which you read in a fugitive journal comes to your eye. All these are young adventurers, who produce their performance to the wise ear of Time, who sits and weighs, and, ten years hence, out of a million of pages reprints one. Again it is judged, it is winnowed by all the winds of opinion, and what terrific selection has not passed on it before it can be reprinted after twenty years; —and reprinted after a century!—it is as if Minos and Rhadamanthus had indorsed the writing. 'T is therefore an economy of time to read old and famed books. Nothing can be preserved which is not good; and I know beforehand that Pindar, Martial, Terence, Galen,

Kepler, Galileo, Bacon, Erasmus, More, will be superior to the average intellect. In contemporaries, it is not so easy to distinguish betwixt notoriety and fame.[1]

Be sure then to read no mean books. Shun the spawn of the press on the gossip of the hour. Do not read what you shall learn, without asking, in the street and the train. Dr. Johnson said " he always went into stately shops ; " and good travellers stop at the best hotels ; for though they cost more, they do not cost much more, and there is the good company and the best information.[2] In like manner the scholar knows that the famed books contain, first and last, the best thoughts and facts. Now and then, by rarest luck, in some foolish Grub Street is the gem we want. But in the best circles is the best information. If you should transfer the amount of your reading day by day from the newspaper to the standard authors —— But who dare speak of such a thing?

The three practical rules, then, which I have to offer, are, — 1. Never read any book that is not a year old. 2. Never read any but famed books. 3. Never read any but what you like ; or, in Shakspeare's phrase, —

> " No profit goes where is no pleasure ta'en:
> In brief, sir, study what you most affect." [3]

Montaigne says, " Books are a languid pleasure;" but I find certain books vital and sper-
matic, not leaving the reader what he was: he
shuts the book a richer man. I would never
willingly read any others than such. And I
will venture, at the risk of inditing a list of old
primers and grammars, to count the few books
which a superficial reader must thankfully use.

Of the old Greek books, I think there are five
which we cannot spare:' 1. Homer, who in spite
of Pope and all the learned uproar of centuries,
has really the true fire and is good for simple
minds, is the true and adequate germ of Greece,
and occupies that place as history which nothing
can supply. It holds through all literature that
our best history is still poetry. It is so in Hebrew, in Sanskrit and in Greek. English history is best known through Shakspeare; how
much through Merlin, Robin Hood and the
Scottish ballads!—the German, through the
Nibelungenlied;—the Spanish, through the Cid.
Of Homer, George Chapman's is the heroic
translation, though the most literal prose version
is the best of all. 2. Herodotus, whose history
contains inestimable anecdotes, which brought it
with the learned into a sort of disesteem; but
in these days, when it is found that what is most

memorable of history is a few anecdotes, and
that we need not be alarmed though we should
find it not dull, it is regaining credit. 3. Æschylus, the grandest of the three tragedians, who
has given us under a thin veil the first plantation of Europe. The Prometheus is a poem of
the like dignity and scope as the Book of Job,
or the Norse Edda.[1] 4. Of Plato I hesitate to
speak, lest there should be no end. You find
in him that which you have already found in
Homer, now ripened to thought, — the poet
converted to a philosopher, with loftier strains
of musical wisdom than Homer reached; as if
Homer were the youth and Plato the finished
man; yet with no less security of bold and perfect song, when he cares to use it, and with some
harp-strings fetched from a higher heaven. He
contains the future, as he came out of the past.
In Plato you explore modern Europe in its
causes and seed, — all that in thought, which
the history of Europe embodies or has yet to
embody. The well-informed man finds himself
anticipated. Plato is up with him too. Nothing
has escaped him. Every new crop in the fertile
harvest of reform, every fresh suggestion of modern humanity, is there. If the student wish to
see both sides, and justice done to the man of

the world, pitiless exposure of pedants, and the supremacy of truth and the religious sentiment, he shall be contented also.[1] Why should not young men be educated on this book? It would suffice for the tuition of the race; to test their understanding, and to express their reason. Here is that which is so attractive to all men, —the literature of aristocracy shall I call it?— the picture of the best persons, sentiments and manners, by the first master, in the best times; portraits of Pericles, Alcibiades, Crito, Prodicus, Protagoras, Anaxagoras and Socrates, with the lovely background of the Athenian and sub- urban landscape. Or who can overestimate the images with which Plato has enriched the minds of men, and which pass like bullion in the cur- rency of all nations? Read the Phædo, the Protagoras, the Phædrus, the Timæus, the Re- public and the Apology of Socrates.[2] 5. Plu- tarch cannot be spared from the smallest library; first because he is so readable, which is much; then that he is medicinal and invigorating. The lives of Cimon, Lycurgus, Alexander, Demos- thenes, Phocion, Marcellus and the rest, are what history has of best. But this book has taken care of itself, and the opinion of the world is expressed in the innumerable cheap editions, which make it as accessible as a newspaper. But Plutarch's Morals is less known, and seldom reprinted. Yet such a reader as I am writing to can as ill spare it as the Lives. He will read in it the essays On the Dæmon of Socrates, On Isis and Osiris, On Progress in Virtue, On Garrulity, On Love; and thank anew the art of printing and the cheerful domain of ancient thinking. Plutarch charms by the facility of his associations; so that it signifies little where you open his book, you find yourself at the Olympian tables. His memory is like the Isthmian Games, where all that was excellent in Greece was assembled; and you are stimulated and recruited by lyric verses, by philosophic sentiments, by the forms and behavior of heroes, by the worship of the gods, and by the passing of fillets, parsley and laurel wreaths, chariots, armor, sacred cups and utensils of sacrifice. An inestimable trilogy of ancient social pictures are the three Banquets respectively of Plato, Xenophòn and Plutarch. Plutarch's has the least approach to historical accuracy; but the meeting of the Seven Wise Masters is a charming portraiture of ancient manners and discourse, and is as clear as the voice of a fife, and entertaining as a French novel. Xenophon's delineation of Athenian manners is an accessory to Plato, and supplies traits of Socrates; whilst Plato's has merits of every kind, — being a repertory of the wisdom of the ancients on the subject of love; a picture of a feast of wits, not less descriptive than Aristophanes; and, lastly, containing that ironical eulogy of Socrates which is the source from which all the portraits of that philosopher current in Europe have been drawn.

Of course a certain outline should be obtained of Greek history, in which the important moments and persons can be rightly set down ; but the shortest is the best, and if one lacks stomach for Mr. Grote's voluminous annals, the old slight and popular summary of Goldsmith or of Gillies will serve. The valuable part is the age of Pericles and the next generation. And here we must read the Clouds of Aristophanes, and what more of that master we gain appetite for, to learn our way in the streets of Athens, and to know the tyranny of Aristophanes, requiring more genius and sometimes not less cruelty than belonged to the official commanders.' Aristophanes is now very accessible, with much valuable commentary, through the labors of Mitchell and Cartwright. An excellent popular book is J. A. St. John's Ancient Greece ;

the Life and Letters of Niebuhr, even more
than his Lectures, furnish leading views; and
Winckelmann, a Greek born out of due time,
has become essential to an intimate knowledge
of the Attic genius. The secret of the recent
histories in German and in English is the discovery, owed first to Wolff and later to Boeckh,
that the sincere Greek history of that period
must be drawn from Demosthenes, especially
from the business orations ; and from the comic
poets.

If we come down a little by natural steps
from the master to the disciples, we have, six or
seven centuries later, the Platonists, who also
cannot be skipped, — Plotinus, Porphyry, Proclus, Synesius, Jamblichus. Of Jamblichus the
Emperor Julian said that " he was posterior to
Plato in time, not in genius."[1] Of Plotinus, we
have eulogies by Porphyry and Longinus, and
the favor of the Emperor Gallienus, indicating
the respect he inspired among his contemporaries. If any one who had read with interest
the Isis and Osiris of Plutarch should then read
a chapter called Providence, by Synesius, translated into English by Thomas Taylor, he will
find it one of the majestic remains of literature,
and, like one walking in the noblest of temples,

will conceive new gratitude to his fellow men, and a new estimate of their nobility. The imaginative scholar will find few stimulants to his brain like these writers.[1] He has entered the Elysian Fields; and the grand and pleasing figures of gods and dæmons and dæmoniacal men, of the " azonic " and the " aquatic gods," dæmons with fulgid eyes, and all the rest of the Platonic rhetoric, exalted a little under the African sun, sail before his eyes. The acolyte has mounted the tripod over the cave at Delphi; his heart dances, his sight is quickened. These guides speak of the gods with such depth and with such pictorial details, as if they had been bodily present at the Olympian feasts. The reader of these books makes new acquaintance with his own mind; new regions of thought are opened. Jamblichus's Life of Pythagoras works more directly on the will than the others; since Pythagoras was eminently a practical person, the founder of a school of ascetics and socialists, a planter of colonies, and nowise a man of abstract studies alone.[2]

The respectable and sometimes excellent translations of Bohn's Library have done for literature what railroads have done for internal intercourse. I do not hesitate to read all the books I have named, and all good books, in translations. What is really best in any book is translatable, — any real insight or broad human sentiment. Nay, I observe that, in our Bible, and other books of lofty moral tone, it seems easy and inevitable to render the rhythm and music of the original into phrases of equal melody. The Italians have a fling at translators, — *i traditori traduttori;* but I thank them. I rarely read any Latin, Greek, German, Italian, sometimes not a French book, in the original, which I can procure in a good version. I like to be beholden to the great metropolitan English speech, the sea which receives tributaries from every region under heaven. I should as soon think of swimming across Charles River when I wish to go to Boston, as of reading all my books in originals when I have them rendered for me in my mother tongue.

For history there is great choice of ways to bring the student through early Rome. If he can read Livy, he has a good book ; but one of the short English compends, some Goldsmith or Ferguson, should be used, that will place in the cycle the bright stars of Plutarch. The poet Horace is the eye of the Augustan age ; Tacitus, the wisest of historians ; and Martial will give him Roman manners, — and some very bad ones, — in the early days of the Empire : but Martial must be read, if read at all, in his own tongue. These will bring him to Gibbon, who will take him in charge and convey him with abundant entertainment down — with notice of all remarkable objects on the way — through fourteen hundred years of time. He cannot spare Gibbon, with his vast reading, with such wit and continuity of mind, that, though never profound, his book is one of the conveniences of civilization, like the new railroad from ocean to ocean, — and, I think, will be sure to send the reader to his Memoirs of Himself, and the Extracts from my Journal, and Abstracts of my Readings, which will spur the laziest scholar to emulation of his prodigious performance.[1]

Now having our idler safe down as far as the fall of Constantinople in 1453, he is in very good courses ; for here are trusty hands waiting for him. The cardinal facts of European history are soon learned. There is Dante's poem, to open the Italian Republics of the Middle Age ; Dante's Vita Nuova, to explain Dante and Beatrice ;[2] and Boccaccio's Life of Dante, a great man to describe a greater. To help us, perhaps a volume or two of M. Sismondi's

Italian Republics will be as good as the entire
sixteen. When we come to Michel Angelo,
his Sonnets and Letters must be read, with his
Life by Vasari, or, in our day, by Herman
Grimm.[1] For the Church and the Feudal Institution, Mr. Hallam's Middle Ages will furnish, if superficial, yet readable and conceivable
outlines.

The Life of the Emperor Charles V., by the
useful Robertson, is still the key of the following age.[2] Ximenes, Columbus, Loyola, Luther,
Erasmus, Melanchthon, Francis I., Henry
VIII., Elizabeth, and Henry IV. of France,
are his contemporaries. It is a time of seeds
and expansions, whereof our recent civilization
is the fruit.

If now the relations of England to European
affairs bring him to British ground, he is arrived
at the very moment when modern history takes
new proportions. He can look back for the
legends and mythology to the Younger Edda
and the Heimskringla of Snorro Sturleson, to
Mallet's Northern Antiquities, to Ellis's Metrical Romances, to Asser's Life of Alfred and
Venerable Bede, and to the researches of Sharon
Turner and Palgrave. Hume will serve him
for an intelligent guide, and in the Elizabethan

era he is at the richest period of the English mind, with the chief men of action and of thought which that nation has produced, and with a pregnant future before him. Here he has Shakspeare, Spenser,[1] Sidney, Raleigh, Bacon, Chapman, Jonson, Ford, Beaumont and Fletcher, Herbert, Donne,[2] Herrick ; and Milton, Marvell and Dryden, not long after.

In reading history, he is to prefer the history of individuals. He will not repent the time he gives to Bacon, — not if he read the Advancement of Learning, the Essays, the Novum Organum, the History of Henry VII., and then all the Letters (especially those to the Earl of Devonshire, explaining the Essex business), and all but his Apophthegms.[3]

The task is aided by the strong mutual light which these men shed on each other. Thus, the works of Ben Jonson are a sort of hoop to bind all these fine persons together, and to the land to which they belong. He has written verses to or on all his notable contemporaries ; and what with so many occasional poems, and the portrait sketches in his Discoveries, and the gossiping record of his opinions in his conversations with Drummond of Hawthornden, he has really illustrated the England of his time, if not to the same extent yet much in the same way, as Walter Scott has celebrated the persons and places of Scotland. Walton, Chapman, Herrick and Sir Henry Wotton write also to the times.

Among the best books are certain *Autobiographies;* as, St. Augustine's Confessions; Benvenuto Cellini's Life; Montaigne's Essays; Lord Herbert of Cherbury's Memoirs; Memoirs of the Cardinal de Retz; Rousseau's Confessions; Linnæus's Diary; Gibbon's, Hume's, Franklin's, Burns's, Alfieri's, Goethe's and Haydon's Autobiographies.

Another class of books closely allied to these, and of like interest, are those which may be called *Table-Talks:* of which the best are Saadi's[1] Gulistan; Luther's Table-Talk; Aubrey's Lives; Spence's anecdotes; Selden's Table-Talk; Boswell's Life of Johnson; Eckermann's Conversations with Goethe; Coleridge's Table-Talk; and Hazlitt's Life of Northcote.

There is a class whose value I should designate as *Favorites:* such as Froissart's Chronicles; Southey's Chronicle of the Cid; Cervantes; Sully's Memoirs; Rabelais; Montaigne; Izaak Walton; Evelyn; Sir Thomas Browne; Aubrey; Sterne; Horace Walpole; Lord Claren-

don; Doctor Johnson; Burke, shedding floods
of light on his times; Lamb; Landor; and De
Quincey;—a list, of course, that may easily be
swelled, as dependent on individual caprice.
Many men are as tender and irritable as lovers
in reference to these predilections. Indeed, a
man's library is a sort of harem, and I observe
that tender readers have a great pudency in
showing their books to a stranger.

The annals of bibliography afford many
examples of the delirious extent to which book-
fancying can go, when the legitimate delight in
a book is transferred to a rare edition or to a
manuscript. This mania reached its height about
the beginning of the present century. For an
autograph of Shakspeare one hundred and fifty-
five guineas were given. In May, 1812, the
library of the Duke of Roxburgh was sold. The
sale lasted forty-two days,—we abridge the
story from Dibdin,—and among the many curi-
osities was a copy of Boccaccio published by
Valdarfer, at Venice, in 1471; the only perfect
copy of this edition. Among the distinguished
company which attended the sale were the Duke
of Devonshire, Earl Spencer, and the Duke of
Marlborough, then Marquis of Blandford. The
bid stood at five hundred guineas. " A thousand

VII

guineas," said Earl Spencer: "And ten," added
the Marquis. You might hear a pin drop. All
eyes were bent on the bidders. Now they talked
apart, now ate a biscuit, now made a bet, but
without the least thought of yielding one to the
other. But to pass over some details, — the con-
test proceeded until the Marquis said, "Two
thousand pounds." Earl Spencer bethought
him like a prudent general of useless bloodshed
and waste of powder, and had paused a quarter
of a minute, when Lord Althorp with long steps
came to his side, as if to bring his father a fresh
lance to renew the fight. Father and son whispered together, and Earl Spencer exclaimed,
"Two thousand two hundred and fifty pounds!"
An electric shock went through the assembly.
"And ten," quietly added the Marquis. There
ended the strife. Ere Evans let the hammer
fall, he paused; the ivory instrument swept the
air; the spectators stood dumb, when the hammer fell. The stroke of its fall sounded on the
farthest shores of Italy. The tap of that hammer was heard in the libraries of Rome, Milan
and Venice. Boccaccio stirred in his sleep of five
hundred years, and M. Van Praet groped in
vain among the royal alcoves in Paris, to detect
a copy of the famed Valdarfer Boccaccio.

Another class I distinguish by the term *Vo-cabularies*. Burton's Anatomy of Melancholy is a book of great learning. To read it is like reading in a dictionary. 'T is an inventory to remind us how many classes and species of facts exist, and, in observing into what strange and multiplex byways learning has strayed, to infer our opulence. Neither is a dictionary a bad book to read. There is no cant in it, no excess of explanation, and it is full of suggestion, — the raw material of possible poems and histories. Nothing is wanting but a little shuffling, sorting, ligature and cartilage. Out of a hundred examples, Cornelius Agrippa On the Vanity of Arts and Sciences is a specimen of that scribatiousness which grew to be the habit of the gluttonous readers of his time. Like the modern Germans, they read a literature while other mortals read a few books. They read voraciously, and must disburden themselves; so they take any general topic, as Melancholy, or Praise of Science, or Praise of Folly, and write and quote without method or end. Now and then out of that affluence of their learning comes a fine sentence from Theophrastus, or Seneca, or Boëthius, but no high method, no inspiring efflux. But one cannot afford to read for a few sentences;

they are good only as strings of suggestive words.

There is another class, more needful to the present age, because the currents of custom run now in another direction and leave us dry on this side; — I mean the *Imaginative.*' A right metaphysics should do justice to the coördinate powers of Imagination, Insight, Understanding and Will. Poetry, with its aids of Mythology and Romance, must be well allowed for an imaginative creature. Men are ever lapsing into a beggarly habit, wherein everything that is not ciphering, that is, which does not serve the tyrannical animal, is hustled out of sight. Our orators and writers are of the same poverty, and in this rag-fair neither the Imagination, the great awakening power, nor the Morals, creative of genius and of men, are addressed. But though orator and poet be of this hunger party, the capacities remain. We must have symbols. The child asks you for a story, and is thankful for the poorest. It is not poor to him, but radiant with meaning. The man asks for a novel, — that is, asks leave for a few hours to be a poet, and to paint things as they ought to be. The youth asks for a poem. The very dunces wish to go to the theatre. What private heavens can

we not open, by yielding to all the suggestion of
rich music! We must have idolatries, mythologies, — some swing and verge for the creative
power lying coiled and cramped here, driving
ardent natures to insanity and crime if it do not
find vent. Without the great arts which speak
to the sense of beauty, a man seems to me a
poor, naked, shivering creature. These are his
becoming draperies, which warm and adorn him.
Whilst the prudential and economical tone of
society starves the imagination, affronted Nature
gets such indemnity as she may. The novel is
that allowance and frolic the imagination finds.
Everything else pins it down, and men flee for
redress to Byron, Scott, Disraeli, Dumas, Sand,
Balzac, Dickens, Thackeray and Reade.[1] Their
education is neglected ; but the circulating library and the theatre, as well as the trout-fishing,
the Notch Mountains, the Adirondack country,
the tour to Mont Blanc, to the White Hills and
the Ghauts, make such amends as they can.

The imagination infuses a certain volatility
and intoxication. It has a flute which sets the
atoms of our frame in a dance, like planets ; and
once so liberated, the whole man reeling drunk
to the music, they never quite subside to their
old stony state. But what is the imagination?

Only an arm or weapon of the interior energy; only the precursor of the reason. And books that treat the old pedantries of the world, our times, places, professions, customs, opinions, histories, with a certain freedom, and distribute things, not after the usages of America and Europe but after the laws of right reason, and with as daring a freedom as we use in dreams, put us on our feet again, enable us to form an original judgment of our duties, and suggest new thoughts for to-morrow.

Lucrezia Floriani, Le Péché de M. Antoine, Jeanne and Consuelo, of George Sand, are great steps from the novel of one termination, which we all read twenty years ago. Yet how far off from life and manners and motives the novel still is! Life lies about us dumb; the day, as we know it, has not yet found a tongue. These stories are to the plots of real life what the figures in La Belle Assemblée, which represent the fashion of the month, are to portraits. But the novel will find the way to our interiors one day, and will not always be the novel of costume merely. I do not think it inoperative now. So much novel-reading cannot leave the young men and maidens untouched; and doubtless it gives some ideal dignity to the day. The young study noble behavior ; and as the player in Consuelo insists that he and his colleagues on the boards have taught princes the fine etiquette and strokes of grace and dignity which they practise with so much effect in their villas and among their dependents, so I often see traces of the Scotch or the French novel in the courtesy and brilliancy of young midshipmen, collegians and clerks. Indeed, when one observes how ill and ugly people make their loves and quarrels, 't is pity they should not read novels a little more, to import the fine generosities and the clear, firm conduct, which are as becoming in the unions and separations which love effects under shingle roofs as in palaces and among illustrious personages.

In novels the most serious questions are beginning to be discussed. What made the popularity of Jane Eyre, but that a central question was answered in some sort? The question there answered in regard to a vicious marriage will always be treated according to the habit of the party. A person of commanding individualism will answer it as Rochester does, — as Cleopatra, as Milton, as George Sand do, — magnifying the exception into a rule, dwarfing the world into an exception. A person of less courage, that is of less constitution, will answer as the heroine does, — giving way to fate, to conventionalism, to the actual state and doings of men and women.

For the most part, our novel-reading is a passion for results. We admire parks, and high-born beauties, and the homage of drawing-rooms and parliaments. They make us skeptical, by giving prominence to wealth and social position.[1]

I remember when some peering eyes of boys discovered that the oranges hanging on the boughs of an orange-tree in a gay piazza were tied to the twigs by thread. I fear 't is so with the novelist's prosperities. Nature has a magic by which she fits the man to his fortunes, by making them the fruit of his character. But the novelist plucks this event here and that fortune there, and ties them rashly to his figures, to tickle the fancy of his readers with a cloying success or scare them with shocks of tragedy. And so, on the whole, 't is a juggle. We are cheated into laughter or wonder by feats which only oddly combine acts that we do every day. There is no new element, no power, no furtherance. 'T is only confectionery, not the raising of new corn. Great is the poverty of their inventions. *She was beautiful and he fell in love.* Money, and killing, and the Wandering Jew, and persuading the lover that his mistress is

betrothed to another, these are the main-springs;
new names, but no new qualities in the men and
women. Hence the vain endeavor to keep any
bit of this fairy gold which has rolled like a
brook through our hands. A thousand thoughts
awoke ; great rainbows seemed to span the sky,
a morning among the mountains ; but we close
the book and not a ray remains in the memory
of evening. But this passion for romance, and
this disappointment, show how much we need
real elevations and pure poetry : that which shall
show us, in morning and night, in stars and
mountains and in all the plight and circumstance
of men, the analogons of our own thoughts, and
a like impression made by a just book and by
the face of Nature.

If our times are sterile in genius, we must
cheer us with books of rich and believing men
who had atmosphere and amplitude about them.
Every good fable, every mythology, every biography from a religious age, every passage of
love, and even philosophy and science, when
they proceed from an intellectual integrity and
are not detached and critical, have the imaginative element. The Greek fables, the Persian
history (Firdusi),¹ the Younger Edda of the
Scandinavians, the Chronicle of the Cid, the

poem of Dante, the Sonnets of Michel Angelo,' the English drama of Shakspeare, Beaumont and Fletcher, and Ford, and even the prose of Bacon and Milton,—in our time the Ode of Wordsworth, and the poems and the prose of Goethe, have this enlargement, and inspire hope and generous attempts.

There is no room left,—and yet I might as well not have begun as to leave out a class of books which are the best: I mean the Bibles of the world, or the sacred books of each nation, which express for each the supreme result of their experience. After the Hebrew and Greek Scriptures, which constitute the sacred books of Christendom, these are, the Desatir of the Persians, and the Zoroastrian Oracles; the Vedas and Laws of Menu; the Upanishads, the Vishnu Purana, the Bhagvat Geeta, of the Hindoos; the books of the Buddhists; the Chinese Classic, of four books, containing the wisdom of Confucius and Mencius.¹ Also such other books as have acquired a semi-canonical authority in the world, as expressing the highest sentiment and hope of nations. Such are the Hermes Trismegistus, pretending to be Egyptian remains; the Sentences of Epictetus; of Marcus Antoninus; the Vishnu Sarma of the Hin-·

doos; the Gulistan of Saadi; the Imitation of
Christ, of Thomas à Kempis; and the Thoughts
of Pascal.

All these books are the majestic expressions
of the universal conscience, and are more to our
daily purpose than this year's almanac or this
day's newspaper. But they are for the closet,
and to be read on the bended knee. Their
communications are not to be given or taken
with the lips and the end of the tongue, but
out of the glow of the cheek, and with the
throbbing heart. Friendship should give and
take, solitude and time brood and ripen, heroes
absorb and enact them. They are not to be held
by letters printed on a page, but are living characters translatable into every tongue and form
of life. I read them on lichens and bark; I
watch them on waves on the beach; they fly in
birds, they creep in worms; I detect them in
laughter and blushes and eye-sparkles of men
and women. These are Scriptures which the
missionary might well carry over prairie, desert
and ocean, to Siberia, Japan, Timbuctoo. Yet
he will find that the spirit which is in them
journeys faster than he, and greets him on his
arrival, — was there already long before him.
The missionary must be carried by it, and find

it there, or he goes in vain. Is there any geography in these things? We call them Asiatic, we call them primeval; but perhaps that is only optical, for Nature is always equal to herself, and there are as good eyes and ears now in the planet as ever were. Only these ejaculations of the soul are uttered one or a few at a time, at long intervals, and it takes millenniums to make a Bible.

These are a few of the books which the old and the later times have yielded us, which will reward the time spent on them. In comparing the number of good books with the shortness of life, many might well be read by proxy, if we had good proxies; and it would be well for sincere young men to borrow a hint from the French Institute and the British Association, and as they divide the whole body into sections, each of which sits upon and reports of certain matters confided to it, so let each scholar associate himself to such persons as he can rely on, in a literary club, in which each shall undertake a single work or series for which he is qualified. For example, how attractive is the whole literature of the Roman de la Rose, the Fabliaux, and the *gaie science* of the French Troubadours! Yet who in Boston has time for that? But one of our company shall undertake it, shall study and master it, and shall report on it as under oath; shall give us the sincere result as it lies in his mind, adding nothing, keeping nothing back. Another member meantime shall as honestly search, sift and as truly report on British mythology, the Round Table, the histories of Brut, Merlin and Welsh poetry; a third on the Saxon Chronicles, Robert of Gloucester and William of Malmesbury; a fourth, on Mysteries, Early Drama, Gesta Romanorum, Collier, and Dyce, and the Camden Society. Each shall give us his grains of gold, after the washing; and every other shall then decide whether this is a book indispensable to him also.[1]

IX

CLUBS

Yet Saadi loved the race of men, —
No churl, immured in cave or den;
In bower and hall
He wants them all;
.   .   .   .

But he has no companion;
Come ten, or come a million,
Good Saadi dwells alone.

Too long shut in strait and few,
Thinly dieted on dew,
I will use the world, and sift it,
To a thousand humors shift it.

CLUBS

WE are delicate machines, and require nice treatment to get from us the maximum of power and pleasure. We need tonics, but must have those that cost little or no reaction. The flame of life burns too fast in pure oxygen, and Nature has tempered the air with nitrogen. So thought is the native air of the mind, yet pure it is a poison to our mixed constitution, and soon burns up the bone-house of man, unless tempered with affection and coarse practice in the material world. Varied foods, climates, beautiful objects, — and especially the alternation of a large variety of objects, — are the necessity of this exigent system of ours. But our tonics, our luxuries, are force-pumps which exhaust the strength they pretend to supply ; and of all the cordials known to us, the best, safest and most exhilarating, with the least harm, is society ; and every healthy and efficient mind passes a large part of life in the company most easy to him.[1]

We seek society with very different aims, and the staple of conversation is widely unlike in its circles. Sometimes it is facts, — running from

VII

those of daily necessity, to the last results of
science, — and has all degrees of importance;
sometimes it is love, and makes the balm of our
early and of our latest days;¹ sometimes it is
thought, as from a person who is a mind only;
sometimes a singing, as if the heart poured out
all like a bird; sometimes experience. With
some men it is a debate; at the approach of a
dispute they neigh like horses. Unless there be
an argument, they think nothing is doing. Some
talkers excel in the precision with which they
formulate their thoughts, so that you get from
them somewhat to remember; others lay criticism asleep by a charm. Especially women use
words that are not words, — as steps in a dance
are not steps, — but reproduce the genius of that
they speak of; as the sound of some bells makes
us think of the bell merely, whilst the church-
chimes in the distance bring the church and its
serious memories before us. Opinions are accidental in people, — have a poverty-stricken air.
A man valuing himself as the organ of this or that
dogma is a dull companion enough; but opinion native to the speaker is sweet and refresh-
ing, and inseparable from his image. Neither
do we by any means always go to people for
conversation. How often to say nothing, — and

yet must go ; as a child will long for his companions, but among them plays by himself. 'T is
only presence which we want. But one thing is
certain, — at some rate, intercourse we must
have. The experience of retired men is positive,
— that we lose our days and are barren of
thought for want of some person to talk with.
The understanding can no more empty itself by
its own action than can a deal box.

The clergyman walks from house to house
all day all the year to give people the comfort
of good talk. The physician helps them mainly
in the same way, by healthy talk giving a right
tone to the patient's mind. The dinner, the
walk, the fireside, all have that for their main
end.[1]

See how Nature has secured the communication of knowledge. 'T is certain that money
does not more burn in a boy's pocket than a
piece of news burns in our memory until we can
tell it. And in higher activity of mind, every
new perception is attended with a thrill of pleasure, and the imparting of it to others is also
attended with pleasure. Thought is the child
of the intellect, and this child is conceived with
joy and born with joy.[2]

Conversation is the laboratory and workshop

of the student. The affection or sympathy helps. The wish to speak to the want of another mind assists to clear your own. A certain truth possesses us which we in all ways strive to utter. Every time we say a thing in conversation, we get a mechanical advantage in detaching it well and deliverly. I prize the mechanics of conversation. 'T is pulley and lever and screw. To fairly disengage the mass, and send it jingling down, a good boulder, — a block of quartz and gold, to be worked up at leisure in the useful arts of life, — is a wonderful relief.[1]

What are the best days in memory? Those in which we met a companion who was truly such. How sweet those hours when the day was not long enough to communicate and compare our intellectual jewels, — the favorite passages of each book, the proud anecdotes of our heroes, the delicious verses we had hoarded! What a motive had then our solitary days! How the countenance of our friend still left some light after he had gone![2] We remember the time when the best gift we could ask of fortune was to fall in with a valuable companion in a ship's cabin, or on a long journey in the old stage-coach, where, each passenger being forced to know every other, and other employments being out of question, conversation naturally flowed, people became rapidly acquainted, and, if well adapted, more intimate in a day than if they had been neighbors for years.

In youth, in the fury of curiosity and acquisition, the day is too short for books and the crowd of thoughts, and we are impatient of interruption. Later, when books tire, thought has a more languid flow; and the days come when we are alarmed, and say there are no thoughts. 'What a barren-witted pate is mine!' the student says; 'I will go and learn whether I have lost my reason.' He seeks intelligent persons, whether more wise or less wise than he, who give him provocation, and at once and easily the old motion begins in his brain: thoughts, fancies, humors flow; the cloud lifts; the horizon broadens; and the infinite opulence of things is again shown him. But the right conditions must be observed. Mainly he must have leave to be himself. Sancho Panza blessed the man who invented sleep. So I prize the good invention whereby everybody is provided with somebody who is glad to see him.

If men are less when together than they are alone, they are also in some respects enlarged. They kindle each other; and such is the power of suggestion that each sprightly story calls out more; and sometimes a fact that had long slept in the recesses of memory hears the voice, is welcomed to daylight, and proves of rare value. Every metaphysician must have observed, not only that no thought is alone, but that thoughts commonly go in pairs; though the related thoughts first appeared in his mind at long distances of time. Things are in pairs: a natural fact has only half its value until a fact in moral nature, its counterpart, is stated.[1] Then they confirm and adorn each other; a story is matched by another story. And that may be the reason why, when a gentleman has told a good thing, he immediately tells it again.

Nothing seems so cheap as the benefit of conversation; nothing is more rare. 'T is wonderful how you are balked and baffled. There is plenty of intelligence, reading, curiosity; but serious, happy discourse, avoiding personalities, dealing with results, is rare: and I seldom meet with a reading and thoughtful person but he tells me, as if it were his exceptional mishap, that he has no companion.

Suppose such a one to go out exploring different circles in search of this wise and genial counterpart, — he might inquire far and wide.

Conversation in society is found to be on a platform so low as to exclude science, the saint and
the poet. Amidst all the gay banter, sentiment
cannot profane itself and venture out. The reply of old Isocrates comes so often to mind, —
" The things which are now seasonable I cannot
say; and for the things which I can say it is
not now the time." Besides, who can resist the
charm of talent? The lover of letters loves
power too. Among the men of wit and learning, he could not withhold his homage from the
gayety, grasp of memory, luck, splendor and
speed; such exploits of discourse, such feats of
society! What new powers, what mines of
wealth! But when he came home, his brave
sequins were dry leaves. He found either that
the fact they had thus dizened and adorned was
of no value, or that he already knew all and
more than all they had told him. He could
not find that he was helped by so much as one
thought or principle, one solid fact, one commanding impulse: great was the dazzle, but the
gain was small. He uses his occasions; he seeks
the company of those who have convivial talent.
But the moment they meet, to be sure they begin to be something else than they were; they
play pranks, dance jigs, run on each other, pun,

tell stories, try many fantastic tricks, under some superstition that there must be excitement and elevation;—and they kill conversation at once. I know well the rusticity of the shy hermit. No doubt he does not make allowance enough for men of more active blood and habit. But it is only on natural ground that conversation can be rich. It must not begin with uproar and violence. Let it keep the ground, let it feel the connection with the battery. Men must not be off their centres.

Some men love only to talk where they are masters. They like to go to school-girls, or to boys, or into the shops where the sauntering people gladly lend an ear to any one. On these terms they give information and please themselves by sallies and chat which are admired by the idlers; and the talker is at his ease and jolly, for he can walk out without ceremony when he pleases. They go rarely to their equals, and then as for their own convenience simply, making too much haste to introduce and impart their new whim or discovery; listen badly or do not listen to the comment or to the thought by which the company strive to repay them; rather, as soon as their own speech is done, they take their hats.[1] Then there are the gladiators, to whom it is always a battle; 'tis no matter on which side, they fight for victory; then the heady men, the egotists, the monotones, the steriles and the impracticables.

It does not help that you find as good or a better man than yourself, if he is not timed and fitted to you. The greatest sufferers are often those who have the most to say, — men of a delicate sympathy, who are dumb in mixed company.[1] Able people, if they do not know how to make allowance for them, paralyze them. One of those conceited prigs who value Nature only as it feeds and exhibits them is equally a pest with the roysterers. There must be large reception as well as giving. How delightful after these disturbers is the radiant, playful wit of — one whom I need not name, — for in every society there is his representative. Good nature is stronger than tomahawks. His conversation is all pictures: he can reproduce whatever he has seen; he tells the best story in the county, and is of such genial temper that he disposes all others irresistibly to good humor and discourse. Diderot said of the Abbé Galiani: " He was a treasure in rainy days; and if the cabinet-makers made such things, everybody would have one in the country." [2]

One lesson we learn early, — that in spite of seeming difference, men are all of one pattern. We readily assume this with our mates, and are disappointed and angry if we find that we are premature, and that their watches are slower than ours. In fact the only sin which we never forgive in each other is difference of opinion. We know beforehand that yonder man must think as we do. Has he not two hands, — two feet, — hair and nails? Does he not eat, — bleed, — laugh, — cry? His dissent from me is the veriest affectation. This conclusion is at once the logic of persecution and of love. And the ground of our indignation is our conviction that his dissent is some wilfulness he practises on himself. He checks the flow of his opinion, as the cross cow holds up her milk. Yes, and we look into his eye, and see that he knows it and hides his eye from ours.

But to come a little nearer to my mark, I am to say that there may easily be obstacles in the way of finding the pure article we are in search of, but when we find it it is worth the pursuit, for beside its comfort as medicine and cordial, once in the right company, new and vast values do not fail to appear. All that man can do for man is to be found in that market. There are great prizes in this game. Our fortunes in the world are as our mental equipment for this competition is. Yonder is a man who can answer the questions which I cannot. Is it so? Hence comes to me boundless curiosity to know his experiences and his wit. Hence competition for the stakes dearest to man. What is a match at whist, or draughts, or billiards, or chess, to a match of mother-wit, of knowledge and of resources? However courteously we conceal it, it is social rank and spiritual power that are compared; whether in the parlor, the courts, the caucus, the senate, or the chamber of science, — which are only less or larger theatres for this competition.[1]

He that can define, he that can answer a question so as to admit of no further answer, is the best man. This was the meaning of the story of the Sphinx. In the old time conundrums were sent from king to king by ambassadors. The seven wise masters at Periander's banquet spent their time in answering them.[2] The life of Socrates is a propounding and a solution of these. So, in the hagiology of each nation, the lawgiver was in each case some man of eloquent tongue, whose sympathy brought him face to face with the extremes of society. Jesus, Menu,

the first Buddhist, Mahomet, Zertusht,[1] Pythagoras, are examples.

Jesus spent his life in discoursing with humble
people on life and duty, in giving wise answers,
showing that he saw at a larger angle of vision,
and at least silencing those who were not generous enough to accept his thoughts. Luther
spent his life so ; and it is not his theologic
works, — his Commentary on the Galatians,
and the rest, but his Table-Talk, which is still
read by men. Dr. Johnson was a man of no
profound mind, — full of English limitations,
English politics, English Church, Oxford philosophy ; yet, having a large heart, mother-wit
and good sense which impatiently overleaped
his customary bounds, his conversation as reported by Boswell has a lasting charm. Conversation is the vent of character as well as of
thought ; and Dr. Johnson impresses his company, not only by the point of the remark, but
also, when the point fails, because *he* makes it.
His obvious religion or superstition, his deep
wish that they should think so or so, weighs
with them, — so rare is depth of feeling, or a
constitutional value for a thought or opinion,
among the light-minded men and women who
make up society ; and though they know that

there is in the speaker a degree of shortcoming, of insincerity and of talking for victory, yet the existence of character, and habitual reverence for principles over talent or learning, is felt by the frivolous.

One of the best records of the great German master who towered over all his contemporaries in the first thirty years of this century, is his conversations as recorded by Eckermann; and the Table-Talk of Coleridge is one of the best remains of his genius.

In the Norse legends, the gods of Valhalla, when they meet the Jotuns, converse on the perilous terms that he who cannot answer the other's questions forfeits his own life. Odin comes to the threshold of the Jotun Wafthrudnir in disguise, calling himself Gangrader; is invited into the hall, and told that he cannot go out thence unless he can answer every question Wafthrudnir shall put. Wafthrudnir asks him the name of the god of the sun, and of the god who brings the night; what river separates the dwellings of the sons of the giants from those of the gods; what plain lies between the gods and Surtur, their adversary, etc.; all which the disguised Odin answers satisfactorily. Then it is his turn to interrogate, and he is answered well for a time by the Jotun. At last he puts a question which none but himself could answer : " What did Odin whisper in the ear of his son Balder, when Balder mounted the funeral pile ?" The startled giant replies : " None of the gods knows what in the old time THOU saidst in the ear of thy son : with death on my mouth have I spoken the fate-words of the generation of the Æsir ; with Odin contended I in wise words. Thou must ever the wisest be." [1]

And still the gods and giants are so known, and still they play the same game in all the million mansions of heaven and of earth ; at all tables, clubs and *tête-à-têtes*, the lawyers in the court-house, the senators in the capitol, the doctors in the academy, the wits in the hotel. Best is he who gives an answer that cannot be answered again. *Omnis definitio periculosa est*, and only wit has the secret. The same thing took place when Leibnitz came to visit Newton ; when Schiller came to Goethe ; when France, in the person of Madame de Staël, visited Goethe and Schiller; when Hegel was the guest of Victor Cousin in Paris ; when Linnæus was the guest of Jussieu. It happened many years ago that an American chemist carried a letter of introduction to Dr. Dalton of Manchester, Eng-

land, the author of the theory of atomic proportions, and was coolly enough received by the
doctor in the laboratory where he was engaged.
Only Dr. Dalton scratched a formula on a scrap
of paper and pushed it towards the guest, —
" Had he seen that? " The visitor scratched on
another paper a formula describing some results
of his own with sulphuric acid, and pushed it
across the table, — " Had he seen that ? " The
attention of the English chemist was instantly
arrested, and they became rapidly acquainted.[1]

To answer a question so as to admit of no
reply, is the test of a man, — to touch bottom
every time. Hyde, Earl of Rochester, asked
Lord-Keeper Guilford, " Do you not think I
could understand any business in England in a
month?" " Yes, my lord," replied the other,
" but I think you would understand it better in
two months." When Edward I. claimed to be
acknowledged by the Scotch (1292) as lord
paramount, the nobles of Scotland replied, " No
answer can be made while the throne is vacant."
When Henry III. (1217) plead duress against
his people demanding confirmation and execution of the Charter, the reply was : " If this were
admitted, civil wars could never close but by the
extirpation of one of the contending parties."

What can you do with one of these sharp respondents? What can you do with an eloquent man? No rules of debate, no contempt of court, no exclusions, no gag-laws can be contrived that his first syllable will not set aside or overstep and annul. You can shut out the light, it may be, but can you shut out gravitation? You may condemn his book, but can you fight against his thought? That is always too nimble for you, anticipates you, and breaks out victorious in some other quarter. Can you stop the motions of good sense? What can you do with Beaumarchais, who converts the censor whom the court has appointed to stifle his play into an ardent advocate? The court appoints another censor, who shall crush it this time. Beaumarchais persuades him to defend it. The court successively appoints three more severe inquisitors; Beaumarchais converts them all into triumphant vindicators of the play which is to bring in the Revolution.¹ Who can stop the mouth of Luther, — of Newton, — of Franklin, — of Mirabeau, — of Talleyrand?

These masters can make good their own place, and need no patron. Every variety of gift — science, religion, politics, letters, art, prudence, war or love — has its vent and exchange in conversation. Conversation is the Olympic games whither every superior gift resorts to assert and approve itself, — and, of course, the inspirations of powerful and public men, with the rest. But it is not this class, whom the splendor of their accomplishment almost inevitably guides into the vortex of ambition, makes them chancellors and commanders of council and of action, and makes them at last fatalists, — not these whom we now consider. We consider those who are interested in thoughts, their own and other men's, and who delight in comparing them ; who think it the highest compliment they can pay a man to deal with him as an intellect, to expose to him the grand and cheerful secrets perhaps never opened to their daily companions, to share with him the sphere of freedom and the simplicity of truth.[1]

But the best conversation is rare. Society seems to have agreed to treat fictions as realities, and realities as fictions ; and the simple lover of truth, especially if on very high grounds, as a religious or intellectual seeker, finds himself a stranger and alien.

It is possible that the best conversation is between two persons who can talk only to each other. Even Montesquieu confessed that in

VII

conversation, if he perceived he was listened to by a third person, it seemed to him from that moment the whole question vanished from his mind. I have known persons of rare ability who were heavy company to good social men who knew well enough how to draw out others of retiring habit; and, moreover, were heavy to intellectual men who ought to have known them. And does it never occur that we perhaps live with people too superior to be seen, — as there are musical notes too high for the scale of most ears? There are men who are great only to one or two companions of more opportunity, or more adapted.

It was to meet these wants that in all civil nations attempts have been made to organize conversation by bringing together cultivated people under the most favorable conditions. 'T is certain there was liberal and refined conversation in the Greek, in the Roman and in the Middle Age. There was a time when in France a revolution occurred in domestic architecture; when the houses of the nobility, which, up to that time, had been constructed on feudal necessities, in a hollow square, — the ground-floor being resigned to offices and stables, and the floors above to rooms of state and to lodging-rooms,

— were rebuilt with new purpose. It was the Marchioness of Rambouillet who first got the horses out of and the scholars into the palaces, having constructed her *hôtel* with a view to society, with superb suites of drawing-rooms on the same floor, and broke through the *morgue* of etiquette by inviting to her house men of wit and learning as well as men of rank, and piqued the emulation of Cardinal Richelieu to rival assemblies, and so to the founding of the French Academy. The history of the Hôtel Rambouillet and its brilliant circles makes an important date in French civilization. And a history of clubs from early antiquity, tracing the efforts to secure liberal and refined conversation, through the Greek and Roman to the Middle Age, and thence down through French, English and German memoirs, tracing the clubs and coteries in each country, would be an important chapter in history. We know well the Mermaid Club, in London, of Shakspeare, Ben Jonson, Chapman, Herrick, Selden, Beaumont and Fletcher; its Rules are preserved, and many allusions to their suppers are found in Jonson, Herrick and in Aubrey. Anthony Wood has many details of Harrington's Club. Dr. Bentley's Club held Newton, Wren, Evelyn and Locke; and we

owe to Boswell our knowledge of the club of
Dr. Johnson, Goldsmith, Burke, Gibbon, Rey-
nolds, Garrick, Beauclerk and Percy. And we
have records of the brilliant society that Edinburgh boasted in the first decade of this century.
Such societies are possible only in great cities,
and are the compensation which these can make
to their dwellers for depriving them of the free
intercourse with Nature. Every scholar is surrounded by wiser men than he — if they cannot
write as well.[1] Cannot they meet and exchange
results to their mutual benefit and delight? It
was a pathetic experience when a genial and accomplished person said to me, looking from his
country home to the capital of New England,
" There is a town of two hundred thousand
people, and not a chair in it for me." If he
were sure to find at No. 2000 Tremont Street
what scholars were abroad after the morning
studies were ended, Boston would shine as the
New Jerusalem to his eyes.

Now this want of adapted society is mutual.
The man of thought, the man of letters, the
man of science, the administrator skilful in
affairs, the man of manners and culture, whom
you so much wish to find, — each of these is
wishing to be found. Each wishes to open his

thought, his knowledge, his social skill to the daylight in your company and affection, and to exchange his gifts for yours; and the first hint of a select and intelligent company is welcome.

But the club must be self-protecting, and obstacles arise at the outset. There are people who cannot well be cultivated; whom you must keep down and quiet if you can. There are those who have the instinct of a bat to fly against any lighted candle and put it out, — marplots and contradictors. There are those who go only to talk, and those who go only to hear: both are bad. A right rule for a club would be, — Admit no man whose presence excludes any one topic. It requires people who are not surprised and shocked, who do and let do and let be, who sink trifles and know solid values, and who take a great deal for granted.

It is always a practical difficulty with clubs to regulate the laws of election so as to exclude peremptorily every social nuisance. Nobody wishes bad manners. We must have loyalty and character. The poet Marvell was wont to say that he " would not drink wine with any one with whom he could not trust his life." But neither can we afford to be superfine. A man of irreproachable behavior and excellent

sense preferred on his travels taking his chance
at a hotel for company, to the charging himself
with too many select letters of introduction.[1]
He confessed he liked low company. He said
the fact was incontestable that the society of
gypsies was more attractive than that of bishops.
The girl deserts the parlor for the kitchen ; the
boy, for the wharf. Tutors and parents cannot
interest him like the uproarious conversation he
finds in the market or the dock. I knew a
scholar, of some experience in camps, who said
that he liked, in a barroom, to tell a few coon
stories and put himself on a good footing with
the company ; then he could be as silent as he
chose. A scholar does not wish to be always
pumping his brains ; he wants gossips. The
black-coats are good company only for black-
coats ; but when the manufacturers, merchants
and shipmasters meet, see how much they have
to say, and how long the conversation lasts !
They have come from many zones ; they have
traversed wide countries ; they know each his
own arts, and the cunning artisans of his craft ;
they have seen the best and the worst of men.
Their knowledge contradicts the popular opinion and your own on many points. Things
which you fancy wrong they know to be right

and profitable ; things which you reckon superstitious they know to be true. They have found
virtue in the strangest homes ; and in the rich
store of their adventures are instances and examples which you have been seeking in vain for
years, and which they suddenly and unwittingly
offer you.[1]

I remember a social experiment in this direction, wherein it appeared that each of the
members fancied he was in need of society, but
himself unpresentable. On trial they all found
that they could be tolerated by, and could toler-
ate, each other. Nay, the tendency to extreme
self-respect which hesitated to join in a club
was running rapidly down to abject admiration
of each other, when the club was broken up by
new combinations.[2]

The use of the hospitality of the club hardly
needs explanation. Men are unbent and social
at table ; and I remember it was explained to
me, in a Southern city, that it was impossible to
set any public charity on foot unless through a
tavern dinner. I do not think our metropolitan
charities would plead the same necessity ; but
to a club met for conversation a supper is a
good basis, as it disarms all parties and puts
pedantry and business to the door. All are in

good humor and at leisure, which are the first conditions of discourse ; the ordinary reserves are thrown off, experienced men meet with the freedom of boys, and, sooner or later, impart all that is singular in their experience.

The hospitalities of clubs are easily exaggerated. No doubt the suppers of wits and philosophers acquire much lustre by time and renown. Plutarch, Xenophon and Plato, who have celebrated each a banquet of their set, have given us next to no data of the viands ; and it is to be believed that an indifferent tavern dinner in such society was more relished by the *convives* than a much better one in worse company. Herrick's verses to Ben Jonson no doubt paint the fact : —

> " When we such clusters had
> As made us nobly wild, not mad;
> And yet, each verse of thine
> Outdid the meat, outdid the frolic wine." [1]

Such friends make the feast satisfying; and I notice that it was when things went prosperously, and the company was full of honor, at the banquet of the Cid, that " the guests all were joyful, and agreed in one thing, — that they had not eaten better for three years."

I need only hint the value of the club for

bringing masters in their several arts to compare and expand their views, to come to an understanding on these points, and so that their united opinion shall have its just influence on public questions of education and politics. It is agreed that in the sections of the British Association more information is mutually and effectually communicated, in a few hours, than in many months of ordinary correspondence and the printing and transmission of ponderous reports. We know that *l'homme de lettres* is a little wary, and not fond of giving away his seed-corn ; but there is an infallible way to draw him out, namely, by having as good as he. If you have Tuscaroora and he Canada, he may exchange kernel for kernel. If his discretion is incurable, and he dare not speak of fairy gold, he will yet tell what new books he has found, what old ones recovered, what men write and read abroad. A principal purpose also is the hospitality of the club, as a means of receiving a worthy foreigner with mutual advantage.

Every man brings into society some partial thought and local culture. We need range and alternation of topics and variety of minds. One likes in a companion a phlegm which it is a triumph to disturb, and, not less, to make in an

old acquaintance unexpected discoveries of scope
and power through the advantage of an inspiring subject. Wisdom is like electricity. There
is no permanently wise man, but men capable
of wisdom, who, being put into certain company, or other favorable conditions, become
wise for a short time, as glasses rubbed acquire
electric power for a while.[1] But while we look
complacently at these obvious pleasures and
values of good companions, I do not forget that
Nature is always very much in earnest, and that
her great gifts have something serious and stern.
When we look for the highest benefits of conversation, the Spartan rule of one to one is
usually enforced. Discourse, when it rises highest and searches deepest, when it lifts us into
that mood out of which thoughts come that
remain as stars in our firmament, is between
two.[2]

X

COURAGE

So nigh is grandeur to our dust,
So near is God to man,
When Duty whispers low, *Thou must,*
The youth replies, *I can.*

Peril around, all else appalling,
Cannon in front and leaden rain,
Him duty, through the clarion calling
To the van, called not in vain.

COURAGE

I OBSERVE that there are three qualities which conspicuously attract the wonder and reverence of mankind : —

1. Disinterestedness, as shown in indifference to the ordinary bribes and influences of conduct, —a purpose so sincere and generous that it cannot be tempted aside by any prospects of wealth or other private advantage. Self-love is, in almost all men, such an over-weight, that they are incredulous of a man's habitual preference of the general good to his own ;[1] but when they see it proved by sacrifices of ease, wealth, rank, and of life itself, there is no limit to their admiration. This has made the power of the saints of the East and West, who have led the religion of great nations. Self-sacrifice is the real miracle out of which all the reported miracles grew. This makes the renown of the heroes of Greece and Rome, — of Socrates, Aristides and Phocion ; of Quintus Curtius, Cato and Regulus ; of Hatem Tai's hospitality ;[2] of Chatham, whose scornful magnanimity gave him immense popularity; of Washington, giving his service to the public without salary or reward.[3]

2. Practical power. Men admire the man who can organize their wishes and thoughts in stone and wood and steel and brass, — the man who can build the boat, who has the impiety to make the rivers run the way he wants them ; who can lead his telegraph through the ocean from shore to shore ; who, sitting in his closet, can lay out the plans of a campaign, sea-war and land-war, such that the best generals and admirals, when all is done, see that they must thank him for success ; the power of better combination and foresight, however exhibited, whether it only plays a game of chess, or whether, more loftily, a cunning mathematician, penetrating the cubic weights of stars, predicts the planet which eyes had never seen ; or whether, exploring the chemical elements whereof we and the world are made, and seeing their secret, Franklin draws off the lightning in his hand ; suggesting that one day a wiser geology shall make the earthquake harmless and the volcano an agricultural resource. Or here is one who, seeing the wishes of men, knows how to come at their end ; whispers to this friend, argues down that adversary, moulds society to his purpose, and looks at all men as wax for his hands ; takes command of them as the wind does of clouds,

as the mother does of the child, or the man that knows more does of the man that knows less, and leads them in glad surprise to the very point where they would be: this man is followed with acclamation.

3. The third excellence is courage, the perfect will, which no terrors can shake, which is attracted by frowns or threats or hostile armies, nay, needs these to awake and fan its reserved energies into a pure flame, and is never quite itself until the hazard is extreme; then it is serene and fertile, and all its powers play well.[1] There is a Hercules, an Achilles, a Rustem, an Arthur or a Cid in the mythology of every nation; and in authentic history, a Leonidas, a Scipio, a Cæsar, a Richard Cœur de Lion, a Cromwell, a Nelson, a Great Condé, a Bertrand du Guesclin, a Doge Dandolo, a Napoleon, a Masséna, and Ney. 'T is said courage is common, but the immense esteem in which it is held proves it to be rare. Animal resistance, the instinct of the male animal when cornered, is no doubt common; but the pure article, courage with eyes, courage with conduct, self-possession at the cannon's mouth, cheerfulness in lonely adherence to the right, is the endowment of elevated characters. I need not show how much it is

esteemed, for the people give it the first rank. They forgive everything to it. What an ado we make through two thousand years about Thermopylæ and Salamis! What a memory of Poitiers and Crécy, and Bunker Hill, and Washington's endurance! And any man who puts his life in peril in a cause which is esteemed becomes the darling of all men. The very nursery-books, the ballads which delight boys, the romances which delight men, the favorite topics of eloquence, the thunderous emphasis which orators give to every martial defiance and passage of arms, and which the people greet, may testify. How short a time since this whole nation rose every morning to read or to hear the traits of courage of its sons and brothers in the field, and was never weary of the theme! We have had examples of men who, for showing effective courage on a single occasion, have become a favorite spectacle to nations, and must be brought in chariots to every mass meeting.

Men are so charmed with valor that they have pleased themselves with being called lions, leopards, eagles and dragons, from the animals contemporary with us in the geologic formations. But the animals have great advantage of us in precocity. Touch the snapping-turtle with a stick, and he seizes it with his teeth. Cut off his head, and the teeth will not let go the stick. Break the egg of the young, and the little embryo, before yet the eyes are open, bites fiercely; these vivacious creatures contriving — shall we say? — not only to bite after they are dead, but also to bite before they are born.

But man begins life helpless. The babe is in paroxysms of fear the moment its nurse leaves it alone, and it comes so slowly to any power of self-protection that mothers say the salvation of the life and health of a young child is a perpetual miracle. The terrors of the child are quite reasonable, and add to his loveliness; for his utter ignorance and weakness, and his enchanting indignation on such a small basis of capital compel every by-stander to take his part. Every moment as long as he is awake he studies the use of his eyes, ears, hands and feet, learning how to meet and avoid his dangers, and thus every hour loses one terror more. But this education stops too soon. A large majority of men being bred in families and beginning early to be occupied day by day with some routine of safe industry, never come to the rough experiences that make the Indian, the soldier or the frontiersman self-subsistent and

VII

fearless. Hence the high price of courage indicates the general timidity. "Mankind," said Franklin, "are dastardly when they meet with opposition." In war even generals are seldom found eager to give battle. Lord Wellington said, "Uniforms were often masks;" and again, "When my journal appears, many statues must come down." The Norse Sagas relate that when Bishop Magne reproved King Sigurd for his wicked divorce, the priest who attended the bishop, expecting every moment when the savage king would burst with rage and slay his superior, said that he "saw the sky no bigger than a calf-skin." And I remember when a pair of Irish girls who had been run away with in a wagon by a skittish horse, said that when he began to rear, they were so frightened that they could not see the horse.

Cowardice shuts the eyes till the sky is not larger than a calf-skin; shuts the eyes so that we cannot see the horse that is running away with us; worse, shuts the eyes of the mind and chills the heart. Fear is cruel and mean. The political reigns of terror have been reigns of madness and malignity, — a total perversion of opinion; society is upside down, and its best men are thought too bad to live. Then the

protection which a house, a family, neighborhood and property, even the first accumulation
of savings gives, go in all times to generate this
taint of the respectable classes. Those political parties which gather in the well-disposed
portion of the community, — how infirm and
ignoble! what white lips they have! always on
the defensive, as if the lead were intrusted to
the journals, often written in great part by
women and boys, who, without strength, wish
to keep up the appearance of strength. They can
do the hurras, the placarding, the flags, — and
the voting, if it is a fair day ; but the aggressive
attitude of men who will have right done, will no
longer be bothered with burglars and ruffians in
the streets, counterfeiters in public offices, and
thieves on the bench ; that part, the part of the
leader and soul of the vigilance committee, must
be taken by stout and sincere men who are
really angry and determined. In ordinary, we
have a snappish criticism which watches and
contradicts the opposite party. We want the
will which advances and dictates. When we
get an advantage, as in Congress the other day,
it is because our adversary has committed a fault,
not that we have taken the initiative and given
the law.[1] Nature has made up her mind that

what cannot defend itself shall not be defended.
Complaining never so loud and with never so
much reason is of no use. One heard much cant
of peace-parties long ago in Kansas and elsewhere,
that their strength lay in the greatness of their
wrongs, and dissuading all resistance, as if to
make this strength greater. But were their
wrongs greater than the negro's? And what
kind of strength did they ever give him?[1] It
was always invitation to the tyrant, and bred
disgust in those who would protect the victim.
What cannot stand must fall; and the measure
of our sincerity and therefore of the respect of
men, is the amount of health and wealth we will
hazard in the defence of our right. An old
farmer, my neighbor across the fence, when I
ask him if he is not going to town-meeting,
says: " No; 't is no use balloting, for it will
not stay; but what you do with the gun will
stay so."[2] Nature has charged every one with
his own defence as with his own support, and
the only title I can have to your help is when I
have manfully put forth all the means I possess
to keep me, and being overborne by odds, the
by-standers have a natural wish to interfere and
see fair play.

But with this pacific education we have no

readiness for bad times. I am much mistaken
if every man who went to the army in the late
war had not a lively curiosity to know how he
should behave in action. Tender, amiable boys,
who had never encountered any rougher play
than a base-ball match or a fishing excursion,
were suddenly drawn up to face a bayonet charge
or capture a battery. Of course they must each
go into that action with a certain despair.¹ Each
whispers to himself: "My exertions must be
of small account to the result; only will the benignant Heaven save me from disgracing myself
and my friends and my State. Die! O yes, I
can well die; but I cannot afford to misbehave;
and I do not know how I shall feel." So great
a soldier as the old French Marshal Montluc
acknowledges that he has often trembled with
fear, and recovered courage when he had said a
prayer for the occasion. I knew a young soldier
who died in the early campaign, who confided to
his sister that he had made up his mind to volunteer for the war. " I have not," he said, " any
proper courage, but I shall never let any one
find it out." And he had accustomed himself
always to go into whatever place of danger,
and do whatever he was afraid to do, setting a
dogged resolution to resist this natural infirmity.

Coleridge has preserved an anecdote of an officer in the British Navy who told him that when
he, in his first boat expedition, a midshipman in
his fourteenth year, accompanied Sir Alexander
Ball, "as we were rowing up to the vessel we
were to attack, amid a discharge of musketry,
I was overpowered with fear, my knees shook
and I was ready to faint away. Lieutenant Ball
seeing me, placed himself close beside me, took
hold of my hand and whispered, 'Courage, my
dear boy! you will recover in a minute or so;
I was just the same when I first went out in this
way.' It was as if an angel spoke to me. From
that moment I was as fearless and as forward as
the oldest of the boat's crew. But I dare not
think what would have become of me, if, at that
moment, he had scoffed and exposed me." [1]

Knowledge is the antidote to fear, — Knowledge, Use and Reason, with its higher aids.
The child is as much in danger from a staircase,
or the fire-grate, or a bath-tub, or a cat, as the
soldier from a cannon or an ambush. Each
surmounts the fear as fast as he precisely
understands the peril and learns the means of
resistance. Each is liable to panic, which is,
exactly, the terror of ignorance surrendered to
the imagination. Knowledge is the encourager,

knowledge that takes fear out of the heart, knowledge and use, which is knowledge in practice. They can conquer who believe they can. It is he who has done the deed once who does not shrink from attempting it again. It is the groom who knows the jumping horse well who can safely ride him. It is the veteran soldier, who, seeing the flash of the cannon, can step aside from the path of the ball. Use makes a better soldier than the most urgent considerations of duty, — familiarity with danger enabling him to estimate the danger. He sees how much is the risk, and is not afflicted with imagination ; knows practically Marshal Saxe's rule, that every soldier killed costs the enemy his weight in lead.

The sailor loses fear as fast as he acquires command of sails and spars and steam ; the frontiersman, when he has a perfect rifle and has acquired a sure aim. To the sailor's experience every new circumstance suggests what he must do. The terrific chances which make the hours and the minutes long to the passenger, he whiles away by incessant application of expedients and repairs. To him a leak, a hurricane, or a waterspout is so much work, — no more. The hunter is not alarmed by bears, catamounts or wolves, nor the grazier by his bull, nor the dog-breeder by his bloodhound, nor an Arab by the simoon, nor a farmer by a fire in the woods. The forest on fire looks discouraging enough to a citizen: the farmer is skilful to fight it. The neighbors run together; with pine boughs they can mop out the flame, and by raking with the hoe a long but little trench, confine to a patch the fire which would easily spread over a hundred acres.[1]

In short, courage consists in equality to the problem before us. The school-boy is daunted before his tutor by a question of arithmetic, because he does not yet command the simple steps of the solution which the boy beside him has mastered. These once seen, he is as cool as Archimedes, and cheerily proceeds a step farther. Courage is equality to the problem, in affairs, in science, in trade, in council, or in action; consists in the conviction that the agents with whom you contend are not superior in strength of resources or spirit to you. The general must stimulate the mind of his soldiers to the perception that they are men, and the enemy is no more. Knowledge, yes; for the danger of dangers is illusion. The eye is easily daunted; and the drums, flags, shining helmets, beard and moustache of the soldier have conquered you long before his sword or bayonet reaches you.   .

But we do not exhaust the subject in the slight analysis ; we must not forget the variety of temperaments, each of which qualifies this power of resistance. It is observed that men with little imagination are less fearful ; they wait till they feel pain, whilst others of more sensibility anticipate it, and suffer in the fear of the pang more acutely than in the pang. 'T is certain that the threat is sometimes more formidable than the stroke, and 't is possible that the beholders suffer more keenly than the victims. Bodily pain is superficial, seated usually in the skin and the extremities, for the sake of giving us warning to put us on our guard ; not in the vitals, where the rupture that produces death is perhaps not felt, and the victim never knew what hurt him. Pain is superficial, and therefore fear is. The torments of martyrdoms are probably most keenly felt by the by-standers. The torments are illusory. The first suffering is the last suffering, the later hurts being lost on insensibility. Our affections and wishes for the external welfare of the hero tumultuously rush to expression in tears and outcries : but we, like him, subside into indifferency and defiance when we perceive how short is the longest arm of malice, how serene is the sufferer.

It is plain that there is no separate essence
called courage, no cup or cell in the brain, no
vessel in the heart containing drops or atoms
that make or give this virtue; but it is the right
or healthy state of every man, when he is free
to do that which is constitutional to him to do.
It is directness, — the instant performing of
that which he ought. The thoughtful man says,
You differ from me in opinion and methods,
but do you not see that I cannot think or act
otherwise than I do? that my way of living
is organic? And to be really strong we must
adhere to our own means. On organic action
all strength depends.' Hear what women say
of doing a task by sheer force of will: it costs
them a fit of sickness. Plutarch relates that
the Pythoness who tried to prophesy without
command in the Temple at Delphi, though she
performed the usual rites, and inhaled the air of
the cavern standing on the tripod, fell into con-
vulsions and died. Undoubtedly there is a temperamental courage, a warlike blood, which loves
a fight, does not feel itself except in a quarrel, as
one sees in wasps, or ants, or cocks, or cats.
The like vein appears in certain races of men
and in individuals of every race. In every school
there are certain fighting boys; in every society,

the contradicting men ; in every town, bravoes
and bullies, better or worse dressed, fancy-men,
patrons of the cock-pit and the ring. Courage
is temperamental, scientific, ideal. Swedenborg
has left this record of his king : " Charles XII.
of Sweden did not know what that was which
others called fear, nor what that spurious valor
and daring that is excited by inebriating draughts,
for he never tasted any liquid but pure water.
Of him we may say that he led a life more remote
from death, and in fact lived more, than any
other man." It was told of the Prince of Condé
that " there not being a more furious man in the
world, danger in fight never disturbs him more
than just to make him civil, and to command
in words of great obligation to his officers and
men, and without any the least disturbance to his
judgment or spirit." Each has his own courage,
as his own talent ; but the courage of the tiger
is one, and of the horse another. The dog that
scorns to fight, will fight for his master. The
llama that will carry a load if you caress him,
will refuse food and die if he is scourged. The
fury of onset is one, and of calm endurance
another. There is a courage of the cabinet as
well as a courage of the field ; a courage of manners in private assemblies, and another in public

assemblies; a courage which enables one man
to speak masterly to a hostile company, whilst
another man who can easily face a cannon's
mouth dares not open his own.

There is a courage of a merchant in dealing
with his trade, by which dangerous turns of
affairs are met and prevailed over. Merchants
recognize as much gallantry, well judged too, in
the conduct of a wise and upright man of business in difficult times, as soldiers in a soldier.

There is a courage in the treatment of every
art by a master in architecture, in sculpture, in
painting or in poetry, each cheering the mind
of the spectator or receiver as by true strokes of
genius, which yet nowise implies the presence
of physical valor in the artist. This is the courage of genius, in every kind. A certain quantity
of power belongs to a certain quantity of faculty.
The beautiful voice at church goes sounding on,
and covers up in its volume, as in a cloak, all the
defects of the choir. The singers, I observe, all
yield to it, and so the fair singer indulges her
instinct, and dares, and dares, because she knows
she can.[1]

It gives the cutting edge to every profession. The judge puts his mind to the tangle of
contradictions in the case, squarely accosts the

question, and by not being afraid of it, by dealing with it as business which must be disposed
of, he sees presently that common arithmetic
and common methods apply to this affair. Perseverance strips it of all peculiarity, and ranges it
on the same ground as other business. Morphy
played a daring game in chess : the daring was
only an illusion of the spectator, for the player
sees his move to be well fortified and safe. You
may see the same dealing in criticism ; a new
book astonishes for a few days, takes itself out of
common jurisdiction, and nobody knows what to
say of it : but the scholar is not deceived. The
old principles which books exist to express are
more beautiful than any book ; and out of love
of the reality he is an expert judge how far
the book has approached it and where it has
come short. In all applications it is the same
power, — the habit of reference to one's own
mind, as the home of all truth and counsel, and
which can easily dispose of any book because
it can very well do without all books. When a
confident man comes into a company magnifying this or that author he has freshly read, the
company grow silent and ashamed of their ignorance. But I remember the old professor, whose
searching mind engraved every word he spoke

on the memory of the class, when we asked if he had read this or that shining novelty, " No, I have never read that book ; " instantly the book lost credit, and was not to be heard of again.[1]

Every creature has a courage of his constitution fit for his duties : — Archimedes, the courage of a geometer to stick to his diagram, heedless of the siege and sack of the city ; and the Roman soldier his faculty to strike at Archimedes. Each is strong, relying on his own, and each is betrayed when he seeks in himself the courage of others.

Captain John Brown, the hero of Kansas, said to me in conversation, that " for a settler in a new country, one good, believing, strong-minded man is worth a hundred, nay, a thousand men without character ; and that the right men will give a permanent direction to the fortunes of a state. As for the bullying drunkards of which armies are usually made up, he thought cholera, small-pox and consumption as valuable recruits." He held the belief that courage and chastity are silent concerning themselves. He said, " As soon as I hear one of my men say, ' Ah, let me only get my eye on such a man, I 'll bring him down,' I don't expect much aid in the fight from that talker. 'T is the quiet, peaceable men, the men of principle, that make the best soldiers."

> " 'T is still observed those men most valiant are
> Who are most modest ere they came to war." [1]

True courage is not ostentatious; men who wish to inspire terror seem thereby to confess themselves cowards. Why do they rely on it, but because they know how potent it is with themselves? [2]

The true temper has genial influences. It makes a bond of union between enemies. Governor Wise of Virginia, in the record of his first interviews with his prisoner, appeared to great advantage. If Governor Wise is a superior man, or inasmuch as he is a superior man, he distinguishes John Brown. As they confer, they understand each other swiftly; each respects the other. If opportunity allowed, they would prefer each other's society and desert their former companions.[3] Enemies would become affectionate. Hector and Achilles, Richard and Saladin, Wellington and Soult, General Daumas and Abdel-Kader, become aware that they are nearer and more alike than any other two, and, if their nation and circumstance did not keep them apart, would run into each other's arms.

See too what good contagion belongs to it.
Everywhere it finds its own with magnetic affinity. Courage of the soldier awakes the courage
of woman. Florence Nightingale brings lint and
the blessing of her shadow.' Heroic women
offer themselves as nurses of the brave veteran.
The troop of Virginian infantry that had marched
to guard the prison of John Brown ask leave to
pay their respects to the prisoner. Poetry and
eloquence catch the hint, and soar to a pitch unknown before. Everything feels the new breath
except the old doting nigh-dead politicians,
whose heart the trumpet of resurrection could
not wake.

The charm of the best courages is that they
are inventions, inspirations, flashes of genius.
The hero could not have done the feat at another
hour, in a lower mood. The best act of the
marvellous genius of Greece was its first act;
not in the statue or the Parthenon, but in the
instinct which, at Thermopylæ, held Asia at bay,
kept Asia out of Europe, — Asia with its antiquities and organic slavery, — from corrupting
the hope and new morning of the West. The
statue, the architecture, were the later and in-
ferior creation of the same genius. In view of
this moment of history, we recognize a certain

prophetic instinct, better than wisdom. Napoleon said well, " My hand is immediately connected with my head ;" but the *sacred* courage is connected with the heart. The head is a half, a fraction, until it is enlarged and inspired by the moral sentiment. For it is not the means on which we draw, as health or wealth, practical skill or dexterous talent, or multitudes of followers, that count, but the aims only. The aim reacts back on the means. A great aim aggrandizes the means. The meal and water that are the commissariat of the *forlorn hope* that stake their lives to defend the pass are sacred as the Holy Grail, or as if one had eyes to see in chemistry the fuel that is rushing to feed the sun.

There is a persuasion in the soul of man that he is here for cause, that he was put down in this place by the Creator to do the work for which he inspires him, that thus he is an overmatch for all antagonists that could combine against him. The pious Mrs. Hutchinson says of some passages in the defence of Nottingham against the Cavaliers, "It was a great instruction that the best and highest courages are beams of the Almighty." And whenever the religious sentiment is adequately affirmed, it must be with dazzling courage. As long as it is cowardly insinuated, as with the wish

to succor some partial and temporary interest, or
to make it affirm some pragmatical tenet which our
parish church receives to-day, it is not imparted,
and cannot inspire or create. For it is always new,
leads and surprises, and practice never comes up
with it. There are ever appearing in the world
men who, almost as soon as they are born, take a
bee-line to the rack of the inquisitor, the axe of
the tyrant, like Giordano Bruno, Vanini, Huss,
Paul, Jesus and Socrates. Look at Fox's Lives
of the Martyrs, Sewel's History of the Quakers,
Southey's Book of the Church, at the folios of
the Brothers Bollandi, who collected the lives of
twenty-five thousand martyrs, confessors, ascetics
and self-tormentors.[1] There is much of fable,
but a broad basis of fact. The tender skin does
not shrink from bayonets, the timid woman is
not scared by fagots; the rack is not frightful,
nor the rope ignominious. The poor Puritan,
Antony Parsons, at the stake, tied straw on his
head when the fire approached him, and said,
"This is God's hat." Sacred courage indicates
that a man loves an idea better than all things
in the world; that he is aiming neither at pelf
nor comfort, but will venture all to put in act
the invisible thought in his mind. He is everywhere a liberator, but of a freedom that is ideal;

not seeking to have land or money or conveniences, but to have no other limitation than that which his own constitution imposes. He is free to speak truth; he is not free to lie. He wishes to break every yoke all over the world which hinders his brother from acting after his thought.

There are degrees of courage, and each step upward makes us acquainted with a higher virtue.[1] Let us say then frankly that the education of the will is the object of our existence. Poverty, the prison, the rack, the fire, the hatred and execrations of our fellow men, appear trials beyond the endurance of common humanity; but to the hero whose intellect is aggrandized by the soul, and so measures these penalties against the good which his thought surveys, these terrors vanish as darkness at sunrise.

We have little right in piping times of peace to pronounce on these rare heights of character; but there is no assurance of security. In the most private life, difficult duty is never far off. Therefore we must think with courage. Scholars and thinkers are prone to an effeminate habit, and shrink if a coarser shout comes up from the street, or a brutal act is recorded in the journals. The Medical College piles up in its museum its grim monsters of morbid anatomy, and there are melancholy skeptics with a taste for carrion who batten on the hideous facts in history, — persecutions, inquisitions, St. Bartholomew massacres, devilish lives, Nero, Cæsar Borgia, Marat, Lopez; men in whom every ray of humanity was extinguished, parricides, matricides and whatever moral monsters. These are not cheerful facts, but they do not disturb a healthy mind; they require of us a patience as robust as the energy that attacks us, and an unresting exploration of final causes. Wolf, snake and crocodile are not inharmonious in Nature, but are made useful as checks, scavengers and pioneers; and we must have a scope as large as Nature's to deal with beast-like men, detect what scullion function is assigned them, and foresee in the secular melioration of the planet how these will become unnecessary and will die out.

He has not learned the lesson of life who does not every day surmount a fear. I do not wish to put myself or any man into a theatrical position, or urge him to ape the courage of his comrade. Have the courage not to adopt another's courage. There is scope and cause and resistance enough for us in our proper work and circumstance. And there is no creed of an honest man, be he Christian, Turk or Gentoo, which does not equally preach it. If you have no faith in beneficent power above you, but see only an adamantine fate coiling its folds about Nature and man, then reflect that the best use of fate is to teach us courage, if only because baseness cannot change the appointed event. If you accept your thoughts as inspirations from the Supreme Intelligence, obey them when they prescribe difficult duties, because they come only so long as they are used; or, if your skepticism reaches to the last verge, and you have no confidence in any foreign mind, then be brave, because there is one good opinion which must always be of consequence to you, namely, your own.[1]

I am permitted to enrich my chapter by adding an anecdote of pure courage from real life, as narrated in a ballad by a lady to whom all the particulars of the fact are exactly known.[2]

GEORGE NIDIVER

Men have done brave deeds,
  And bards have sung them well:
I of good George Nidiver
  Now the tale will tell.

In Californian mountains
  A hunter bold was he:
Keen his eye and sure his aim
  As any you should see.

A little Indian boy
  Followed him everywhere,
Eager to share the hunter's joy,
  The hunter's meal to share.

And when the bird or deer
  Fell by the hunter's skill,
The boy was always near
  To help with right good will.

One day as through the cleft
  Between two mountains steep,
Shut in both right and left,
  Their questing way they keep,

They see two grizzly bears
  With hunger fierce and fell
Rush at them unawares
  Right down the narrow dell.

The boy turned round with screams,
  And ran with terror wild;
One of the pair of savage beasts
  Pursued the shrieking child.

The hunter raised his gun, —
  He knew *one* charge was all, —

And through the boy's pursuing foe
  He sent his only ball.

The other on George Nidiver
  Came on with dreadful pace:
The hunter stood unarmed,
  And met him face to face.

I say *unarmed* he stood.
  Against those frightful paws
The rifle butt, or club of wood,
  Could stand no more than straws.

George Nidiver stood still
  And looked him in the face;
The wild beast stopped amazed,
  Then came with slackening pace.

Still firm the hunter stood,
  Although his heart beat high;
Again the creature stopped,
  And gazed with wondering eye.

The hunter met his gaze,
  Nor yet an inch gave way;
The bear turned slowly round,
  And slowly moved away.

What thoughts were in his mind
  It would be hard to spell:
What thoughts were in George Nidiver
  I rather guess than tell.

But sure that rifle's aim,
   Swift choice of generous part,
Showed in its passing gleam
   The depths of a brave heart.

XI

SUCCESS

One thing is forever good;
That one thing is Success, —
Dear to the Eumenides,
And to all the heavenly brood.
Who bides at home, nor looks abroad,
Carries the eagles and masters the sword.

But if thou do thy best,
Without remission, without rest,
And invite the sunbeam,
And abhor to feign or seem
Even to those who thee should love
And thy behavior approve;
If thou go in thine own likeness,
Be it health or be it sickness;
If thou go as thy father's son,
If thou wear no mask or lie,
Dealing purely and nakedly; —

    •   •   •   •   •

SUCCESS

OUR American people cannot be taxed with slowness in performance or in praising their performance. The earth is shaken by our engineries. We are feeling our youth and nerve and bone. We have the power of territory and of seacoast, and know the use of these. We count our census, we read our growing valuations, we survey our map, which becomes old in a year or two. Our eyes run approvingly along the lengthened lines of railroad and telegraph. We have gone nearest to the Pole. We have discovered the Antarctic continent. We interfere in Central and South America, at Canton and in Japan ; we are adding to an already enormous territory. Our political constitution is the hope of the world, and we value ourselves on all these feats.

'T is the way of the world; 't is the law of youth, and of unfolding strength. Men are made each with some triumphant superiority, which, through some adaptation of fingers or ear or eye or ciphering or pugilistic or musical or literary craft, enriches the community with a new art; and not only we, but all men of European stock, value these certificates. Giotto could draw a perfect circle: Erwin of Steinbach could build a minster; Olaf, king of Norway, could run round his galley on the blades of the oars of the rowers when the ship was in motion; Ojeda ' could run out swiftly on a plank projected from the top of a tower, turn round swiftly and come back; Evelyn writes from Rome: "Bernini, the Florentine sculptor, architect, painter and poet, a little before my coming to Rome, gave a public opera, wherein he painted the scenes, cut the statues, invented the engines, composed the music, writ the comedy and built the theatre."

"There is nothing in war," said Napoleon, "which I cannot do by my own hands. If there is nobody to make gunpowder, I can manufacture it. The gun-carriages I know how to construct. If it is necessary to make cannons at the forge, I can make them. The details of working them in battle, if it is necessary to teach, I shall teach them. In administration, it is I alone who have arranged the finances, as you know."

It is recorded of Linnæus, among many proofs of his beneficent skill, that when the timber in the shipyards of Sweden was ruined by rot, Linnæus was desired by the government to find a remedy.

He studied the insects that infested the timber, and found that they laid their eggs in the logs within certain days in April, and he directed that during ten days at that season the logs should be immersed under water in the docks; which being done, the timber was found to be uninjured.

Columbus at Veragua found plenty of gold; but leaving the coast, the ship full of one hundred and fifty skilful seamen, — some of them old pilots, and with too much experience of their craft and treachery to him, — the wise admiral kept his private record of his homeward path. And when he reached Spain he told the King and Queen that "they may ask all the pilots who came with him where is Veragua. Let them answer and say if they know where Veragua lies. I assert that they can give no other account than that they went to lands where there was abundance of gold, but they do not know the way to return thither, but would be obliged to go on a voyage of discovery as much as if they had never been there before. There is a mode of reckoning," he proudly adds, "derived from astronomy, which is sure and safe to any one who understands it." [1]

Hippocrates in Greece knew how to stay the

devouring plague which ravaged Athens in his time, and his skill died with him. Dr. Benjamin Rush, in Philadelphia, carried that city heroically through the yellow fever of the year 1793. Leverrier carried the Copernican system in his head, and knew where to look for the new planet. We have seen an American woman write a novel of which a million copies were sold, in all languages, and which had one merit, of speaking to the universal heart, and was read with equal interest to three audiences, namely, in the parlor, in the kitchen and in the nursery of every house. We have seen women who could institute hospitals and schools in armies. We have seen a woman who by pure song could melt the souls of whole populations. And there is no limit to these varieties of talent.[1]

These are arts to be thankful for, — each one as it is a new direction of human power. We cannot choose but respect them. Our civilization is made up of a million contributions of this kind. For success, to be sure we esteem it a test in other people, since we do first in ourselves. We respect ourselves more if we have succeeded. Neither do we grudge to each of these benefactors the praise or the profit which accrues from his industry.

Here are already quite different degrees of moral merit in these examples. I don't know but we and our race elsewhere set a higher value on wealth, victory and coarse superiority of all kinds, than other men, — have less tranquillity of mind, are less easily contented. The Saxon is taught from his infancy to wish to be first. The Norseman was a restless rider, fighter, free-booter. The ancient Norse ballads describe him as afflicted with this inextinguishable thirst of victory. The mother says to her son:—

> "Success shall be in thy courser tall,
> Success in thyself, which is best of all,
> Success in thy hand, success in thy foot,
> In struggle with man, in battle with brute:—
> The holy God and Saint Drothin dear
> Shall never shut eyes on thy career;
> Look out, look out, Svend Vonved!" [1]

These feats that we extol do not signify so much as we say. These boasted arts are of very recent origin. They are local conveniences, but do not really add to our stature. The greatest men of the world have managed not to want them. Newton was a great man, without telegraph, or gas, or steam-coach, or rubber shoes, or lucifer-matches, or ether for his pain; so was Shakspeare and Alfred and Scipio and Socrates.

These are local conveniences, but how easy to go now to parts of the world where not only all these arts are wanting, but where they are despised. The Arabian sheiks, the most dignified people in the planet, do not want them; yet have as much self-respect as the English, and are easily able to impress the Frenchman or the American who visits them with the respect due to a brave and sufficient man.

These feats have to be sure great difference of merit, and some of them involve power of a high kind. But the public values the invention more than the inventor does. The inventor knows there is much more and better where this came from. The public sees in it a lucrative secret. Men see the reward which the inventor enjoys, and they think, 'How shall we win that?' Cause and effect are a little tedious; how to leap to the result by short or by false means? We are not scrupulous. What we ask is victory, without regard to the cause; after the Rob Roy rule, after the Napoleon rule, to be the strongest to-day, — the way of the Talleyrands, prudent people, whose watches go faster than their neighbors', and who detect the first moment of decline and throw themselves on the instant on the winning side. I have heard that Nelson used to say,

" Never mind the justice or the impudence, only let me succeed." Lord Brougham's single duty of counsel is, " to get the prisoner clear." Fuller says 't is a maxim of lawyers that " a crown once worn cleareth all defects of the wearer thereof." *Rien ne réussit mieux que le succès.* And we Americans are tainted with this insanity, as our bankruptcies and our reckless politics may show. We are great by exclusion, grasping and egotism. Our success takes from all what it gives to one. 'T is a haggard, malignant, careworn running for luck.[1]

Egotism is a kind of buckram that gives momentary strength and concentration to men, and seems to be much used in Nature for fabrics in which local and spasmodic energy is required. I could point to men in this country, of indispensable importance to the carrying on of American life, of this humor, whom we could ill spare; any one of them would be a national loss. But it spoils conversation. They will not try conclusions with you. They are ever thrusting this pampered self between you and them.[2] It is plain they have a long education to undergo to reach simplicity and plain-dealing, which are what a wise man mainly cares for in his companion. Nature knows how to convert evil to

VII

good; Nature utilizes misers, fanatics, show-men, egotists, to accomplish her ends; but we must not think better of the foible for that. The passion for sudden success is rude and puerile, just as war, cannons and executions are used to clear the ground of bad, lumpish, irreclaimable savages, but always to the damage of the conquerors.

I hate this shallow Americanism which hopes to get rich by credit, to get knowledge by raps on midnight tables, to learn the economy of the mind by phrenology, or skill without study, or mastery without apprenticeship, or the sale of goods through pretending that they sell, or power through making believe you are powerful, or through a packed jury or caucus, bribery and " repeating " votes, or wealth by fraud. They think they have got it, but they have got something else, — a crime which calls for another crime, and another devil behind that; these are steps .to suicide, infamy and the harming of mankind. We countenance each other in this life of show, puffing, advertisement and manufacture of public opinion; and excellence is lost sight of in the hunger for sudden performance and praise.

There was a wise man, an Italian artist, Michel

Angelo, who writes thus of himself: "Meanwhile the Cardinal Ippolito, in whom all my best hopes were placed, being dead, I began to understand that the promises of this world are for the most part vain phantoms, and that to confide in one's self, and become something of worth and value, is the best and safest course." Now, though I am by no means sure that the reader will assent to all my propositions, yet I think we shall agree in my first rule for success, — that we shall drop the brag and the advertisement, and take Michel Angelo's course, " to confide in one's self, and be something of worth and value."

Each man has an aptitude born with him. Do your work. I have to say this often, but Nature says it oftener. 'T is clownish to insist on doing all with one's own hands, as if every man should build his own clumsy house, forge his hammer, and bake his dough; but he is to dare to do what he can do best; not help others as they would direct him, but as he knows his helpful power to be. To do otherwise is to neutralize all those extraordinary special talents distributed among men. Yet whilst this self-truth is essential to the exhibition of the world and to the growth and glory of each mind, it is rare to find a man who believes his own thought or who speaks that which he was created to say.[1] As nothing astonishes men so much as common sense and plain dealing, so nothing is more rare in any man than an act of his own. Any work looks wonderful to him, except that which he can do. We do not believe our own thought; we must serve somebody; we must quote somebody; we dote on the old and the distant; we are tickled by great names; we import the religion of other nations; we quote their opinions; we cite their laws. The gravest and learnedest courts in this country shudder to face a new question, and will wait months and years for a case to occur that can be tortured into a precedent, and thus throw on a bolder party the *onus* of an initiative. Thus we do not carry a counsel in our breasts, or do not know it; and because we cannot shake off from our shoes this dust of Europe and Asia, the world seems to be born old, society is under a spell, every man is a borrower and a mimic, life is theatrical and literature a quotation; and hence that depression of spirits, that furrow of care, said to mark every American brow.[2]

Self-trust is the first secret of success, the belief that if you are here the authorities of the universe put you here, and for cause, or with

some task strictly appointed you in your constitution, and so long as you work at that you
are well and successful. It by no means consists
in rushing prematurely to a showy feat that shall
catch the eye and satisfy spectators. It is enough
if you work in the right direction. So far from
the performance being the real success, it is
clear that the success was much earlier than
that, namely, when all the feats that make our
civility were the thoughts of good heads.[1] The
fame of each discovery rightly attaches to the
mind that made the formula which contains all
the details, and not to the manufacturers who
now make their gain by it; although the mob
uniformly cheers the publisher, and not the inventor. It is the dulness of the multitude that
they cannot see the house in the ground-plan;
the working, in the model of the projector.
Whilst it is a thought, though it were a new
fuel, or a new food, or the creation of agriculture,
it is cried down, it is a chimera; but when it is
a fact, and comes in the shape of eight per cent.,
ten per cent., a hundred per cent., they cry, ' It
is the voice of God.'[2] Horatio Greenough the
sculptor said to me of Robert Fulton's visit to
Paris: " Fulton knocked at the door of Napoleon with steam, and was rejected; and Napoleon

lived long enough to know that he had excluded a greater power than his own."

Is there no loving of knowledge, and of art, and of our design, for itself alone? Cannot we please ourselves with performing our work, or gaining truth and power, without being praised for it? I gain my point, I gain all points, if I can reach my companion with any statement which teaches him his own worth. The sum of wisdom is, that the time is never lost that is devoted to work. The good workman never says, 'There, that will do;' but, 'There, that is it: try it, and come again, it will last always.' If the artist, in whatever art, is well at work on his own design, it signifies little that he does not yet find orders or customers. I pronounce that young man happy who is content with having acquired the skill which he had aimed at, and waits willingly when the occasion of making it appreciated shall arrive, knowing well that it will not loiter. The time your rival spends in dressing up his work for effect, hastily, and for the market, you spend in study and experiments towards real knowledge and efficiency. He has thereby sold his picture or machine, or won the prize, or got the appointment; but you have raised yourself into a higher school of

art, and a few years will show the advantage
of the real master over the short popularity
of the showman. I know it is a nice point to
discriminate this self-trust, which is the pledge
of all mental vigor and performance, from the
disease to which it is allied, — the exaggeration
of the part which we can play; — yet they are
two things. But it is sanity to know that, over
my talent or knack, and a million times better
than any talent, is the central intelligence which
subordinates and uses all talents; and it is
only as a door into this, that any talent or the
knowledge it gives is of value. He only who
comes into this central intelligence, in which
no egotism or exaggeration can be, comes into
self-possession.

My next point is that in the scale of powers
it is not talent but sensibility which is best: talent
confines, but the central life puts us in relation to
all. How often it seems the chief good to be born
with a cheerful temper and well adjusted to the
tone of the human race. Such a man feels himself in harmony, and conscious by his receptivity
of an infinite strength. Like Alfred, "good fortune accompanies him like a gift of God."¹ Feel
yourself, and be not daunted by things. 'T is
the fulness of man that runs over into objects,

and makes his Bibles and Shakspeares and
Homers so great. The joyful reader borrows
of his own ideas to fill their faulty outline, and
knows not that he borrows and gives.[1]

There is something of poverty in our criticism. We assume that there are few great men,
all the rest are little; that there is but one
Homer, but one Shakspeare, one Newton, one
Socrates. But the soul in her beaming hour
does not acknowledge these usurpations. We
should know how to praise Socrates, or Plato,
or Saint John, without impoverishing us. In
good hours we do not find Shakspeare or Homer
over-great, only to have been translators of the
happy present, and every man and woman
divine possibilities. 'T is the good reader that
makes the good book; a good head cannot read
amiss, in every book he finds passages which
seem confidences or asides hidden from all else
and unmistakably meant for his ear.[2]

The light by which we see in this world comes
out from the soul of the observer. Wherever
any noble sentiment dwelt, it made the faces and
houses around to shine. Nay, the powers of
this busy brain are miraculous and illimitable.
Therein are the rules and formulas by which
the whole empire of matter is worked. There is

no prosperity, trade, art, city, or great material wealth of any kind, but if you trace it home, you will find it rooted in a thought of some individual man.

Is all life a surface affair ? 'T is curious, but our difference of wit appears to be only a difference of impressionability, or power to appreciate faint, fainter and infinitely faintest voices and visions.[1] When the scholar or the writer has pumped his brain for thoughts and verses, and then comes abroad into Nature, has he never found that there is a better poetry hinted in a boy's whistle of a tune, or in the piping of a sparrow, than in all his literary results ? We call it health. What is so admirable as the health of youth? — with his long days because his eyes are good, and brisk circulations keep him warm in cold rooms, and he loves books that speak to the imagination ; and he can read Plato, covered to his chin with a cloak in a cold upper chamber, though he should associate the Dialogues ever after with a woollen smell.[2] 'T is the bane of life that natural effects are continually crowded out, and artificial arrangements substituted. We remember when in early youth the earth spoke and the heavens glowed ; when an evening, any evening, grim and wintry, sleet and snow, was enough for us; the houses were in the air. Now it costs a rare combination of clouds and lights to overcome the common and mean. What is it we look for in the landscape, in sunsets and sunrises, in the sea and the firmament? what but a compensation for the cramp and pettiness of human performances?[1] We bask in the day, and the mind finds somewhat as great as itself. In Nature all is large massive repose. Remember what befalls a city boy who goes for the first time into the October woods. He is suddenly initiated into a pomp and glory that brings to pass for him the dreams of romance. He is the king he dreamed he was; he walks through tents of gold, through bowers of crimson, porphyry and topaz, pavilion on pavilion, garlanded with vines, flowers and sunbeams, with incense and music, with so many hints to his astonished senses; the leaves twinkle and pique and flatter him, and his eye and step are tempted on by what hazy distances to happier solitudes.[2] All this happiness he owes only to his finer perception. The owner of the wood-lot finds only a number of discolored trees, and says, 'They ought to come down; they are n't growing any better; they should be cut and corded before spring.'

Wordsworth writes of the delights of the boy
in Nature : —

> "For never will come back the hour
>   Of splendor in the grass, of glory in the flower." [1]

But I have just seen a man, well knowing what
he spoke of, who told me that the verse was not
true for him ; that his eyes opened as he grew
older, and that every spring was more beautiful
to him than the last. *compare*

X— We live among gods of our own creation.
Does that deep-toned bell, which has shortened
many a night of ill nerves, render to you nothing
but acoustic vibrations ? Is the old church
which gave you the first lessons of religious life,
or the village school, or the college where you
first knew the dreams of fancy and joys of
thought, only boards or brick and mortar? [2] Is
the house in which you were born, or the house
in which your dearest friend lived, only a piece
of real estate whose value is covered by the
Hartford insurance ? You walk on the beach and
enjoy the animation of the picture. Scoop up a
little water in the hollow of your palm, take up
a handful of shore sand ; well, these are the elements. What is the beach but acres of sand?
what is the ocean but cubic miles of water? a
little more or less signifies nothing. No, it is

that this brute matter is part of somewhat not brute. It is that the sand floor is held by spheral gravity, and bent to be a part of the round globe, under the optical sky, — part of the astonishing astronomy, and existing at last to moral ends and from moral causes.[1]

The world is not made up to the eye of figures, that is, only half; it is also made of color. How that element washes the universe with its enchanting waves! The sculptor had ended his work, and behold a new world of dream-like glory. 'T is the last stroke of Nature; beyond color she cannot go.[2] In like manner, life is made up, not of knowledge only, but of love also. If thought is form, sentiment is color. It clothes the skeleton world with space, variety and glow. The hues of sunset make life great; so the affections make some little web of cottage and fireside populous, important, and filling the main space in our history.

The fundamental fact in our metaphysic constitution is the correspondence of man to the world, so that every change in that writes a record in the mind.[3] The mind yields sympathetically to the tendencies or law which stream through things and make the order of Nature; and in the perfection of this correspondence or

expressiveness, the health and force of man consist. If we follow this hint into our intellectual
education, we shall find that it is not propositions, not new dogmas and a logical exposition
of the world that are our first need; but to
watch and tenderly cherish the intellectual and
moral sensibilities, those fountains of right
thought, and woo them to stay and make their
home with us. Whilst they abide with us we
shall not think amiss. Our perception far out-
runs our talent. We bring a welcome to the
highest lessons of religion and of poetry out of
all proportion beyond our skill to teach. And,
further, the great hearing and sympathy of men
is more true and wise than their speaking is
wont to be. A deep sympathy is what we require for any student of the mind; for the chief
difference between man and man is a difference of impressionability. Aristotle or Bacon
or Kant propound some maxim which is the
key-note of philosophy thenceforward. But I
am more interested to know that when at last
they have hurled out their grand word, it is
only some familiar experience of every man in
the street. If it be not, it will never be heard
of again.[1]

Ah! if one could keep this sensibility, and live

in the happy sufficing present, and find the day
and its cheap means contenting, which only ask
receptivity in you, and no strained exertion and
cankering ambition, overstimulating to be at the
head of your class and the head of society, and
to have distinction and laurels and consumption !
We are not strong by our power to penetrate,
but by our relatedness.¹ The world is enlarged
for us, not by new objects, but by finding more
affinities and potencies in those we have.

This sensibility appears in the homage to
beauty which exalts the faculties of youth; in
the power which form and color exert upon the
soul; when we see eyes that are a compliment
to the human race, features that explain the
Phidian sculpture. Fontenelle said : "There
are three things about which I have curiosity,
though I know nothing of them, — music,
poetry and love." The great doctors of this
science are the greatest men, — Dante, Petrarch,
Michel Angelo and Shakspeare. The wise Socrates treats this matter with a certain archness,
yet with very marked expressions. "I am
always," he says, "asserting that I happen to
know, I may say, nothing but a mere trifle relating to matters of love; yet in that kind of
learning I lay claim to being more skilled than

any one man of the past or present time." They may well speak in this uncertain manner of their knowledge, and in this confident manner of their will, for the secret of it is hard to detect, so deep it is ; and yet genius is measured by its skill in this science.[1]

Who is he in youth or in maturity or even in old age, who does not like to hear of those sensibilities which turn curled heads round at church, and send wonderful eye-beams across assemblies, from one to one, never missing in the thickest crowd? The keen statist reckons by tens and hundreds ; the genial man is interested in every slipper that comes into the assembly. The passion, alike everywhere, creeps under the snows of Scandinavia, under the fires of the equator, and swims in the seas of Polynesia. Lofn is as puissant a divinity in the Norse Edda as Camadeva in the red vault of India, Eros in the Greek, or Cupid in the Latin heaven. And what is specially true of love is that it is a state of extreme impressionability ; the lover has more senses and finer senses than others ; his eye and ear are telegraphs ; he reads omens on the flower, and cloud, and face, and form, and gesture, and reads them aright. In his surprise at the sudden and entire understanding that is between him and the beloved person, it occurs to him that they might somehow meet independently of time and place. How delicious the belief that he could elude all guards, precautions, ceremonies, means and delays, and hold instant and sempiternal communication! In solitude, in banishment, the hope returned, and the experiment was eagerly tried. The supernal powers seem to take his part. What was on his lips to say is uttered by his friend. When he went abroad, he met, by wonderful casualties, the one person he sought.[1] If in his walk he chanced to look back, his friend was walking behind him. And it has happened that the artist has often drawn in his pictures the face of the future wife whom he had not yet seen.

But also in complacencies nowise so strict as this of the passion, the man of sensibility counts it a delight only to hear a child's voice fully addressed to him, or to see the beautiful manners of the youth of either sex. When the event is past and remote, how insignificant the greatest compared with the piquancy of the present! To-day at the school examination the professor interrogates Sylvina in the history class about Odoacer and Alaric. Sylvina can't remember, but suggests that Odoacer was defeated; and the professor tartly replies, " No, he defeated the Romans." But 't is plain to the visitor that 't is of no importance at all about Odoacer and 't is a great deal of importance about Sylvina, and if she says he was defeated, why he had better a great deal have been defeated than give her a moment's annoy. Odoacer, if there was a particle of the gentleman in him, would have said, Let me be defeated a thousand times.[1]

And as our tenderness for youth and beauty gives a new and just importance to their fresh and manifold claims, so the like sensibility gives welcome to all excellence, has eyes and hospitality for merit in corners. An Englishman of marked character and talent, who had brought with him hither one or two friends and a library of mystics, assured me that nobody and nothing of possible interest was left in England,—he had brought all that was alive away. I was forced to reply: " No, next door to you probably, on the other side of the partition in the same house, was a greater man than any you had seen." [2] Every man has a history worth knowing, if he could tell it, or if we could draw it from him. Character and wit have their own magnetism. Send a deep man into any town, and he will find another

VII

deep man there, unknown hitherto to his neighbors. That is the great happiness of life,— to add to our high acquaintances. The very law of averages might have assured you that there will be in every hundred heads, say ten or five good heads. Morals are generated as the atmosphere is. 'T is a secret, the genesis of either ; but the springs of justice and courage do not fail any more than salt or sulphur springs.

The world is always opulent,[1] the oracles are never silent; but the receiver must by a happy temperance be brought to that top of condition, that frolic health, that he can easily take and give these fine communications. Health is the condition of wisdom, and the sign is cheerfulness, —an open and noble temper. There was never poet who had not the heart in the right place. The old trouveur, Pons Capdueil,[2] wrote,—

> " Oft have I heard, and deem the witness true,
> Whom man delights in, God delights in too."

All beauty warms the heart, is a sign of health, prosperity and the favor of God. Everything lasting and fit for men the Divine Power has marked with this stamp. What delights, what emancipates, not what scars and pains us, is wise and good in speech and in the arts.[3] For, truly, the heart at the centre of the universe with every throb hurls the flood of happiness into every artery, vein and veinlet, so that the whole system is inundated with the tides of joy. The plenty of the poorest place is too great: the harvest cannot be gathered. Every sound ends in music. The edge of every surface is tinged with prismatic rays.

One more trait of true success. The good mind chooses what is positive, what is advancing, —embraces the affirmative. Our system is one of poverty. 'T is presumed, as I said, there is but one Shakspeare, one Homer, one Jesus, — not that all are or shall be inspired. But we must begin by affirming. Truth and goodness subsist forevermore. It is true there is evil and good, night and day: but these are not equal. The day is great and final. The night is for the day, but the day is not for the night. What is this immortal demand for more, which belongs to our constitution? this enormous ideal? There is no such critic and beggar as this terrible Soul. No historical person begins to content us. We know the satisfactoriness of justice, the sufficiency of truth.[1] We know the answer that leaves nothing to ask. We know the Spirit by its victorious tone. The searching tests to apply to every new pretender are amount

and quality, — what does he add? and what is
the state of mind he leaves me in? Your theory
is unimportant; but what new stock you can add
to humanity, or how high you can carry life?[1]
A man is a man only as he makes life and nature
happier to us.

I fear the popular notion of success stands in
direct opposition in all points to the real and
wholesome success. One adores public opinion,
the other private opinion;[2] one fame, the other
desert; one feats, the other humility; one lucre,
the other love; one monopoly, and the other
hospitality of mind.

We may apply this affirmative law to letters,
to manners, to art, to the decorations of our
houses, etc. I do not find executions or tortures
or lazar-houses, or grisly photographs of the field
on the day after the battle, fit subjects for cabinet
pictures. I think that some so-called "sacred
subjects" must be treated with more genius
than I have seen in the masters of Italian or
Spanish art to be right pictures for houses and
churches.[3] Nature does not invite such exhibition. Nature lays the ground-plan of each creature accurately, sternly fit for all his functions;
then veils it scrupulously. See how carefully she
covers up the skeleton. The eye shall not see

it; the sun shall not shine on it. She weaves her tissues and integuments of flesh and skin and hair and beautiful colors of the day over it, and forces death down underground, and makes haste to cover it up with leaves and vines, and wipes carefully out every trace by new creation. Who and what are you that would lay the ghastly anatomy bare?

Don't hang a dismal picture on the wall, and do not daub with sables and glooms in your conversation. Don't be a cynic and disconsolate preacher. Don't bewail and bemoan. Omit the negative propositions. Nerve us with incessant affirmatives. Don't waste yourself in rejection,[1] nor bark against the bad, but chant the beauty of the good. When that is spoken which has a right to be spoken, the chatter and the criticism will stop. Set down nothing that will not help somebody; —

> "For every gift of noble origin
> Is breathed upon by Hope's perpetual breath." [2]

The affirmative of affirmatives is love. As much love, so much perception. As caloric to matter, so is love to mind; so it enlarges, and so it empowers it. Good will makes insight, as one finds his way to the sea by embarking on a river. I have seen scores of people who can silence me, but I seek one who shall make me forget or overcome the frigidities and imbecilities into which I fall. The painter Giotto, Vasari tells us, renewed art because he put more goodness into his heads. To awake in man and to raise the sense of worth, to educate his feeling and judgment so that he shall scorn himself for a bad action, that is the only aim.

'T is cheap and easy to destroy. There is not a joyful boy or an innocent girl buoyant with fine purposes of duty, in all the street full of eager and rosy faces, but a cynic can chill and dishearten with a single word. Despondency comes readily enough to the most sanguine. The cynic has only to follow their hint with his bitter confirmation, and they check that eager courageous pace and go home with heavier step and premature age. They will themselves quickly enough give the hint he wants to the cold wretch. Which of them has not failed to please where they most wished it? or blundered where they were most ambitious of success? or found themselves awkward or tedious or incapable of study, thought or heroism, and only hoped by good sense and fidelity to do what they could and pass unblamed? And this witty malefactor makes their little hope less with satire and skepticism, and slackens the springs of endeavor. Yes, this is easy; but to help the young soul, add energy, inspire hope and blow the coals into a useful flame; to redeem defeat by new thought, by firm action, that is not easy, that is the work of divine men.[1]

We live on different planes or platforms. There is an external life, which is educated at school, taught to read, write, cipher and trade; taught to grasp all the boy can get, urging him to put himself forward, to make himself useful and agreeable in the world, to ride, run, argue and contend, unfold his talents, shine, conquer and possess.

But the inner life sits at home, and does not learn to do things, nor value these feats at all. 'Tis a quiet, wise perception. It loves truth, because it is itself real; it loves right, it knows nothing else; but it makes no progress; was as wise in our first memory of it as now; is just the same now in maturity and hereafter in age, it was in youth. We have grown to manhood and womanhood; we have powers, connection, children, reputations, professions: this makes no account of them all. It lives in the great present; it makes the present great. This tranquil, well-founded, wide-seeing soul is no express-rider, no attorney, no magistrate: it lies in the sun and broods on the world. A person of this temper once said to a man of much activity, "I will pardon you that you do so much, and you me that I do nothing." And Euripides says that "Zeus hates busybodies and those who do too much."[1]

XII

OLD AGE

‘Once more,’ the old man cried, ‘ye clouds,
Airy turrets purple-piled,
Which once my infancy beguiled,
Beguile me with the wonted spell.
I know ye skilful to convoy
The total freight of hope and joy
Into rude and homely nooks,
Shed mocking lustres on shelf of books,
On farmer’s byre, on pasture rude,
And stony pathway to the wood.
I care not if the pomps you show
Be what they soothfast appear,
Or if yon realms in sunset glow
Be bubbles of the atmosphere.
And if it be to you allowed
To fool me with a shining cloud,
So only new griefs are consoled
By new delights, as old by old,
Frankly I will be your guest,
Count your change and cheer the best.
The world hath overmuch of pain, —
If Nature give me joy again,
Of such deceit I ’ll not complain.’

'As the bird trims her to the gale,
  I trim myself to the storm of time,
  I man the rudder, reef the sail,
  Obey the voice at eve obeyed at prime:
  Lowly faithful, banish fear,
  Right onward drive unharmed;
  The port, well worth the cruise, is near
  And every wave is charmed.'

OLD AGE

ON the anniversary of the Phi Beta Kappa
Society at Cambridge in 1861, the venerable President Quincy, senior member of the
Society, as well as senior alumnus of the University, was received at the dinner with peculiar
demonstrations of respect. He replied to these
compliments in a speech, and, gracefully claiming the privileges of a literary society, entered at
some length into an Apology for Old Age, and,
aiding himself by notes in his hand, made a sort
of running commentary on Cicero's chapter De
Senectute. The character of the speaker, the
transparent good faith of his praise and blame,
and the naïveté of his eager preference of Cicero's
opinions to King David's, gave unusual interest
to the College festival. It was a discourse full of
dignity, honoring him who spoke and those who
heard.

The speech led me to look over at home —
an easy task — Cicero's famous essay, charming
by its uniform rhetorical merit; heroic with
Stoical precepts, with a Roman eye to the claims
of the State; happiest perhaps in his praise of
life on the farm; and rising at the conclusion to

a lofty strain. But he does not exhaust the subject; rather invites the attempt to add traits to
the picture from our broader modern life.

Cicero makes no reference to the illusions
which cling to the element of time, and in which
Nature delights. Wellington, in speaking of
military men, said, "What masks are these uniforms to hide cowards!" I have often detected
the like deception in the cloth shoe, wadded
pelisse, wig, spectacles and padded chair of Age.
Nature lends herself to these illusions, and adds
dim sight, deafness, cracked voice, snowy hair,
short memory and sleep. These also are masks,
and all is not Age that wears them. Whilst we
yet call ourselves young and our mates are yet
youths with even boyish remains, one good fellow in the set prematurely sports a gray or a bald
head, which does not impose on us who know
how innocent of sanctity or of Platonism he is,
but does deceive his juniors and the public, who
presently distinguish him with a most amusing
respect: and this lets us into the secret that the
venerable forms that so awed our childhood were
just such impostors. Nature is full of freaks,
and now puts an old head on young shoulders,
and then a young heart beating under fourscore
winters.

For if the essence of age is not present, these
signs, whether of Art or Nature, are counterfeit
and ridiculous : and the essence of age is intellect. Wherever that appears, we call it old. If
we look into the eyes of the youngest person we
sometimes discover that here is one who knows
already what you would go about with much
pains to teach him ; there is that in him which
is the ancestor of all around him : which fact the
Indian Vedas express when they say, " He that
can discriminate is the father of his father." And
in our old British legends of Arthur and the
Round Table, his friend and counsellor, Merlin
the Wise, is a babe found exposed in a basket by the river-side, and, though an infant of
only a few days, speaks articulately to those who
discover him, tells his name and history, and
presently foretells the fate of the by-standers.
Wherever there is power, there is age. Don't
be deceived by dimples and curls. I tell you
that babe is a thousand years old.¹

Time is indeed the theatre and seat of illusion :
nothing is so ductile and elastic. The mind
stretches an hour to a century and dwarfs an
age to an hour.² Saadi found in a mosque at
Damascus an old Persian of a hundred and fifty
years, who was dying, and was saying to him-

self, "I said, coming into the world by birth, 'I will enjoy myself for a few moments.' Alas! at the variegated table of life I partook of a few mouthfuls, and the Fates said, '*Enough!*'" That which does not decay is so central and controlling in us, that, as long as one is alone by himself, he is not sensible of the inroads of time, which always begin at the surface-edges. If, on a winter day, you should stand within a bell-glass, the face and color of the afternoon clouds would not indicate whether it were June or January; and if we did not find the reflection of ourselves in the eyes of the young people, we could not know that the century-clock had struck seventy instead of twenty. How many men habitually believe that each chance passenger with whom they converse is of their own age, and presently find it was his father and not his brother whom they knew![1]

But not to press too hard on these deceits and illusions of Nature, which are inseparable from our condition, and looking at age under an aspect more conformed to the common sense, if the question be the felicity of age, I fear the first popular judgments will be unfavorable. From the point of sensuous experience, seen from the streets and markets and the haunts of pleasure and gain, the estimate of age is low, melancholy and skeptical. Frankly face the facts, and see the result. Tobacco, coffee, alcohol, hashish, prussic acid, strychnine, are weak dilutions: the surest poison is time. This cup which Nature puts to our lips, has a wonderful virtue, surpassing that of any other draught. It opens the senses, adds power, fills us with exalted dreams, which we call hope, love, ambition, science: especially, it creates a craving for larger draughts of itself. But they who take the larger draughts are drunk with.it, lose their stature, strength, beauty and senses, and end in folly and delirium. We postpone our literary work until we have more ripeness and skill to write, and we one day discover that our literary talent was a youthful effervescence which we have now lost.[1] We had a judge in Massachusetts who at sixty proposed to resign, alleging that he perceived a certain decay in his faculties; he was dissuaded by his friends, on account of the public convenience at that time. At seventy it was hinted to him that it was time to retire; but he now replied that he thought his judgment as robust and all his faculties as good as ever they were. But besides the self-deception, the strong and hasty laborers of the street do not work well with the chronic valetudinarian. Youth is everywhere in

place. Age, like woman, requires fit surround-
ings. Age is comely in coaches, in churches,
in chairs of state and ceremony, in council-
chambers, in courts of justice and historical
societies. Age is becoming in the country. But
in the rush and uproar of Broadway, if you look
into the faces of the passengers there is dejection
or indignation in the seniors, a certain concealed
sense of injury, and the lip made up with a heroic
determination not to mind it. Few envy the
consideration enjoyed by the oldest inhabitant.
We do not count a man's years, until he has
nothing else to count. The vast inconvenience
of animal immortality was told in the fable of
Tithonus.[1] In short, the creed of the street is,
Old Age is not disgraceful, but immensely dis-
advantageous. Life is well enough, but we shall
all be glad to get out of it, and they will all be
glad to have us.

This is odious on the face of it. Universal
convictions are not to be shaken by the whim-
seys of overfed butchers and firemen, or by the
sentimental fears of girls who would keep the
infantile bloom on their cheeks. We know the
value of experience. Life and art are cumulative;
and he who has accomplished something in any
department alone deserves to be heard on that

subject. A man of great employments and excellent performance used to assure me that he did not think a man worth anything until he was sixty; although this smacks a little of the resolution of a certain " Young Men's Republican Club," that all men should be held eligible who are under seventy. But in all governments, the councils of power were held by the old; and patricians or *patres*, senate or *senes*, *seigneurs* or seniors, *gerousia*, the senate of Sparta, the presbytery of the Church, and the like, all signify simply old men.

The cynical creed or lampoon of the market is refuted by the universal prayer for long life, which is the verdict of Nature and justified by all history. We have, it is true, examples of an accelerated pace by which young men achieved grand works; as in the Macedonian Alexander, in Raffaelle, Shakspeare, Pascal, Burns and Byron; but these are rare exceptions. Nature, in the main, vindicates her law. Skill to do comes of doing; knowledge comes by eyes always open, and working hands; and there is no knowledge that is not power. Béranger said, "Almost all the good workmen live long."[1] And if the life be true and noble, we have quite another sort of seniors than the frowzy, timorous, peevish dotards who are falsely old, —namely, the men who fear no city, but by whom cities stand; who appearing in any street, the people empty their houses to gaze at and obey them : as at " My Cid, with the fleecy beard," in Toledo; or Bruce, as Barbour reports him; as blind old Dandolo, elected doge at eighty-four years, storming Constantinople at ninety-four, and after the revolt again victorious and elected at the age of ninety-six to the throne of the Eastern Empire, which he declined, and died doge at ninety-seven. We still feel the force of Socrates, "whom well-advised the oracle pronounced wisest of men ;" of Archimedes, holding Syracuse against the Romans by his wit, and himself better than all their nation ; of Michel Angelo, wearing the four crowns of architecture, sculpture, painting and poetry; of Galileo, of whose blindness Castelli said, " The noblest eye is darkened that Nature ever made, — an eye that hath seen more than all that went before him, and hath opened the eyes of all that shall come after him ;" of Newton, who made an important discovery for every one of his eighty-five years; of Bacon, who " took all knowledge to be his province ;" of Fontenelle, " that precious porcelain vase laid up in the centre of France to be guarded with the utmost care for a hundred years ; " of Franklin, Jefferson and Adams, the wise and heroic statesmen ; of Washington, the perfect citizen ; of Wellington, the perfect soldier; of Goethe, the all-knowing poet ; of Humboldt, the encyclopædia of science.[1]

Under the general assertion of the well-being of age, we can easily count particular benefits of that condition. It has weathered the perilous capes and shoals in the sea whereon we sail, and the chief evil of life is taken away in removing the grounds of fear. The insurance of a ship expires as she enters the harbor at home. It were strange if a man should turn his sixtieth year without a feeling of immense relief from the number of dangers he has escaped. When the old wife says, ' Take care of that tumor in your shoulder, perhaps it is cancerous,' — he replies, ' I am yielding to a surer decomposition.' The humorous thief who drank a pot of beer at the gallows blew off the froth because he had heard it was unhealthy ; but it will not add a pang to the prisoner marched out to be shot, to assure him that the pain in his knee threatens mortification. When the pleuro-pneumonia of the cows raged, the butchers said that though the acute degree was novel, there never was a time

when this disease did not occur among cattle.
All men carry seeds of all distempers through
life latent, and we die without developing them;
such is the affirmative force of the constitution;
but if you are enfeebled by any cause, some of
these sleeping seeds start and open. Meantime,
at every stage we lose a foe. At fifty years, 't is
said, afflicted citizens lose their sick-headaches.
I hope this hegira is not as movable a feast as
that one I annually look for, when the horti-
culturists assure me that the rose-bugs in our
gardens disappear on the tenth of July; they
stay a fortnight later in mine.[1] But be it as it
may with the sick-headache, — 't is certain that
graver headaches and heart-aches are lulled once
for all as we come up with certain goals of time.
The passions have answered their purpose: that
slight but dread overweight with which in each
instance Nature secures the execution of her aim,
drops off. To keep man in the planet, she impresses the terror of death. To perfect the commissariat, she implants in each a certain rapacity
to get the supply, and a little oversupply, of his
wants. To insure the existence of the race, she
reinforces the sexual instinct, at the risk of dis-
order, grief and pain.[2] To secure strength, she
plants cruel hunger and thirst, which so easily

overdo their office, and invite disease. But these temporary stays and shifts for the protection of the young animal are shed as fast as they can be replaced by nobler resources. We live in youth amidst this rabble of passions, quite too tender, quite too hungry and irritable. Later, the interiors of mind and heart open, and supply grander motives. We learn the fatal compensations that wait on every act. Then, one after another, this riotous time-destroying crew disappear.

I count it another capital advantage of age, this, that a success more or less signifies nothing. Little by little it has amassed such a fund of merit that it can very well afford to go on its credit when it will.[1] When I chanced to meet the poet Wordsworth, then sixty-three years old, he told me that " he had just had a fall and lost a tooth, and when his companions were much concerned for the mischance, he had replied that he was glad it had not happened forty years before." Well, Nature takes care that we shall not lose our organs forty years too soon. A lawyer argued a cause yesterday in the Supreme Court, and I was struck with a certain air of levity and defiance which vastly became him. Thirty years ago it was a serious concern to him whether his pleading

was good and effective. Now it is of importance
to his client, but of none to himself. It has
been long already fixed what he can do and
cannot do, and his reputation does not gain or
suffer from one or a dozen new performances.
If he should on a new occasion rise quite beyond
his mark and achieve somewhat great and extraordinary, that, of course, would instantly tell;
but he may go below his mark with impunity,
and people will say, 'O, he had headache,' or
' He lost his sleep for two nights.' What a lust
of appearance, what a load of anxieties that once
degraded him he is thus rid of! Every one is
sensible of this cumulative advantage in living.
All the good days behind him are sponsors, who
speak for him when he is silent, pay for him
when he has no money, introduce him where
he has no letters, and work for him when he
sleeps.

A third felicity of age is that it has found
expression. The youth suffers not only from
ungratified desires, but from powers untried, and
from a picture in his mind of a career which has
as yet no outward reality. He is tormented with
the want of correspondence between things and
thoughts. Michel Angelo's head is full of mas-
culine and gigantic figures as gods walking, which

make him savage until his furious chisel can render them into marble; and of architectural dreams, until a hundred stone-masons can lay them in courses of travertine. There is the like tempest in every good head in which some great benefit for the world is planted. The throes continue until the child is born. Every faculty new to each man thus goads him and drives him out into doleful deserts until it finds proper vent. All the functions of human duty irritate and lash him forward, bemoaning and chiding, until they are performed. He wants friends, employment, knowledge, power, house and land, wife and children, honor and fame; he has religious wants, æsthetic wants, domestic, civil, humane wants. One by one, day after day, he learns to coin his wishes into facts. He has his calling, homestead, social connection and personal power, and thus, at the end of fifty years, his soul is appeased by seeing some sort of correspondence between his wish and his possession. This makes the value of age, the satisfaction it slowly offers to every craving. He is serene who does not feel himself pinched and wronged, but whose condition, in particular and in general, allows the utterance of his mind. In old persons, when thus fully expressed, we often observe a fair, plump, perennial, waxen complexion, which indicates that all the ferment of earlier days has subsided into serenity of thought and behavior.

The compensations of Nature play in age as in youth. In a world so charged and sparkling with power, a man does not live long and actively without costly additions of experience, which, though not spoken, are recorded in his mind. What to the youth is only a guess or a hope, is in the veteran a digested statute. He beholds the feats of the juniors with complacency, but as one who having long ago known these games, has refined them into results and morals. The Indian Red Jacket, when the young braves were boasting their deeds, said, " But the sixties have all the twenties and forties in them."

For a fourth benefit, age sets its house in order, and finishes its works, which to every artist is a supreme pleasure.' Youth has an excess of sensibility, before which every object glitters and attracts. We leave one pursuit for another, and the young man's year is a heap of beginnings. At the end of a twelvemonth, he has nothing to show for it, — not one completed work. But the time is not lost. Our instincts drove us to hive innumerable experiences, that are yet of no visible value, and which we may

keep for twice seven years before they shall be
wanted. The best things are of secular growth.
The instinct of classifying marks the wise and
healthy mind. Linnæus projects his system, and
lays out his twenty-four classes of plants, before
yet he has found in Nature a single plant to justify
certain of his classes. His seventh class has not
one. In process of time, he finds with delight the
little white *Trientalis,* the only plant with seven
petals and sometimes seven stamens, which constitutes a seventh class in conformity with his
system.[1] The conchologist builds his cabinet
whilst as yet he has few shells. He labels shelves
for classes, cells for species: all but a few are
empty. But every year fills some blanks, and
with accelerating speed as he becomes knowing
and known. An old scholar finds keen delight
in verifying the impressive anecdotes and cita-
tions he has met with in miscellaneous reading
and hearing, in all the years of youth. We carry
in memory important anecdotes, and have lost
all clew to the author from whom we had them.
We have a heroic speech from Rome or Greece,
but cannot fix it on the man who said it. We
have an admirable line worthy of Horace, ever
and anon resounding in our mind's ear, but have
searched all probable and improbable books for

it in vain. We consult the reading men: but,
strangely enough, they who know everything
know not this. But especially we have a certain
insulated thought, which haunts us, but remains
insulated and barren. Well, there is nothing for
all this but patience and time. Time, yes, that
is the finder, the unweariable explorer, not subject to casualties, omniscient at last. The day
comes when the hidden author of our story is
found; when the brave speech returns straight
to the hero who said it; when the admirable
verse finds the poet to whom it belongs; and
best of all, when the lonely thought, which
seemed so wise, yet half-wise, half-thought, because it cast no light abroad, is suddenly matched
in our mind by its twin, by its sequence, or next
related analogy, which gives it instantly radiating power, and justifies the superstitious instinct
with which we have hoarded it. We remember
our old Greek Professor at Cambridge, an ancient bachelor, amid his folios, possessed by this
hope of completing a task, with nothing to break
his leisure after the three hours of his daily
classes, yet ever restlessly stroking his leg and
assuring himself "he should retire from the University and read the authors." [1] In Goethe's
Romance, Makaria, the central figure for wisdom

and influence, pleases herself with withdrawing
into solitude to astronomy and epistolary correspondence. Goethe himself carried this comple-
tion of studies to the highest point. Many of
his works hung on the easel from youth to age,
and received a stroke in every month or year.
A literary astrologer, he never applied himself
to any task but at the happy moment when all
the stars consented. Bentley thought himself
likely to live till fourscore, — long enough to
read everything that was worth reading, — "*Et
tunc magna mei sub terris ibit imago.*" [1] Much
wider is spread the pleasure which old men take
in completing their secular affairs, the inventor
his inventions, the agriculturist his experiments,
and all old men in finishing their houses, round-
ing their estates, clearing their titles, reducing
tangled interests to order, reconciling enmities
and leaving all in the best posture for the future.
It must be believed that there is a proportion
between the designs of a man and the length of
his life : there is a calendar of his years, so of his
performances. [2]

America is the country of young men, and
too full of work hitherto for leisure and tranquillity ; yet we have had robust centenarians,
and examples of dignity and wisdom. I have

lately found in an old note-book a record of a
visit to ex-President John Adams, in 1825, soon
after the election of his son to the Presidency.
It is but a sketch, and nothing important passed
in the conversation; but it reports a moment
in the life of a heroic person, who, in extreme
old age, appeared still erect and worthy of his
fame.

———, *Feb., 1825.* To-day at Quincy, with
my brother, by invitation of Mr. Adams's family. The old President sat in a large stuffed arm-
chair, dressed in a blue coat, black small-clothes,
white stockings; a cotton cap covered his bald
head. We made our compliment, told him he
must let us join our congratulations to those of
the nation on the happiness of his house. He
thanked us, and said: " I am rejoiced, because
the nation is happy. The time of gratulation and
congratulations is nearly over with me; I am
astonished that I have lived to see and know of
this event. I have lived now nearly a century
[he was ninety in the following October]; a long,
harassed and distracted life." I said, "The world
thinks a good deal of joy has been mixed with
it." — " The world does not know," he replied,
" how much toil, anxiety and sorrow I have suf-

fered." — I asked if Mr. Adams's letter of acceptance had been read to him. — "Yes," he said, and added, " My son has more political prudence than any man that I know who has existed in my time ; he never was put off his guard ; and I hope he will continue such : but what effect age may work in diminishing the power of his mind, I do not know ; it has been very much on the stretch, ever since he was born. He has always been laborious, child and man, from infancy." — When Mr. J. Q. Adams's age was mentioned, he said, " He is now fifty-eight, or will be in July ;" and remarked that "all the Presidents were of the same age : General Washington was about fifty-eight, and I was about fifty-eight, and Mr. Jefferson, and Mr. Madison, and Mr. Monroe." — We inquired when he expected to see Mr. Adams. — He said : " Never : Mr. Adams will not come to Quincy but to my funeral. It would be a great satisfaction to me to see him, but I don't wish him to come on my account." He spoke of Mr. Lechmere, whom he " well remembered to have seen come down daily, at a great age, to walk in the old town-house," adding, " And I wish I could walk as well as he did. He was Collector of the Customs for many years under the Royal Government." — E. said:

" I suppose, sir, you would not have taken his place, even to walk as well as he." — " No," he replied, "that was not what I wanted." — He talked of Whitefield,¹ and remembered when he was a Freshman in College to have come into town to the *Old South* church [I think] to hear him, but could not get into the house; — " I, however, saw him," he said, "through a window, and distinctly heard all. He had a voice such as I never heard before or since. He cast it out so that you might hear it at the meeting-house [pointing towards the Quincy meeting-house], and he had the grace of a dancing-master, of an actor of plays. His voice and manner helped him more than his sermons. I went with Jonathan Sewall." — "And you were pleased with him, sir?" — "Pleased ! I was delighted beyond measure." — We asked if at Whitefield's return the same popularity continued. — " Not the same fury," he said, " not the same wild enthusiasm as before, but a greater esteem, as he became more known. He did not terrify, but was admired."

We spent about an hour in his room. He speaks very distinctly for so old a man, enters bravely into long sentences, which are interrupted by want of breath, but carries them invariably to a conclusion, without correcting a word.

He spoke of the new novels of Cooper, and Peep at the Pilgrims, and Saratoga, with praise, and named with accuracy the characters in them. He likes to have a person always reading to him, or company talking in his room, and is better the next day after having visitors in his chamber from morning to night.

He received a premature report of his son's election, on Sunday afternoon, without any excitement, and told the reporter he had been hoaxed, for it was not yet time for any news to arrive. The informer, something damped in his heart, insisted on repairing to the meeting-house, and proclaimed it aloud to the congregation, who were so overjoyed that they rose in their seats and cheered thrice. The Reverend Mr. Whitney dismissed them immediately.

When life has been well spent, age is a loss of what it can well spare, — muscular strength, organic instincts, gross bulk, and works that belong to these. But the central wisdom, which was old in infancy, is young in fourscore years, and, dropping off obstructions, leaves in happy subjects the mind purified and wise. I have heard that

whoever loves is in no condition old.[1] I have
heard that whenever the name of man is spoken,
the doctrine of immortality is announced; it
cleaves to his constitution. The mode of it
baffles our wit, and no whisper comes to us from
the other side. But the inference from the working of intellect, hiving knowledge, hiving skill,
— at the end of life just ready to be born, —
affirms the inspirations of affection and of the
moral sentiment.[2]

NOTES

NOTES

SOCIETY AND SOLITUDE

IT may be well to recall some of the outward events which occurred and conditions which existed during the decade intervening between the publication of *The Conduct of Life* and of Mr. Emerson's next volume of essays, *Society and Solitude,* which did not appear until 1870. In those years a crisis in which the life or death of the United States hung long in what seemed a doubtful issue had been safely passed. Statesmen, "practical" politicians who ridiculed the higher law which the scholars and simple folk believed in, and merchants who strove to silence them for the sake of trade, were suddenly overwhelmed by the logic of events.

> Destiny sat by and said,
> 'Pang for pang your seed shall pay,
> Hide in false peace your coward head,
> I bring round the harvest day.'

This triumph of Right to

> Redress the eternal scales

brought to Emerson relief and joy; but he had not, like Jonah, sat still watching for the destruction of the wicked. Before the war, in speaking for the slave, he had steadily braved unpopularity, and once or twice perhaps danger; yet, seeing the distress that sudden loss of slave property would cause in the South, had urged compensation when few Northern abolitionists could make allowance for the unfortunate condition into which the slaveholders were born, but regarded them only as criminals. He wished to deliver the white man from his curse even more than the negro. When after Lincoln's inauguration the issue was forced by the slaveholding interest, Mr. Emerson could not bear arms, but did better service to his country after his kind. Through the long, cruel conflict he strove, not only in special patriotic meetings, but in his lectures on the great and permanent themes, to keep the hearts of his hearers up and lift their standard higher. Many of these essays, as lectures, had exordiums fit for the day. "Civilization" is but a part of a lecture given at the Smithsonian Institution in Washington, in January, 1862, called "Civilization at a Pinch," in which the duty of the hour, Emancipation, was urged. The "Boston Hymn" a year later celebrated its proclamation, and "Voluntaries" was a proud dirge for Colonel Robert Shaw and his officers and soldiers killed on the slopes of Fort Wagner.

But the war made great demands on the resources of those who stayed at home, as taxes and prices rose, and the "hard times" outlasted the four years of actual hostilities. Strictest economies and increased work were required to meet them. Mr. Emerson derived little income from his books, and lecturing was his main resource. Fortunately the awakened heart and mind of the people demanded encouragement and instruction. Not only the lyceums of the older States, where his voice had long been heard, wished to hear his word of hope, but calls came from the new country beyond the Mississippi.

Mr. Emerson's name was now widely known. Many guests from both sides of the ocean came to his door. His children had grown up, and in 1865 his younger daughter was happily married to a brave soldier whose release from a Southern prison came just in time to enable him to be present at the closing scene of the war. Mr. Emerson's delight in children appears in the lecture on Domestic Life and, though it was written in 1859, it very possibly was improved before printing because of the birth of his grandchildren.

In 1866 Harvard College invited him, after twenty-nine years, again to deliver the Phi Beta Kappa Oration. Next year he was chosen an Overseer, and in 1870 was asked to deliver a course on Philosophy there.

In this decade two near friends were taken from him by death, Henry Thoreau and Mrs. Sarah Ripley. In 1860 Theodore Parker, respected and valued by Mr. Emerson, died, and for several years thereafter he was frequently called by Mr. Parker's Society to speak to them on Sundays at the Music Hall and on week-days at their " Fraternity Lectures."

To one who heard Emerson lecture, the printed essays recall the spoken word and the speaker's presence. They were all thus first tested on the average American audience in town and country. The earlier addresses show more of the priest, the later of the lecturer who was also a poet, though the characteristics only vary in proportion.

The testimony of two of the hearers may be adduced. Mr. John Albee in his " Emerson as an Essayist " [1] says: —

" Most of them were prepared for public delivery. Some profess to detect this in their style. I should never discover it, had I not heard some of them and since been unable to forget the tones of voice, the manner and the total effect of the delivery. For it certainly cannot be discovered by any resemblances to writing that we do know was prepared for public delivery, which has for its prevailing qualities nothing in the 'east like the qualities of Emerson's page.

" The old lecture platform witnessed every sort of performance with an impartial eye. It listened to eloquence, to nonsense and to thought; it was not greatly moved by any; it was, perhaps, made a little more eager for the next lecture, which might demolish the ideas of the last. The audiences had their

[1] *Remembrances of Emerson*, by John Albee.

favorites, usually the more eloquent speakers. But it is painful to recall and still more so to read what went under the name of eloquence in Emerson's day; that which was selected for school-readers, spouted by collegians and admired by everybody."

Lowell said in an article in the *Nation*: —

" I have heard some great speakers, and some accomplished orators, but never any that so moved and persuaded men as he. There is a kind of undertone in that rich baritone of his that sweeps our minds from their foothold into deep waters with a drift we cannot and would not resist. And how artfully (for Emerson is a long-studied artist in these things) does the deliberate utterance, that seems waiting for the first word, seem to admit us partners in the labor of thought, and make us feel as if the glance of humor were a sudden suggestion; as if the perfect phrase lying written there on the desk were as unexpected to him as to us ! "

Two extracts from Mr. Emerson's letters to Carlyle may be here introduced to bring up the picture of the raw young country in those days, as seen through the hopeful eyes of the New England idealist.

28 July, 1851: " ' The Far West ' is the right name for these verdant deserts. On all the shores interminable silent forest. If you land, there is prairie beyond prairie, forest behind forest, sites of nations, no nations. The raw bullion of nature; what we call ' moral ' value not yet stamped on it. But in a thousand miles the immense material values will show twenty or fifty Californias; that a good ciphering head will make one where he is. Thus at Pittsburg, on the Ohio, the Iron City, whither, from want of railroads, few Yankees have penetrated, every acre of land has three or four bottoms: first of rich soil; then nine feet of bituminous coal; a little lower

fourteen feet of coal; then iron, or salt; salt springs, with a valuable oil called petroleum floating on their surface. Yet this acre sells for the price of any tillage acre in Massachusetts; and, in a year, the railroads will reach it, east and west. I came home by the great Northern Lakes and Niagara."

19 April, 1853: "I went lately to St. Louis and saw the Mississippi again. The powers of the River, the insatiate craving for nations of men to reap and cure its harvests, the conditions it imposes, — for it yields to no engineering, — are interesting enough. The Prairie exists to yield the greatest possible quantity of adipocere. For corn makes pig, pig is the export of all the land, and you shall see the instant dependence of aristocracy and civility on the fat four-legs. Workingmen, ability to do the work of the River, abounded. Nothing higher was to be thought of. America is incomplete. Room for us all, since it has not ended, nor given sign of ending, in bard or hero. 'T is a wild democracy, the riot of mediocrities, and none of your selfish Italies and Englands, when an age sublimates into a genius."

In a letter written to Carlyle in the end of January, 1870, Mr. Emerson gives the following account of the making of this volume: "I received your first letter with pure joy, but in the midst of extreme inefficiency. I had suddenly yielded to a proposition of Fields & Co. to manufacture a book for a given day. The book was planned and going on passably, when it was found better to divide the matter, and separate and postpone the purely literary portion (criticism chiefly), and therefore to modify and swell the elected part. The attempt proved more difficult than I had believed. Meantime the publication day was announced and the printer at the door. Then came your letter in the shortening days. When I drudged to keep my word, *invita Minerva*, I could not write in my book and I

could not write a letter. To-morrow and many morrows made
things worse, for we have indifferent health in the house, and,
as it chanced, unusual strain of affairs — which always come
when they should not. . . . But I will leave the bad month,
which I hope will not match itself in my lifetime. Only
't is pathetic and remorseful to me that any purpose of yours,
especially a purpose so inspired, should find me imbecile.''

The '' purely literary portion '' mentioned as omitted from
the book probably refers to the '' Poetry and Criticism '' and
'' Persian Poetry,'' which were included in the next volume,
Letters and Social Aims.

When the volume reached England it brought back this
response from his old friend: —

APRIL 6TH, 1870.

The '' little Book'' I read here, . . . with great attention,
clear assent for most part, and admiring recognition. It seems
to me you are all your old self here, and something more. A
calm insight, piercing to the very centre; a beautiful sympathy,
a beautiful epic humor; a soul peaceably irrefragable in this loud-
jangling world, of which it sees the ugliness, but notices only
the huge new opulences (still so anarchic); knows the electric
telegraph, with all its vulgar botherations and impertinences,
accurately for what it is, and ditto ditto the oldest eternal Theo-
logies of men. All this belongs to the Highest Class of thought
(you may depend upon it); and again seemed to me as, in
several respects, the one perfectly Human Voice I had heard
among my fellow creatures for a long time. And then the
'' style,'' the treatment and expression, — yes, it is inimitable,
best, — Emersonian throughout. Such brevity, simplicity,
softness, homely grace; with such a penetrating meaning, soft
enough, but irresistible, going down to the depths and up to the
heights, as silent electricity goes. You have done very well;

and many will know it ever better by degrees. Only one thing
farther I will note: How you go as if altogether on the "Over-
Soul," the Ideal, the Perfect or Universal and Eternal in this
life of ours; and take so little heed of the frightful quantities
of friction and perverse impediment there everywhere are; the
reflections upon which in my own poor life made me now and
then very sad, as I read you. Ah me, ah me; what a vista it
is, mournful, beautiful, unfathomable as Eternity itself, these
last fifty years of Time to me.

All or nearly all the essays included in this book existed in
some form as lectures in 1858 or 1859. What is known of
their first delivery will be told in the notes to each essay. Yet
they underwent much change during the long period of re-
hearsal, and sheets from them often did duty in other lectures,
before the final crystallization.

Page 3, note 1. One may guess that this humorist inter-
preted the Medusa as a Memory because, though her face was
calm, it was ever encircled by snakes. This passage may be a
parable in which are figured "those infinite compunctions
which embitter in mature life the remembrances of budding
joy, and cover every beloved name. Everything is beautiful
seen from the point of the intellect, or as truth. But all is sour
if seen as experience." [1]

Mr. Emerson believed himself so unfitted for society, in his
younger years, that his memories were mortifications, and he
turned his face resolutely away from them. He felt the want
of animal spirits. He early wrote: "There is no more indifferent companion, Heaven knows, in ordinary society than
myself. I profoundly pity my right and left hand men. But

[1] "Love," *Essays, First Series*, p. 171.

do not blame my dulness. As soon as I have done my studies
I collapse. 'T is my hygeia and natural restorative.''

In those days he was not strong, and perhaps memories of
his awkwardness in his parochial duties distressed him.

Journal, 1835. '' Is it because I am such a bigot to my own
whims, that I distrust the ability of a man who insists much
on the advantage to be derived from literary *conversazioni*.
Above is wisdom, above is happiness. Society nowadays
makes us low-spirited, hopeless; above is heaven.''

In Concord woods he found healing for body, and oracles
for the soul. The following is an extract from a lecture called
''Country Life,'' given in 1857: —

'' The place where a thoughtful man in the country feels
the joy of eminent domain is his wood-lot. If he suffer from
accident or low spirits, his spirits rise when he enters it. I
could not find it in my heart to chide the citizen who should
ruin himself to buy a patch of heavy oak-timber. A walk in
the woods is the consolation of mortal men. I think no pursuit has more breath of immortality in it.''

Page 5, note 1. But the wood-life had no exemption from
the law of Compensation. The virtue that there came in to
him must go out from him, the messages be delivered. In
family, village and public life he did his part and reaped his
reward.

Journal, 1840. '' Would it not be a good cipher for the
seal of the Lonely Society which forms so fast in these days, —
Two porcupines meeting, with all their spines erect, and the
motto, ' We converse at the quills' end ' ? ''

Page 7, note 1. During Mr. Emerson's ministry in Boston in 1828 he wrote in his journal, '' A wise man in certain
society is a magnet among shavings.''

Of the Poet he later wrote, —

In cities he was low and mean;
The mountain waters washed him clean
And by the sea-waves he was strong.

"Fragments on the Poet," *Poems*, Appendix.

Page 8, note 1. Of himself Mr. Emerson would say,
"My doom and my strength is to be solitary."

Page 9, note 1. In a lecture on Society, in the course in
Boston, 1836–37, he said: "A man should live among those
with whom he can act naturally, who permit and provoke the
expression of all his thoughts and emotions. Yet the course of
events does steadily thwart any attempt at very dainty and
select fellowship, and he who would live as a man in the world
must not wait too proudly for the presence of the gifted and the
good. The unlike mind can teach him much."

Page 9, note 2. The soul's solitude may be read in his
parable, the fragment on Nature, —

Atom from atom yawns as far
As moon from earth or star from star.

Journal, 1835. "'T is very strange how much we owe the
perception of the absolute solitude of the spirit to the affections.
I sit alone, and cannot arouse myself to thoughts. I go and sit
with my friend and in the endeavour to explain my thought to
him or her, I lay bare the awful mystery to myself as never
before, and start at the total loneliness and infinity of one
man."

In the lecture on Society above mentioned he wrote with
regard to the societies which claimed his aid: —

"Philanthropic association aims to increase the efficiency of
individuals by organization. But the gain of power is much
less than it seems, since each brings only a mechanical aid; does
not apply to the enterprise the infinite force of one man; and

in some proportion to the material growth is the spiritual decay."

Page 10, note 1. Now comes the counter-statement. In a lecture on Private Life, in the course of 1839–40 on the Present Age, Mr. Emerson said, "Nothing but God is self-dependent. Man is powerful only by the multitude of his affinities."

Mr. Emerson writes in his journal of 1852: —

"Of Francis Potter Aubrey says, ''T was pity that such a delicate inventive wit should be staked in an obscure corner from whence men rarely emerge to higher preferment, but contract a moss on them, like an old pale in an orchard, for want of ingenious conversations, which is a great want even to the deepest thinking men; as Mr. Hobbes hath often said to me.'"

The new home in Concord after Mr. Emerson's marriage, its hospitalities and the new friends who visited him there, altered his half-resolves to be a hermit, "since it was from eternity a settled thing that he and society were to be nothing to each other."

Page 11, note 1. The rapidly increasing demand through the country for instruction by the serious lyceum-lecture justified this statement. Mr. Emerson, remembering that "the light of the public square tests the statue," saw the value of testing his lectures on self-made men and brave women and earnest youths struggling for an education.

Page 12, note 1. The allusion here is to a happy experience, always remembered with pleasure. On his journey to Florida for health, when a student, Mr. Emerson fell in with Achille Murat, the son of Napoleon's great leader of cavalry, afterwards king of Naples. The son was a man of thought and of great charm, then a planter at Tallahassee.

He and Mr. Emerson exchanged some thoughtful letters, but never met again. Apropos of the first part of the paragraph is the following extract: —

Journal, 1862. "In manners, how impossible to overcome an unlucky temperament, unless by living with the well-bred from the start !

.   .   .   .

"Intellectual men pass for vulgar, and are timid and heavy with the elegant; but exhibit the best style if the elegant are intellectual. But the dancers' violin, or Beethoven's music even, degrades them instantly in manners, if they are not also musical.

"Laws of society, a forever engaging topic. At Sir Wm. Molesworth's house, I asked Milnes to get me safely out: he behaved very well. An impassive temperament is a great fortune. Que de choses dont je peux me passer ! even dancing and music, if I had that."

Page 13, note 1. The heights of an austere nobility in friendship and love are pictured in the end of the poems "Rhea" and "The Celestial Love." The poem "Friendship" is more human and no less noble.

Page 14, note 1. Mr. Emerson used to say, "Whom God hath put asunder let not man join together."

Page 15, note 1.

> If Love his moment overstay,
> Hatred's swift repulsions play.
> > "The Visit," *Poems.*

Page 16, note 1. The balancing necessity of these complementary conditions is set forth in a stray sheet, perhaps from the course on the Present Age, in 1839–40: —

"We have a double consciousness. We go to school, we

learn to read, write, cipher and trade. We have talents, arts, success; we buy and sell, have wives, children, possessions, humours; we unfold and earn and prosper and possess.

"But there is another element in us which does not learn or study or make gain, or value these things at all. It broods on all that is done, but does not; it makes no progress; is as wise at our earliest remembrance, as it is now. Others may come and go, fetch and carry, travel and govern. It lies in the sun and broods on the world."

Yet in turn Thought must become Action to justify itself. The following is from the lecture "Morals," given in 1859:

"Meantime let no man imagine that the ends of the soul can be attained by intellectual exercises. Contemplation is an office of man, but contemplation is not man. Let him obey the melodious voice of Duty, which vibrates through the universe, calling him always to act. The moral sentiment so profound, and which seems the nearest vision we have of the face of the Creator, reveals itself still in actions. The heart in us is orphan and forlorn until it finds virtue. Beside a duty, beside humility, beside courage, self-denial, and laborious love, how cold and dreary seem to us the gifts of mere genius. Go and deal with persons who are just and benevolent, not in the vulgar and moderate sense, but religiously so, and you feel at home, though in another land or another world."

Mr. Emerson elsewhere thus summarized his conclusion:
"A man must ride alternately on the horses of his public and private nature, —

"Like vaulters in a circus round
Who leap from horse to horse but never touch the ground."

CIVILIZATION

In April, 1861, Mr. Emerson began a course of lectures on Life and Literature at the Meionaon in Boston. He had probably prepared the lecture on Civilization in much the same form that it is printed here. But the outbreak of the Rebellion turned all thought on the crisis in the life of the Nation. Four days before this lecture was delivered he had seen the young men of Concord mustered in arms on the village green and, with the prayers of their townsfolk, march to the defence of constitutional liberty.

It seemed a fated day for Concord, the Nineteenth of April, for this was the third time in her history that her sons had been summoned for that duty on that day. The news of the attack of the Baltimore mob on the Sixth Massachusetts Regiment on that same day had also come, and again, as at Concord Bridge, a soldier from Acton was the first victim of the war. With a lapse towards barbarism threatening the country, and yet a new hope springing up with the awakening of the North, the lecture written in less stirring days had to be remodelled for the hour. Mr. Emerson named it " Civilization at a Pinch." This was, without doubt, the basis for the lecture which, with the addition of an earnest appeal to the Administration for emancipation of the slaves, was read by him before the Smithsonian Institution at Washington in January, 1862. Under the title there used, " American Civilization," it was printed in the *Atlantic Monthly* for April, 1862. It was afterwards separated into the essay here printed, treating of the general theme, only referring to the times in the last paragraph, and the appeal for the political exigency of the hour, "American Civilization," included in the *Miscel-lanies.*

Page 19, note 1. The civilized man in the best sense is described in the poem which serves also as motto for "Culture" and bears that name, beginning, —

> Can rules or tutors educate
> The semigod whom we await ?

Page 20, note 1. Less well known than that of Cadmus in the mythology, the inventor of the alphabet, is the name of Pytheas, the Massilian Greek who, in the fourth century B. C., first explored the shores of Northern Europe and described them and the midnight sun. He discovered the inclination of the ecliptic, the circuit of the Pole-star and the relation of the tides to the moon. Manco Capac, according to tradition, was the first of the Incas, the son of the sun, and gave to the savage Peruvians the arts of life.

Page 21, note 1.

> Rich are the sea-gods: — who gives gifts but they ?
> They grope the sea for pearls, but more than pearls;
> They pluck Force thence and give it to the wise.
> For every wave is wealth to Dædalus,
> Wealth to the cunning artist who can work
> This matchless strength.
> > "Sea-Shore," *Poems.*

Page 22, note 1. By comparing this paragraph with the ending of "The Adirondacs" in the Poems, when, after the celebration of the wild forest life, and the men it breeds, Civilization yet receives its dues, the date of the composition can be fixed. For in the summer of 1858 Mr. Emerson enjoyed with his friends, yet, as ever, much alone, two weeks in the primæval woods around Follansbee Pond. William J. Still-man, the all-accomplished captain of the party, has told its story in his Autobiography.[1] His excellent painting of the forest camp and the company is in the Concord Public Library.

Page 23, note 1. Journal, 1854. "Roads, the wafer on letters, and the position of woman are good tests of civilization." Until the second half of the century envelopes were little used, and the letter-sheet was folded and sealed with one wafer.

Page 23, note 2. Dr. Thomas Brown, physician and philosopher, wrote *An Inquiry into the Relation of Cause and Effect*, supporting Hume's Theory of Causation.

Page 24, note 1. Dr. Holmes in his book on Emerson thus refers to this evident quotation from memory by his friend from his poem "The Steamboat": "My attention was called to one paragraph for a reason which my reader will readily understand and, I trust, look upon good-naturedly." He quotes the passage, including the lines of verse, and goes on, "I cannot be wrong, it seems to me, in supposing these two lines to be an incorrect version of these two from a poem of my own called 'The Steamboat': —

> " ' The beating of her restless heart
> Still sounding through the storm.'

"It is never safe to quote poetry from memory, at least while the writer lives, for he is ready to ' cavil on the ninth part of a hair,' where his verses are concerned. But extreme accuracy was not one of Emerson's special gifts, and vanity whispers to the misrepresented versifier that

> " ' 'T is better to be quoted wrong
> Than to be quoted not at all.' "

[1] *The Autobiography of a Journalist.* Houghton, Mifflin & Co., 1901.

VII

Page 26, note 1. In the poem " Voluntaries," the second stanza, the greater favor of Freedom for the Northman is told.

Page 28, note 1.

> He planted where the Deluge ploughed,
> His hired hands were wind and cloud.
>
>   " Fragments on the Poet," *Poems*, Appendix.

Page 28, note 2. Again Dr. Holmes's charming book must be quoted with regard to this passage: " This Essay of Emerson's is irradiated by a single precept that is worthy to stand by the side of that which Juvenal says came from heaven. How could the man in whose thought such a meteoric expression suddenly announced itself fail to recognize it as divine ? It is not strange that he repeats it on the page next the one where we first see it. Not having any golden letters to print it in, I will underscore it for italics, and doubly underscore it in the second extract for small capitals." And he did so.

Page 30, note 1. From the poem of Samuel Daniel " To the Countess of Cumberland." There is a passage to this purpose on page 307 of " Circles," in the first series of Essays.

Page 30, note 2. The wife of Colonel John Hutchinson.

Page 31, note 1.

> But he, the man-child glorious, —
> Where tarries he the while ?
>
>   " Song of Nature," *Poems*.

Page 33, note 1. Journal, 1847. " Civilization is symbolized (how wittily) by a cake, in the hierological cipher of the Egyptians."

Page 33, note 2. A proper perspective of the important

and the unimportant in life was early taught to her sons by Madam Emerson. To her oldest son William, who wrote to her at the age of thirteen about his college room, his mother answered: —

My DEAR SON, —

You did right to give me so early a proof of your affection as to write to me the first week of your college life. Everything respecting you is doubtless interesting to me, but your domestic arrangements the least of anything, as these make no part of the man or the character any further than he learns humility from his dependence on such trifles as *convenient accommodations* for his happiness. You, I trust, will rise superior to these little things, for, though small indeed, they consume much time that might be appropriated to better purpose and far nobler pursuits. What most excites my solicitude is your moral improvement and your progress in virtue. . . . Let your whole life reflect honor on the name you bear. . . . Should Paul plant and Apollos water, it is God alone who can give the increase.

Page 34, note 1. This concluding passage alone in the essay retains the impress of the feeling, due to the long reign of bad politics, of a doubtful issue to the great struggle just begun. Hence Emerson's word of warning to his countrymen was plain and strong.

Page 34, note 2. The journal for 1864 has the following memorandum: —

"In my paper on Civilization I omitted an important trait, namely, the increased respect for human life. The difference between the oriental nations, on one side, and Europe and America, on the other, lies mainly herein. The Japanese in France are astonished, 'tis said, at the vast apparatus and extent of a capital trial: . . . Remember General Scott's maxim, too, about the sacrifice of one life more than necessity requires.''

And in the first months of the war, relieved by the clearing of the moral atmosphere of the country, Mr. Emerson gladly noted: —

'' War civilizes; for it forces individuals and tribes to combine, and act with larger views, and under the best heads, and keeps the population together, producing the effect of cities; for camps are wandering cities.''

ART

Mr. Emerson's first lecture on Art seems to have been that given in Boston in December, 1836, in the course on the Philosophy of History. In that and the succeeding lecture Art and Literature were compared.

'' Art delights in carrying thought into action. Literature is the conversion of action into thought. The architect executes his dream in stone. The poet enchants you by idealizing your life and fortunes. In both the highest charm comes from that which is inevitable in the work, a divine necessity overpowering individual effort, and expressing the thought of mankind in the time and place.'' The chapter on Art in the first series of Essays contains part of that lecture.

The present essay is, with a few slight changes, mostly verbal, the paper called '' Thoughts on Art,'' printed in the *Dial* by Mr. Emerson in January, 1841. It is probable that it was essentially the second lecture in the course on Life

and Literature given in Boston in April, 1861. It possibly
contained some passages from a lecture on Art and Criticism, given in a course at Freeman Place Chapel in Boston in
the spring of 1859.

Mr. Emerson had never received any instruction in art.
The heads which he carelessly drew on the margins and fly-
leaves of early journals show that he had a good eye and
some native skill of hand. His poems everywhere show that,
for him

> Ever the spell of beauty came
> And turned the drowsy world to flame.
> By lake and stream and gleaming hall
> And modest copse and forest tall,
> Where'er he went, the magic guide
> Kept its place by the poet's side.

But he could express beauty only in life and words.

Journal, 1841. "I frequently find the best part of my ride
in the Concord coach from my house to Winthrop Place to
be in Prince Street, Charter Street, Ann Street and the like
places at the North End of Boston. The *deshabille* of both
men and women, their unrestrained attitudes and manners
make pictures greatly more interesting than the clean-shaved
and silk-robed procession in Washington and Tremont streets.
I often see that the attitudes of both men and women engaged
in hard work are more picturesque than any which art and
study could contrive, for the Heart is in these first. I say
picturesque, because when I pass these groups I instantly
know whence all the fine pictures I have seen had their
origin; I feel the painter in me; these are the traits which
make us feel the force and eloquence of form and the sting of
color. But the painter is only *in* me, and does not come to
the fingers' ends."

In Greek sculpture he delighted, for its calm and temperate beauty. After this he cared most for the work of Michel Angelo in the Sistine Chapel, and Raphael's works, especially his Transfiguration.

He read what Goethe had to say on Art, and took pleasure in Vasari's Lives and Winckelmann's writings on Ancient Art, and read Ruskin and Haydon. Fergusson's and Garbett's works on Architecture were studied by him.

He wrote to a friend in 1839: "There are fewer painters than poets. Ten men can awaken me by words to new hope and fruitful musing for one that can achieve the miracle of forms. Besides, I think the pleasure of the poem lasts me longer."

It is hard to realize that Art, except for portrait painting, was little more than a name in America in the first half of the nineteenth century. What opportunities Boston offered may be learned from Mr. Emerson's own account in the *Memoirs of Margaret Fuller Ossoli*: —

"There are persons to whom a gallery is everywhere a home. In this country the antique is known only by plaster casts and by drawings. The Boston Athenæum, — on whose sunny roof and beautiful chambers may the benedictions of centuries of students rest with mine! — added to its library in 1823 a small but excellent museum of the antique sculpture in plaster; — the selection being dictated, it is said, by no less an adviser than Canova. The Apollo, Laocoòn, the Venuses, Diana, the head of the Phidian Jove, Bacchus, Antinoüs, the Torso Hercules, the Discobolus, the Gladiator Borghese, the Apollino, — all these, and more, the sumptuous gift of Augustus Thorndike. It is much that one man should have power to confer on so many, who never saw him, a benefit so pure and enduring.

"To these were soon added a heroic line of antique busts, and at last, by Horatio Greenough, the Night and Day of Michel Angelo. Here was old Greece and old Italy brought bodily to New England, and a verification given to all our dreams and readings. It was easy to collect from the drawing-rooms of the city a respectable picture-gallery for a summer exhibition. This was also done, and a new pleasure was invented for the studious, and a new home for the solitary. The Brimmer Donation, in 1838, added a costly series of engravings, chiefly of the French and Italian museums, and the drawings of Guercino, Salvator Rosa and other masters."

Page 37, note 1. Through this chapter and that on the same theme in the first book of Essays, what is best in the useful and the fine arts is shown to be that part which is inevitable, the working through the artist of the Universal Soul. In connection with this opening paragraph may be read the last page in the essay on Fate in *Conduct of Life,* where comes in the consoling doctrine of "the Beautiful Necessity" offsetting the drag of temperament and race.

Page 38, note 1. Two other of his definitions may here be given: —

1851. "To describe adequately is the high power and one of the highest enjoyments of man. This is Art."

1863. "My definition of Art is the inspiration of a just design working through all the details. Art is the path of the Creator to his work."

Page 40, note 1. Mr. Emerson expounds, better than in either of the essays on Art, the divine necessity of the best art in his early poem "The Problem."

Page 41, note 1. Mr. Emerson might have mentioned in connection with Smeaton's (the third) Eddystone Lighthouse, that the first, built by Winstanley on that terrible reef, was, at the top, a whimsical and almost pagoda-like structure, unable long to resist the upward dash of the seas.

Page 42, note 1. In one of the fragments in the Appendix to the Poems he makes Nature say, —

> He lives not who can refuse me;
> All my force saith, Come and use me.

Page 43, note 1. In his second poem on Nature Mr. Emerson wrote: —

> And what they call their city way
> Is not their way, but hers,
> And what they say they made to-day,
> They learned of the oaks and firs.
>
> .　　.　　.　　.　　.　　.　　.
>
> What 's most theirs is not their own,
> But borrowed in atoms from iron and stone,
> And in their vaunted works of Art
> The master-stroke is still her part.

Page 46, note 1. This consideration is the theme of the poem "Each and All."

Page 46, note 2. Homer said of the ten years' war around Troy, —

> "Thus the gods fated and such ruin wove
> That song might flourish for posterity."

Page 48, note 1. "Thus to him, to this schoolboy under the bending dome of day, is suggested that he and it proceed from one root; one is leaf and one is flower; relation, sympathy, stirring in every vein. . . . He shall see that Nature is the opposite of the soul, answering to it part for part. One is seal and one is print. Its beauty is the beauty

of his own mind." — "The American Scholar," *Nature,
Addresses and Lectures.*

Page 48, note 2. "The Genius of the Hour sets his ineffaceable seal on the work, and gives it an inexpressible charm for the imagination. As far as the spiritual character of the period overpowers the artist and finds expression in his work, so far will it retain a certain grandeur, and will represent to future beholders the Unknown, the Inevitable, the Divine." — "Art," *Essays, First Series.*

Page 49, note 1. Journal, 1835. "The Arts languish now because all their scope is exhibition; when they originated it was *to serve* the Gods. The Catholic Religion has turned them to continual account in its service. Now they are mere flourishes. Is it strange they perish ?

"Poetry to be sterling must be more than a show, must have or be an earnest meaning. Chaucer, Wordsworth, — per contra, Moore and Byron."

Page 50, note 1. The following is from some loose sheets on Beauty (1866 ?): —

"Beauty was never locked up in Vaticans. It is there, but it is not less here. The seat of beauty is in the truth and health of the Soul. It is the incessant creation of the spirit of man, whenever bad affections and falsehoods do not paralyze his plastic power; places and materials are indifferent to it, and subject to it; a beautiful soul dwells always in a beautiful world."

Page 52, note 1. The following extract is from Mr. Emerson's journal in Florence, in April, 1834 : —

"I revisited the Tribune this morning to see the Venus and the Fornarina and the rest of that attractive company. I reserve my admiration as much as I can: I make a continual effort not to be pleased except by that which ought to please me, and I walked coolly round and round the marble lady, but, when I planted myself at the iron gate which leads into the chamber of Dutch paintings, and looked at the statue, I saw and felt that mankind had had good reason for their preference."

" There is anything but time in my idea of the antique." From a lecture on Art and Criticism, 1839.

Page 53, note 1. The first sentence of this paragraph is thus rendered in his poem " The Rhodora ":—

> If eyes were made for seeing,
> Then Beauty is its own excuse for being;—

and the ideas of the remaining portion of this passage are found in " The Problem ":—

> The hand that rounded Peter's dome
> And groined the aisles of Christian Rome
> Wrought in a sad sincerity;
> Himself from God he could not free;
>
> .   .   .   .
>
> For out of Thought's interior sphere
> These wonders rose to upper air.

Page 53, note 2. Also compare, in *Essays, First Series,* page 17 in " History," and several passages in " Art."
How astonished Art may

> Mimic in slow structures, stone by stone,
>
> .   .   .   .
>
> The frolic architecture of the snow, —

is told by Mr. Emerson in his poem " The Snow-Storm."

Page 54, note 1. Here followed in the original lecture as printed in the *Dial* the paragraphs on the Gothic churches in " History," pp. 20, 21, in the *Essays, First Series.*

Page 56, note 1.

Whilst love and terror laid the tiles.

"The Problem," *Poems.*

Journal, 1848. "I believe in the admirableness of art. I expect it to be miraculous, and find it so. The combinations of the Gothic building are not now attainable, and the Phidian friezes with reason affect us as the forest does."

I copy from a later journal, as appropriate here, the definition of Beauty by Mr. Emerson's friend, Mr. James Elliot Cabot: "*The complete incarnation of spirit,* which is the definition of Beauty, demands equally that there be no point it does not inhabit, and none in which it abides."

Page 56, note 2. Journal, 1863. "The measure in art and in intellect is one: To what end ? Is it yours to do ? Are you bound by character and conviction to that part you take ? . . . But the forsaking the design to produce effects by showy details is the ruin of any work. Then begins shallowness of effect; intellectual bankruptcy of the artist. All goes wrong. Artist and public corrupt each other."

Page 57, note 1. Here Mr. Emerson states again the doctrine of the Trinity, older than the Christian Church. It appears in many places in his writings, especially in " The Transcendentalist," page 354, in *Nature, Addresses and Lectures,* and in "The Poet," page 6, in the second series of Essays.

John Sterling, the friend and correspondent of Carlyle and Emerson, wrote a noble poem on Greek Art, under the title of " Dædalus." It is included in Mr. Emerson's *Parnassus.* Some lines from it might fitly end this chapter: —

"Ever thy phantoms arise before us,
   Our loftier brothers, but one in blood;
   By bed and table they lord it o'er us,
   With looks of beauty and words of good

Calmly they show us mankind victorious
O'er all that's aimless, blind and base;
Their presence has made our nature glorious,
Unveiling our night's illumined face."

ELOQUENCE

In February, 1847, Mr. Emerson gave a lecture on Eloquence before the Boston Mercantile Library Association. It seems to have been much the same as the present essay. Just three years earlier, after reading his lecture on The Young American before the same body, he wrote in his journal as follows: —

FEBRUARY, 1844.

When I address a large assembly, as last Wednesday, I am always apprised that an opportunity is there; not for reading to them, as I do, lively miscellanies, but for painting in fire my thought, and being agitated to agitate. One must dedicate himself to it and think with his audience in his mind, so as to keep the perspective and symmetry of the oration, and enter into all the easily forgotten secrets of a great nocturnal assembly and their relation to the speaker.

But it would be fine music and in the present well rewarded; that is, he should have his audience at his devotion, and all other fames would hush before his. Now, eloquence is merely fabulous. When we talk of it we draw on our fancy. It is one of many things which I should like to do, but it requires a seven years' wooing.

Eloquence, in boyhood and youth, had been his idol. He

had used every opportunity to hear the finished speakers of that day, when rhetoric and oratory were more prized than now. In those days apparently the great body of the students at Cambridge voluntarily went to hear the Seniors declaim. The florid and fervid oratory of the young Southerners had a great charm for the Northern boys. The young Emerson himself took the Boylston prize for speaking. Writing to his Aunt Mary, at the age of twenty, concerning his choice of the ministry as a profession, he said: " I inherit from my sire a formality of manners and speech, but I derive from him or his patriotic parent a passionate love for the strains of eloquence. I burn after the *aliquid immensum infinitumque* which Cicero desired. What we ardently love, we burn to imitate. But the most prodigious genius, a seraph's eloquence, will shamefully defeat its own end, if it has not first won the heart of the defender to the cause he defends." In those days he expressed the hope that he might " put on eloquence like a robe."

After leaving the ministry, on his return from Europe to the new life, he resolved to " say, at public lectures and the like, those things which I have meditated for their own sake, and not for the first time with a view to that occasion." He charged himself to make his writings " as pure of all dross as if thou wert to speak to sages and demigods." Before he learned from his experience in country lyceums how to interest and quicken uncultivated hearers without lowering the thought, an acquaintance prescribed for him " a course of mobs to correct my quaintness and transcendentalism. And I might have found it as good for me as a water-cure for paralyzed stomachs." In the lyceum he drew a lesson from this story of antiquity: " When Anaximander sang, the boys derided him, whereupon he said, ' We must learn to sing better for the boys.' "

In the years between 1840 and 1850 Mr. Emerson's growing desire to express himself in poetry began to be fulfilled. He gave a lecture in London in 1848 before the Portman Square Literary and Scientific Institution, in the exordium of which he said, "I have ventured to name my topic 'Poetry and Eloquence,' though what I have to say is chiefly on the last. There is much that is common to the two." The best prose should be poetic, but the highest eloquence should be a poem.

The present lecture naturally follows that on Art, Eloquence, including Poetry, being the art that the author most loved.

The subject was not easily exhausted, and Mr. Emerson wrote another lecture, which was read in Chicago in 1867. This last is included in the volume *Letters and Social Aims*.

Page 62, note 1. Plato, *Republic*, Book 1. At town-meetings and other public gatherings Mr. Emerson seldom spoke unless the call was urgent. He felt his unfitness for debate or extempore speech; but he listened and watched the disputants with great interest and often admiration.

Page 63, note 1. Among Mr. Emerson's notes on Eloquence he wrote as a sort of motto some lines from the ancient version of "Thomas the Rhymer," called "Thomas of Ersseldoune," a legend that was a favorite with him.

The Queen of Elfland says to Thomas at parting, —

> " ' Fare wele, Thomas, I wend my waye,
>   I may no lengere stande with the: '
> ' Gyff me a tokynynge, lady gaye,
>   That I may saye I spake with the.'

" ' To harpe or carpe whereso thou gose,
    Thomas, thou sall hafe the chose sothely: '
And he saide, ' Harpynge kepe I none,
    For tonge is chefe of minstrelsye.' "

Page 63, note 2. See Plutarch's " Lives of the Ten Orators " in the *Morals.* Antiphon of Rhamnus in Attica (480–
411 B. C.), was the first of the Ten Attic Orators to introduce
the new rhetoric into politics. He was a leader in the Revolution of the Four Hundred, and when they fell was put to death.

Page 65, note 1.

" But now the blood of twenty thousand men
    Did triumph in my face."
        Shakspeare, *Richard II.,* Act III., Scene 2.

Page 65, note 2.

" Un jour, sous sa fenêtre
    Passe un entreterrement:
    Le cortège et le prêtre
    Entendent l'instrument.
    Ils sautent; la prière
    Cede aux joyeux accords;
    Et, jusqu'à cimetière
    On danse autour du corps."
      Béranger, " Ménétrier de Meudon."

Page 67, note 1. In writing in his journal the resolve to
give his best thoughts to all classes of hearers he said, " And
be no whit ashamed if not one, yea, not one in the assembly,
should give sign of intelligence. Is it not pleasant to you —
unexpected wisdom ? depth of sentiment in middle life ? persons that in the thick of the crowd are true kings and gentlemen without the harness and envy of the throne ? "

Page 68, note 1. Yet with all the pleasure he took in the

torrent of Celtic eloquence when Kate, the housemaid, described accidents that befel her, he praises in the essay on The Superlative the cautious understatement of the Yankee.

Page 69, note 1. Colonel Thomas Wentworth Higginson relates that he heard Mr. Emerson speak thus in praise of Southern eloquence, to the content of students from that section, in the audience; a content that was lessened when he went on, "The negro too is eloquent."

Page 70, note 1. Knowing how children learn through stories, Mr. Emerson when a teacher wrote out many good anecdotes from Plutarch and other sources for his scholars, which are still preserved.

Page 71, note 1. The ballad of Glenkindie, the minstrel, is in Professor Child's collection of English and Scottish Ballads.

Page 72, note 1. Mr. Emerson had this description of Ulysses from the Iliad, (Book III. 191) written out for declamation, perhaps for his own speaking when in college. He gave it to his son for this purpose, but he was much disturbed when some one corrected the last sentence to the form here given. His own mistranslation or "acting version" was far more effective and majestic in his delivery: "But when he sent his great voice forth from his breast, and words fell like to the winter snows, not then would any mortal have wished to contend with Ulysses, *and we rejoice not, beholding the son of Laertes here.*"

Page 74, note 1. Journal, 1856. "I last night remembered what fools a few sounding sentences made of me and my mates at Cambridge, as in Lee's and John Everett's orations. . . . I still remember a sentence in Carter Lee's oration: 'And there was a band of heroes, and round their mountains was a wreath of light, and, in the midst, on the mountain-top, stood Liberty feeding her eagle.' "

Page 75, note 1. Daniel Webster.

Page 79, note 1. "My hand of iron," said Napoleon, "was not at the extremity of my arm, it was immediately connected with my head."

Page 80, note 1. In "Natural Aristocracy" (in *Lectures and Biographical Sketches*) the power of a commanding personality is set forth at length.

Page 83, note 1. All this paragraph, as far as the quotation from Pepys's *Diary*, Mr. Emerson took from his notebook of 1830.

Page 83, note 2. The Rev. Joseph Stevens Buckminster, born in 1784, ordained pastor of Brattle Street Church in Boston before he was twenty-one years old, who died at the age of twenty-eight. He was a cultivated, thoughtful and eloquent man. He preached the funeral sermon of Mr. Emerson's father, the Rev. William Emerson.

Page 85, note 1. From his youth upward Mr. Emerson lost no opportunity of hearing Daniel Webster speak. In his Phi Beta Kappa Poem in 1834 he introduced a description of Webster's commanding personality and in praise of his gifts and services. This passage may be found in the Appendix to the *Poems*. In 1843, when Mr. Webster was retained in an important case in Concord, Mr. Emerson wrote in his journal: —

"Mr. Webster loses nothing by comparison with brilliant men in the legal profession; he is as much before them as before the ordinary lawyer. At least, I thought he appeared, among these best lawyers of the Suffolk Bar, like a schoolmaster among his boys. His wonderful organization, the perfection of his elocution, and all that thereto belongs, voice, accent, intonation, attitude, manner, are such as one cannot hope to see again in a century: then he is so thoroughly

VII

simple and wise in his rhetoric. Understanding language and the use of the positive degree, all his words tell, and his rhetoric is perfect, so homely, so fit, so strong. Then he manages his matter so well, he hugs his fact so close, and will not let it go, and never indulges in a weak flourish, though he knows perfectly well how to make such exordiums and episodes and perorations as may give perspective to his harangue without in the least embarrassing his plan or confounding his transitions. What is small he shows as small, and makes the great great. In speech he sometimes roars and his words are like blows of an axe.''

Page 86, note 1. In his poem `` The Adirondacs'' Mr. Emerson celebrates the skill and powers of the guides, to the disadvantage of the gentlemen.

Page 88, note 1. Mr. Emerson honored Lord Mansfield for his decision in the case of Somerset the slave, and contrasted him in his journals with the Boston judges who gave the decision under the Fugitive Slave Law returning Sims and Burns to bondage. Mr. Emerson here and elsewhere shows his liking for the word `` common-sense,'' in its larger sense, being almost an equivalent for the `` universal mind '' found everywhere in his writings. In the journal of 1836–37, after speaking of the mob, he says: —

`` A contrast is seen in the effect of eloquence, the power which one man in an age possesses of uniting men by addressing the common soul of them all: if, ignorantly or wilfully, he seeks to uphold a falsehood, his inspiration and, ere long, his weight with men is lost; instead of leading the whole man, he leads only appetites and passions.''

Page 91, note 1. This definition of the eloquent man suggests the definition of eloquence in the essay of that name in the next volume: `` Eloquence is the power to translate a truth into language perfectly intelligible to the person to whom you speak."

Page 91, note 2. This passage refers to the Rev. Edward Taylor, the pastor of the Seamen's Bethel at the North End in Boston, whose rugged and searching eloquence Mr. Emerson greatly admired.

Journal, 1845. "What an eloquence Taylor suggests! Ah, could he guide those grand sea-horses of his with which he caracoles on the waves of the sunny ocean. But no, he is drawn up and down the ocean currents by the strong sea-monsters only on that condition, that he shall not guide."

Page 92, note 1. See the last part of stanza i. of the "Voluntaries" in the *Poems*.

Page 92, note 2.

> One who having nectar drank
> Into blissful orgies sank;
> He takes no mark of night or day,
> He cannot go, he cannot stay,
> He would, yet would not, counsel keep,
> But, like a walker in his sleep
> With staring eye that seeth none,
> Ridiculously up and down
> Seeks how he may fitly tell
> The heart-o'erlading miracle.
>
> "The Poet," *Poems*, Appendix.

Page 93, note 1.

> "As in a theatre, the eyes of men,
> After a well-graced actor leaves the stage,
> Are idly bent on him that enters next,
> Thinking his prattle to be tedious."
>
> Shakspeare, *Richard II.*, Act V., Scene 2.

Page 94, note 1. When Mr. Emerson, a young divinity

student, was writing his first sermon, he thus cautioned himself: "Take care, take care that your sermon is not a recitation; that it is a sermon to Mr. A and Mr. B and Mr. C."

A few years after leaving the ministry he came home distressed at the preaching he heard on Sunday morning: —

"At church to-day I felt how unequal is this match of words against things. Cease, O thou unauthorized talker, to prate of consolation, and resignation, and spiritual joys in neat and balanced sentences. For I know these men who sit below and on hearing of these *words* look up. Hush quickly! for care and calamity are *things* to them. . . . O speak things then, or hold thy tongue."

Page 95, note 1. Mr. Emerson used to say laughingly, "Eloquence is dog-cheap at an Anti-Slavery meeting."

Page 96, note 1. Evidently Theodore Parker was in Mr. Emerson's mind here. Mr. Lowell's remarkable description of Mr. Parker's omniscient pugnacity in his *Fable for Critics* might be read in this connection.

Page 98, note 1. Mr. Emerson, in writing to his revered friend the Rev. Henry Ware, after the Divinity School Address, had said as to arguments by which he might justify his position, "I do not know what arguments mean in reference to any expression of a thought." On another occasion he said, "Truth ceases to be such when polemically stated." He ignored attacks and left the thought to make its way. This is the counsel given in his poem "Saadi."

Page 98, note 2.

> The rules to men made evident
> By Him who built the day,
> The columns of the firmament
> Not firmer based than they.

"Fragments on the Poet," *Poems,* Appendix.

The speech of John Brown before receiving his death-sentence is an example of eloquence based on the great principles. In the essay on this subject in *Letters and Social Aims*, Mr. Emerson speaks of it, classing it as one of "the two best specimens of eloquence we have had in this country."

Page 98, note 3. Mr. Emerson acted on the counsel he gave to the American Scholar in the Phi Beta Kappa Address, in 1837: "Let him not quit his belief that a popgun is a popgun, though the ancient and honorable of the earth affirm it to be the crack of doom." — *Nature, Addresses and Lectures,* p. 102.

Page 99, note 1. Arnold Ludwig Heeren was a writer whose works on ancient history and civilization, particularly of Greece, translated by George Bancroft, interested Mr. Emerson.

Page 99, note 2. The reference here is to Kurroglou the Kurd, a robber-minstrel. Mr. Emerson was greatly interested in the romantic story of him and his horse Kyrat, told in *Specimens of Ancient Persian Poetry* by Chodzko. Kurroglou is the hero of Longfellow's poem "The Leap of Roushan Beg."

Page 100, note 1. The following note from the journal of 1850 is appropriate: —

"And let it be well considered in eloquence, that what we praise and allow is only relatively good, and that perhaps a person is there present who, if he would, could unsettle all that we have just now agreed on. We have fallen into a poor, beggarly way of living, and our orators are of the same poverty, and deal in rags and cold. The imagination, the great awakening power, the morals, the great creator of genius and men, are not addressed. But though the orators and poets are of this jejune rule of three faction, the capacities remain. The child asks you for a story and is thankful for the poorest. It is not poor to him, but a symbol all radiant with meaning. The man asks you for leave to be a poet and to paint things as they ought to be for a few hours. The youth asks for a poem. The stupidest wish to go to the theatre. We must have idolatries, mythologies, some swing and verge for the eternal and creative power lying coiled and cramped here, driving us to insanity and crime if it do not find vent.''

DOMESTIC LIFE

Mr. Emerson seems to have first treated this subject in a lecture called " Home " in the course on Human Life given in Boston in the winter of 1838–39. A passage from this lecture survives in the present essay and another in that on Education, in *Lectures and Biographical Sketches*. Probably the same, with suitable changes for an English audience, was the lecture called " Domestic Life," one of the three given in Exeter Hall.

The lecture in its present form was read to Mr. Parker's Society in the Music Hall in Boston, November 13, 1859.

Mr. Emerson was an eminently domestic man, more so than might be inferred from his writings, unless perhaps where in them he speaks of little children. In his home he was loved and loving, a good householder, if a poor farmer. His housekeeping was simple but hospitable. He was esteemed by his neighbors, and, though he served himself by preference, was cared for by servants with affectionate respect.

But by force of character and will he succeeded in keeping

to his task and avoiding domestic entanglement, although his study was close by the front door and separated but by thin doors from the parlor.

To show the good school of domesticity in which Mr. Emerson was reared, this picture of the home after his father's death may be given. The letter was written to his Aunt Mary when Ralph was not quite ten years old.

BOSTON, APRIL 16, 1813.

DEAR AUNT, — . . . I mean now to give you an account of what I do commonly in one day, if that is what you mean by giving an account of one single day in my life. Friday, 9th, I choose for the day of telling what I did. In the Morning I rose, as I commonly do, about five minutes before six. I then help Wm. in making the fire, after which I set the table for Prayers. I then call Mamma about quarter after six. We spell as we did before you went away. I confess I often feel an angry passion start in one corner of my heart when one of my Brothers gets above me, which I think sometimes they do by unfair means, after which we eat our breakfast; then I have from about quarter after seven to play or read. I think I am rather inclined to the former. I then go to school where I hope I can say I study more than I did a little while ago. I am in another book called Virgil, and our class are even with another which came to the Latin School one year before us. After attending this school I go to Mr. Webb's private school where I write and cipher. I go to this place at eleven and stay till one o'clock.[1] After I come home I eat my dinner and at two o'clock I resume my studies at the Latin School

[1] He did not think it worth while to mention to his aunt that he found it pleasanter to spend these two hours on the Common until Discovery and Retribution overtook him.

where I do the same except in studying grammar. After I come home I do Mamma her little errands if she has any; then I bring in my wood to supply the breakfast-room. I then have some time to play and eat my supper. After that we say our hymns or chapters, and then take our turns in reading Rollin, as we did before you went.[1] We retire to bed at different times. I go at a little after eight, and retire to my private devotions, and then close my eyes in sleep, and there end the toils of the day.

From Mr. Emerson's note-book: —

"On the back of Alexander's portrait of my mother, taken in 1825, at the age of 57, Edward B. E., who ordered the picture, wrote, —

"Feminae, uxoris, viduae, matris optimae, laudatae, benedictae vita pulchra, similitudo tam similis pretiosa. Ipsa mulier ad coelum ibit: umbra picta inter amicos, Deo volente, numquam inter inimicos, quia tales non sunt, vivis descriptionem sine errore mortalis quondam, tunc angeli dabit.

"Charles C. E. proposes an improved reading of the second sentence : —

"Ipsa mulier in coelum ibit: umbra picta inter amicos, Deo volente, non unquam, cum tales nulli sint, inter inimicos, errore purae mortalis quondam, tunc animae beatae imaginem servabit."

Page 103, note 1. "The babe in arms is a channel through which the energies we call fate, love and reason visibly stream." — "Considerations by the Way," *Conduct of Life.*

Pliny's charming and condensed description of a baby was

[1] An abridged translation in five volumes of the *Histoire Ancienne* by Charles Rollin (1661–1741).

noted by Mr. Emerson before he had children of his own: *Flens animal, cæteris imperaturum*, a crying creature which will give the law to others.

Page 104, note 1. The last three sentences were written soon after the birth of Mr. Emerson's first child, Waldo, who died when five years old.

Page 105, note 1. Mr. Thoreau served as horse and in every other way as delightful friend and companion to the children of his friend.

Page 105, note 2. The following is from an early journal: —

"Blessed is the child: the unconscious is ever the act of God himself. Nobody can reflect upon his unconscious period, or any particular word or act in it, with regret or contempt. Bard or hero cannot look down upon the word or gesture of a child: it is as great as they."

Page 105, note 3. Dr. Holmes wrote: "'Domestic Life' begins with a picture of childhood so charming that it sweetens all the good counsel which follows like honey round the rim of the goblet which holds some tonic draught."

Page 106, note 1. In the early poem "Peter's Field," only published after Mr. Emerson's death, in the Appendix to the *Poems*, he told of the enchanted wood which the oaks and hemlocks behind the Ripley Hill in Concord seemed to him and his brothers.

Page 107, note 1. "We rightly speak of the guardian angels of children. How superior in their security from infusions of evil persons, from vulgarity and second thought! They shed their own abundant beauty on the objects they behold. Therefore they are not at the mercy of such poor educators as we adults. If we huff and chide them, they soon come not to mind it, and get a self-reliance; and if we

indulge them to folly, they learn the limitation elsewhere.'
— "Uses of Great Men," *Representative Men.*

Page 107, note 2. Journal, 1842. "I was a little chubby
boy trundling a hoop in Chauncy Place and spouting poetry
from Scott and Campbell at the Latin School. But Time, the
little gray man, has taken out of his vest pocket a great awkward house (in a corner of which I sit and write of him), some
acres of land, several full grown and several very young persons, and seated them close beside me; then he has taken that
chubbiness and that hoop quite away (to be sure he has left
the declamation and the poetry) and here left a long lean
person threatening soon to be a little gray man like himself."

Page 108, note 1. A similar amusing passage is in the essay
on Beauty (*Conduct of Life*, p. 298): "But our bodies do
not fit us, but caricature and satirize us," etc.

Page 110, note 1. "There are not in the world at any
one time more than a dozen persons who read and understand
Plato, — never enough to pay for an edition of his works; yet
to every generation these come duly down, for the sake of
those few persons, as if God brought them in his hand."—
"Spiritual Laws," *Essays, First Series,* p. 154.

Page 111, note 1.

"None is so wasteful as the scraping dame;
She loseth three for one, her soul, rest, fame."
Herbert, "The Church Porch."

Page 112, note 1.

'T is the day of the chattel,
Web to weave, and corn to grind;
Things are in the saddle,
And ride mankind.
"Ode," inscribed to W. H. Channing, *Poems.*

Page 113, note 1. Journal, 1850. "Hear what the morning says and believe that. The house is full of noise and contradicts all that the morning hints."

Also a passage on the unworthiness of much of our daily employment is called to mind in "Lecture on the Times," *Nature, Addresses and Lectures.*

Page 115, note 1. In the concluding verses of "The Celestial Love" in the *Poems* this aspect of our debt to our kind is treated. In the journal of 1842, speaking of the self-denying ordinances of the reformers in abjuring flesh and wine and civic responsibilities, he concludes, "By none of these ways can he free himself, no, nor by paying his debts with money; only by obedience to his own genius, only by the fresh activity in the way constitutional to him, does an angel seem to arise and lead him by the hand out of all wards of the prison."

Page 117, note 1. His house gave hospitality, simple but comfortable, to the bodies of the many who came, but even more to the ideas. Sometimes the person did not come, only the earnest question or thought, and an answer giving light or refreshment returned. Mr. Emerson said, "I will assume that a stranger is judicious and benevolent. If he is, I will thereby keep him so. If he is not, it will tend to instruct him."

Page 119, note 1.

Thou shalt make thy house
The temple of a nation's vows.
Spirits of a higher strain
Who sought thee once shall seek again.
I detected many a god
Forth already on the road,
Ancestors of beauty come
In thy breast to make a home.
"Fragments on Life," *Poems,* Appendix.

Page 119, note 2. On his return to his own country in 1848, from the conventional life and fixed standards of England, he felt the relief and the opportunity, and wrote: —

"The dinner, the wine, the homes of England look attractive to the traveller, but they are the poor utmost that liberal wealth can perform. Alas! the halls of England are musty, the land is full of coal-smoke and carpet-smell: not a breath of mountain air dilates the languishing lungs."

Page 121, note 1. "The household is a school of power. There, within the door, learn the tragi-comedy of human life. Here is the sincere thing, the wondrous composition for which day and night go round. In that routine are the sacred relations, the passions that bind and sever. Here is poverty and all the wisdom its hated necessities can teach, here labor drudges, here affections glow, here the secrets of character are told, the guards of man, the guards of woman, the compensations which, like angels of justice, pay every debt: the opium of custom, whereof all drink and many go mad. Here is Economy, and Glee, and Hospitality, and Ceremony, and Frankness, and Calamity, and Death, and Hope." — "Education," *Lectures and Biographical Sketches.*

Page 121, note 2. This picture of the home of Mr. Emerson's childhood is well supplemented by those in Mr. Cabot's *Memoir,* vol. i. chapter i., and in the pleasant little book written by his cousin, the Rev. David Greene Haskins.[1] The book of another kinsman, George Barrell Emerson, the distinguished teacher and a much valued friend, contains this account of the Emerson household: —

"The longing for a home led me to apply to a very noble lady whom I had long known, and to beg her to let me

[1] *Ralph Waldo Emerson; his Maternal Ancestors, with some Reminiscences of him.* Boston: Cupples, Upham & Co., 1887.

become one of her family. She granted my request in the kindest manner possible. She was the widow of Rev. William Emerson, and among her sons I found William, whom I had long known and loved, the best reader, and with the sweetest voice I ever heard, and a pleasant talker; Ralph Waldo, whom I had known and admired, and whom all the world now knows almost as well as I do; Edward Bliss, the most modest and genial, the most beautiful and the most graceful speaker, a universal favorite; and Charles Chauncy, bright and ready, full of sense, ambitious of distinction, and capable of it." [1]

Of the religious atmosphere in that home Mr. Emerson thus speaks in his journal of 1837: " I cannot hear the young men whose theological instruction is exclusively owed to Cambridge and to public institutions without feeling how much happier was my star, which rained on me influences of ancestral religion. The depth of the religious sentiment which I knew in my Aunt Mary, imbuing all her genius and derived to her from such hoarded family traditions, from so many godly lives and godly deaths of sainted kindred, at Concord, at Malden, York, was itself a culture, an education. I heard with awe her tales."

Page 123, note 1. In former editions this name has been printed Genelas, but I can learn of no authority for any other spelling than Venelas. The name does not appear in the common English ballad on the same theme, " The Boy and the Mantle." Venelas appears in the " Fabliau du Mantel mantaillé " in the Collection by Montaiglon and Raynaud, and the *Archæologia Cambrensis,* 3d series, vol. ix.

Page 126, note 1. " We give up the past to the objector, and yet we hope. We grant that human life is mean, but how

---

[1] *Reminiscences of an Old Teacher.* Boston: Alfred Mudge & Son, 1878.

did we find out that it was mean?'' — ''The Over-Soul,'' *Essays, First Series*, p. 267.

See also on the last page of '' Poetry and Imagination,'' in *Letters and Social Aims*, '' The grandeur of our life exists in spite of us,'' etc. Also the lines in '' Woodnotes,'' II., beginning, —

> And thou shalt say to the Most High,
> '' Godhead! all this astronomy,'' etc.

Page 127, note 1. The idealized friend appears in the poem '' Friendship,'' the motto of that essay: —

> O friend, my bosom said,
> Through thee alone the sky is arched,
> Through thee the rose is red;
> All things through thee take nobler form
> And look beyond the earth,
> The mill-round of our fate appears
> A sun-path in thy worth.

Page 128, note 1. Quoted by Plutarch in the essay '' Of Brotherly Love'' in the *Morals.*

Page 130, note 1.

> If Thought unlock her mysteries,
> If Friendship on me smile,
> I walk in marble galleries,
> I talk with kings the while.
> '' Walden,'' *Poems,* Appendix.

Page 132, note 1.

> Let statue, picture, park and hall,
> Ballad, flag and festival,
> The past restore, the day adorn,
> And make to-morrow a new morn.

So shall the drudge in dusty frock
Spy behind the city clock
Retinues of airy kings,
Skirts of angels, starry wings,
His fathers shining in bright fables,
His children fed at heavenly tables.

" Art," *Poems.*

Page 132, note 2. Mr. Emerson once said of Gibbon, after praising his power of labor and his stately writing, that the trouble with the man was " that he had no shrine," a man's most needful possession.

Page 133, note 1.

God only knew how Saadi dined;
Roses he ate, and drank the wind.
" Fragments on the Poet," *Poems,* Appendix.

FARMING

This essay, originally called " The Man with the Hoe," was the oration delivered by Mr. Emerson at the annual exhibition of the Middlesex Agricultural Society — " Cattle-show " in the vernacular — September 29, 1858. His towns-man, John S. Keyes, Esquire, the sheriff of Middlesex and the president of the Society, invited him to give the address, knowing well that Mr. Emerson would present the larger and nobler view of their occupation to the farmers and gardeners of the county. For Concord, then a shire-town, was mainly agricultural, its lands still in the hands of the descendants of the early settlers. The two ministers, three doctors, six lawyers, two manufacturers, and the shop-keepers were all gardeners also, as were even the few residents who did business in Boston. So was Mr. Emerson, though in his essay on Prudence he admitted that "whoever sees my garden discovers that I must have some other garden." His poem "My Garden" tells of the latter, which yielded abundantly, but, that he had a right to talk to farmers as one of them, witness the printed Report of the Agricultural Society of 1858, which contains not only the Address in its first form, but the recommendation that R. W. Emerson and O. Farnsworth each receive $1.00 as a gratuity for single dishes of pears; better yet, R. W. Emerson is awarded third premium of $3.00 for Sage grapes. His neighbors, the Concord farmers, returned his salute with courtesy and respect when they met him on the roads or in their wood-lots, and most of them liked to hear him read one or more lectures in the Lyceum each winter, as did the people of the villages around. Mr. Emerson once said that his farming, "like the annual ploughing of the Emperor of China, had a certain emblematic air," but he knew how to find emblems and parables in the field, and proved in his lecturing that common people loved symbols. His neighbors gathered in their crops, but he, unknown to them, had reaped a harvest in their fields of which he tells in his poem "The Apology." This was his best crop, for he was unhandy with the spade. While his garden was small, he worked it with advice and help of his good friends George Bradford and Henry Thoreau, but as his farm increased, it was managed for a time by Mr. Edmund Hosmer. Of this neighbor Mr. Emerson gave a pleasant account in the *Dial* paper "Agriculture of Massachusetts," included in the volume *Natural History of Intellect*. After 1850 the ten-acre farm was managed and worked for him in succession by two excellent and devoted Irishmen, who left him free from its care to mind his own affairs as the interpreter.

['] In the journal of 1838 he wrote: —

"If my garden had only made me acquainted with the muck-worm, the bugs, the grasses and the swamp of plenty in August, I should willingly pay a free tuition. But every process is lucrative to me far beyond its economy."

In the essay on Wealth in *Conduct of Life* is the amusing account of how the weeds insidiously betrayed Mr. Emerson into the loss of his morning, and in *Nature, Addresses and Lectures* the advantages and to some extent the drawbacks of farming are set forth in the early pages of "The American Scholar," and "Man the Reformer," pp. 237–242.

The exordium of the Cattle-show Address was as follows: —

"Mr. President, Ladies and Gentlemen: — I suppose there is no anniversary that meets from all parties a more entire good will than this rural festival. Town and country, trader and manufacturer, clerk and layman, sailor and soldier, men and women, all have an equal stake in the prosperity of the farmer. It is well with all when it is well with him. He has no enemy, and all are loud in his praise. Every wise State has favored him, and the best men have held him highest. Cato said, when it was said that such or such a man was a good husbandman, it was looked upon as the very highest compliment. Of all the rewards given by the Romans to great public benefactors, the most valued and the rarest bestowed was the crown of grass, given only by the acclamation of the army for the preservation of the army by the valor of one man. Since the dependence, not of the whole army, but of the whole state, rests on the tiller of the ground, the *arval* crown, the crown of grass, should be more rightfully awarded to the farmer. Let us then look at the condition of the farmer, or the Man with the Hoe, at his strength and weakness, at his aids and servants, at his greater and lesser means, and his share in the great future which opens before the people of this country.''

Page 137, note 1. In the autumn following his Address to the Divinity Students in 1838, Mr. Emerson had been so much denounced for his dangerous heresies that it almost seemed to him that his lecture courses, on which he largely depended for support, might not be attended. He evidently began to consider man's primitive means of support, for he wrote in the journal of September 30, immediately in connection with some entries, suggested by the attacks made upon him: —

"It seems as if a man should learn to fish, to plant or to hunt that he might be secure if he were cast out from society and not be painful to his friends and fellow men.''

While planting his potatoes this comforting thought occurred: "A great fact of much import to the new philosophical opinions is the garden discovery that a potato put into a hole, in six weeks becomes ten. This is the miracle of the multiplication of loaves.''

And again, May, 1839: "I think we ought to have manual labor, each man. Why else this rapid impoverishing which brings every man continually to the presence of the fact that bread is by the sweat of the face.''

Page 139, note 1. It should be remembered that this address was written at the period when the old New England farming had not yet quite passed into the new. The farmer and his boys were still working together on many farms, and the mother and daughters doing dairy and household work. The farmer was less of a trader than he must be now to succeed, for he and his family mainly lived off the farm. The machine-farming was but beginning, and most farm-work, and even marketing, was done at the pace of the ox, and the horse was only beginning to supersede him. To offset this, the working-day was often sixteen hours long. The bread was still often made of rye and Indian meal, and vegetables, fruit, pork and beef raised on the farm, with cider for drink, made the principal diet. Grocery bills were partly paid in produce, and there was little cash for clothing, household adornment and amusement. The Irishman, whose industry and frugal living has since made him master of half of our farms, was a hired laborer newly come, and the Scandinavian had not arrived.

Page 140, note 1. The unfitness of the amateur farmers of Brook Farm and Fruitlands was in Mr. Emerson's mind.

Page 141, note 1.

> What prizes the town and the tower ?
> Only what the pine-tree yields;
> Sinew that subdued the fields;
> The wild-eyed boy, who in the woods
> Chants his hymn to hills and floods,
> Whom the city's poisoning spleen
> Made not pale, or fat, or lean.
>
> " Woodnotes," II., *Poems.*

Page 142, note 1. Thoreau's plan, by which he became a truly rich man, was to diminish his wants instead of increasing his income.

Page 142, note 2. In the Cattle-show Address, to these servants were added " the winds that have blown in the interminable succession of years before he was born." The paragraph suggests several passages in the *Poems,* as that in the " Song of Nature " beginning

> Time and Thought were my surveyors, —

and in the " Fragments on Nature," where she says : —

He lives not who can refuse me;
All my force saith, Come and use me.

Page 144, note 1.

No ray is dimmed, no atom worn,
My oldest force is good as new,
And the fresh rose on yonder thorn
Gives back the bending heavens in dew.

" Song of Nature."

Page 145, note 1. " They do not believe, what is true, that one half of the weight of the rocks which compose the crust of the globe, . . . of the houses, of the stones of the pavement, of the soils we cultivate, and much more than half by weight of all living animals and plants, consists of oxygen." — Cattle-show Address.

Ever the Rock of Ages melts
Into the mineral air,
To be the quarry whence to build
Thought and its mansions fair.

" Fragments on Life," *Poems.*

Page 145, note 2. This passage suggests the lines in the second " Woodnotes " beginning

Onward and on, the eternal Pan.

The concluding portion of the paragraph is found in metrical form in the little poem " Pan " among the " Fragments on Nature."

This whole theme of the farmer's servants is treated in a few lines in the poem " Guy."

Page 146, note 1.

Put in, drive home the sightless wedges
And split to flakes the crystal ledges.

" Fragments on Nature," *Poems.*

In the Address the paragraph is concluded as follows: —

"Water, the daily miracle — a substance as explosive as gunpowder — the electric force contained in a drop of water being equal in amount to that which is discharged from a thunder-cloud. I quote from the exact Faraday."

Then follows a passage about the farmer's doubtful competence to control these majestic forces: —

"His servants are sometimes too strong for him. His tools are too sharp. But this inequality finds its remedy in practice. Experience gradually teaches him, and he is thoughtful. The farmer hates innovation; he hates the hoe till he tries it, preferring to scratch with a stick; he will walk till he has tried the railway car; but the oldest fogy among us, now that the Atlantic Cable is laid to London, will not send a man to swim across with his letter in his mouth."

Page 147, note 1. It may be interesting to see this passage in the garb in which it was presented to the Middlesex farmers.

"Plant a fruit-tree by the roadside and it will not produce, although it receives many hints, from projected stones and sticks, that fruit is desired to come down, and though it has been swallowed crude into the robust bowels of small boys. But draw a low fence about it to keep out the cow and pig, and for thirty, forty, perhaps a hundred years, it ripens peacefully its delicate fruit, — every pear, every nectarine, every cluster of grapes inviting you to have its picture taken, before being sent to the Horticultural Fair."

Apropos of orchards, I will give here two allusions to apples from the journals: —

1848. "I have planted a Pumpkin-sweeting near my summer house, — I believe out of agreeable recollections of that fruit in my childhood at Newton. It grew in Mr. Greenough's pasture, and I thought it solid sunshine.

    " Ere boyhood with quick glance had ceased to spy
      The doubtful apple 'mid the yellow leaves.''

1853. " The Newtown Pippins, Gentlemen, are they not the *Newton* Pippins ? or, is not this the very pippin that demonstrated to Sir Isaac Newton the fall of the world, not the fall of Adam, but of the moon to the earth, and universal gravity. Well, here they are, a barrel of them; every one of them good to show gravitation, and good to eat; every one as sound as the moon. What will you give me for a barrel of moons ? ''

Page 148, note 1. From " The Mower against Gardens '' by Andrew Marvell (1621–1678).

Page 151, note 1. Henry Charles Carey, a remarkable student and writer on Political Economy. In 1836 he published *The Harmony of the World, as exhibited in the Laws which regulate the Increase of Population and of the Means of Sustenance, and in the Identity of the Interests of the Sovereign and the Subject, the Landlord and the Tenant, the Capitalist and the Workman, the Master and the Slave.*

In support of Mr. Carey's theory it may be said that the Great Meadows of Concord, Bedford, Sudbury and Wayland, bare of trees and waving with coarse grass, are said to have been the bait which lured the first settlers here. They hoped thus to have fertile fields without the long and arduous work of clearing primæval forest. But neither they nor their descendants have ever been able to get anything better than meadow-hay of poor quality from them.

Page 152, note 1. Mr. Emerson, in the Historical Discourse which he gave in Concord in 1835, at the celebration of the two hundredth year of the settlement of the town, gave an amusing if piteous account of the sufferings of the first settlers. See *Miscellanies.*

Page 153, note 1. This sentence recalls Mr. Emerson's wise treatment of his children if they cried at table. He always quietly sent the unhappy one to see whether the front gate were latched, or whether there were perhaps a rain-cloud coming. He knew that the change of scene and the quiet face of Nature would calm the child, who returned and duly reported, wondering why the fear of cows getting in, or a storm coming, had so suddenly come over his father.

Page 153, note 2. The following picture of the Nine-Acre Corner farms along the river, and of the old-time Concord farmers, is from the journal of 1848: —

"The cranberry meadow yonder is that where Darius Hubbard picked one hundred bushels in one season worth 200 dollars, and no labor whatever is bestowed on the crop, not so much as to mow the grass or cut down the bushes. Much more interesting is the wood-lot, which yields its gentle rent of six per cent. without any care or thought when the owner sleeps or travels, and fears no enemy but fire. But E. declares that the railroad has proved too strong for all our farmers and has corrupted them like a war, or the incursion of another race; — has made them all amateurs, given the young men an air their fathers never had; they look as if they might be railroad agents any day. We shall never see Cyrus Hubbard or Ephraim Wheeler or Grass-and-oats or Oats-and-grass, old Barrett or Hosmer, in the next generation. These old Saxons have the look of pine-trees and apple-trees, and might be the sons got between the two; conscientious labourers with a science born with them from out the sap-vessels of these savage sires. This savagery is natural to man, and polished England cannot do without it."

The Cattle-show Address concluded thus: —

"I congratulate the farmer of Massachusetts on his advantages. I congratulate him that he is set down in a good place, where the soil and climate yield a larger Flora than any other. A greater variety of important plants grow here than in any southern or northern latitude. We are on the northern boundary of many tropical trees, and on the southern boundary of the arctic plants. We can raise almost all crops, and if we lack the orange and palm, we have the apple and peach and pear. In Illinois, it is often said, although it is more the voice of their scorn than of their pity, that they reckon it a singular leading of Divine Providence that Massachusetts was settled before the prairie was known, else it would never have been settled. But the Massachusetts farmer may console himself that if he has not as rich a soil, he has the advantage of a market at his own door, the manufactory in the same town. I congratulate you, then, on the advantage of your position. Next, I congratulate you on the new territory which you have discovered, and not annexed but subnexed to Middlesex and to Massachusetts. I congratulate you at being born at a happy time, when the old slow ways of culture must go out with the sharp stick and the bow and arrow, when the steam-engine is in full use, and new plants and new culture are daily brought forward. I congratulate you on the fact that the year that has just witnessed the successful employment of new machines, of the mower and reaper, on the plains and prairies, has also witnessed the laying of the Atlantic Cable. The Cable is laid, and the courage of man is confirmed. All that used to look like vagary and castle-building is to be solid sense henceforth. Who shall ever dare to say impossible again? Henceforth, if a thing is really desirable, it is in that degree really practicable, and the farm you have dreamed of — go instantly and begin to make it. I congratulate you, lastly, on the new political economy which takes off the crape from farms and towns and nations, and lets in the light on all we do and all we gain, and teaches that whatever is really good and useful for one man to do, is good and useful for all.''

WORKS AND DAYS

The lecture "Works and Days" appears to have been first given in Cincinnati and probably other cities and towns in 1857. It followed "Country Life" as the second lecture in the course called the *Natural Method of Mental Philosophy* in the spring of the following year. It opened then with the following passage: —

"One of the oldest remains of literature is the poem of Hesiod, called *Works and Days*. It is not much read in these times crowded with books and manifold spiritual influences; but it has had its day, and has furnished its share of the general culture; in as much as passages from it have passed into the public mind, and make part of the proverbs of mankind. I borrow from it only its title, to offer from this text a lesson to this day and hour.''

Page 157, note 1. Sir Charles Bell quotes Galen as saying, "Did man possess the natural armor of the brutes, he would no longer work as an artificer, nor protect himself with a breast-plate, nor fashion a sword or spear, nor invent a bridle to mount the horse and hunt the lion. Neither would he follow the arts of peace, construct the pipe and lyre, erect houses, place altars, inscribe laws and through letters commune with the wisdom of antiquity.''

Page 157, note 2. This was Thoreau's experience with

some of those who helped him in his land-surveying. He could verify their work by pacing.

Page 161, note 1. At the time when this lecture was written the vast undertaking of connecting by submarine cable the Old World with the New excited the hopes of civilized mankind. The apparent triumph of human wit and hands over stupendous difficulties was celebrated by Mr. Emerson in his poem "The Adirondacs," for it was there that the good news reached him, but that was in August, 1858, more than a year after this lecture was written. It was, of course, adapted to the times when later delivered, and, when the essay was published as part of this volume, the Atlantic Cable had been in successful operation nearly five years.

Page 162, note 1.

My paths lead out
The exodus of nations: I disperse
Men to all shores that front the hoary main.
"Sea-Shore," *Poems.*

Page 162, note 2. This paragraph from the lecture here followed in the essay: —

"Vulgar progress is in extending yourself, claiming and fencing a great deal of land; conquering and counting by continents and by millions. True progress is in making the most of that you have; in disclosing the arsenal of powers that belong to an acre of ground; in unlocking the irresistible faculties that belong to a cultivated man; that control over mankind which belongs to him who controls himself; the knowledge of all men which belongs to self-knowledge; the inevitable radiation of centrality."

Mr. Emerson was speaking in high and general themes, but their special application to the hour was the moral he would point. He was impatient of the leading orators who in those dark days before the war were praising the patriots of " seven-ty-six; " yet showing themselves apostates to their great prin-ciples, applicable as ever to the problems of 1858. An omitted sheet, from the lecture, runs as follows: " Greatness is to live in the present, to magnify the present, to know its duties and carry up the present knot of affairs over Greece, or Rome, or Palestine. But we live as these paltry politicians live; we are absurdly historical: we neglect the plain duty of the moment, to honor the memory of some dead duty, — of some dead body in some dead moment. We praise Washington, but perform Lord North. We keep the fourth of July, and our eyes always nailed on mouldering escutcheons. I dreamed I stood in a city of beheaded men, where the decapitated trunks continued to walk."

Page 164, note 1.

> It cannot conquer folly, —
>   Time-and-space-conquering steam, —
> And the light-outspeeding telegraph
>   Bears nothing on its beam.
>   " The World-Soul," *Poems.*

Page 164, note 2.

>   " Wealth is the conjurer's devil,
> Whom when he thinks he hath, the devil hath him."
>   George Herbert, " The Church Porch."

Page 165, note 1. Mr. Emerson, like others, was feeling the " hard times " of the great financial panic of 1857.

Page 167, note 1. His poem " Days " Mr. Emerson once spoke of as the one which he thought the best. It is not unlikely that he meant it for the purpose for which it is used in this edition, as motto to this essay, but, as he was hurried in preparing the book, could not write mottoes for all and so omitted any. The editor has, however, ventured to supply them from the poems or fragments of verse.

Page 168, note 1. Dr. Holmes, in his interesting chapter on Emerson's poems, quotes this prose sentence from the " Works and Days," and then says, " Now see the thought in full dress," and gives the poem " Days," adding the comment, " Cinderella at the fireside, and Cinderella at the prince's ball! "

This image of the masquerading days appears also in " May-Day," and in a youthful poem, never printed, and also in several essays or lectures; for instance: " The Times are the Masquerade of the Eternities, trivial to the dull, tokens of noble and majestic agents to the wise; . . . the quarry out of which the genius of to-day is building up the Future."

Page 170, note 1. In the original form this sentence ran: " One must look long before he finds the Timæus weather; but at last the high, cold, silent morning arrives, the early dawn," etc.

Page 171, note 1.

Yet whirl the glowing wheels once more,
    And mix the bowl again;
Seethe, Fate! the ancient elements,
    Heat, cold, wet, dry, and peace and pain.

Let war and trade and creeds and song
    Blend, ripen race on race,
The sunburnt world a man shall breed
    Of all the zones and countless days.
                 " Song of Nature," *Poems.*

Page 171, note 2. Milton, *Paradise Lost,* IV. 477.

Page 172, note 1. " The young mortal enters the hall of the firmament. . . . On the instant, and incessantly, fall snowstorms of illusions," etc. — " Illusions," *Conduct of Life*.

Page 173, note 1. Compare the poem " Xenophanes."

Page 174, note 1.

> Who bides at home, nor looks abroad,
> Carries the eagles and masters the sword.
> > " Destiny," *Poems*.

Page 175, note 1. This sentence suggests the ending of the second " Woodnotes."

Page 175, note 2.

> Shines the last age, the next with hope is seen,
> To-day slinks poorly off unmarked between:
> Future or Past no richer secret folds,
> O friendless Present, than thy bosom holds.
> > " Heri, Cras, Hodie," *Poems*, Quatrains.

Page 176, note 1. Letter to Marshal Saint Cyr.

Page 177, note 1. In the lecture this sentence follows: " Beware of affronting the Genius who has covered up under these low haunts your private passage to the council-chamber of the great Gods."

Page 177, note 2. Compare the opening passage of the first essay in this volume.

Page 178, note 1. In the lecture, here follows, " Some mellow, satisfying seasons we have in the woods in cool summer days."

Page 178, note 2.

> τοῖος γὰρ νόος ἐστὶν ἐπιχθονίων ἀνθρώπων,
> οἷον ἐπ' ἦμαρ ἄγῃσι πατὴρ ἀνδρῶν τε θεῶν τε.
> > *Odyssey*, XVIII. 136, 137.

This passage has been much discussed by scholars, but the

view as held at present gives it a different signification from that given in the essay, viz.: *The mind of men on earth is like the day which the Father of gods and men brings to them.*

Page 179, note 1. The elder Pliny's dedication of his Natural History to Titus Vespasian: "I have included in thirty-six books 20,000 topics, all worthy of attention, . . . and to these I have made considerable additions of things which were either not known to my predecessors or which have been lately discovered. Nor can I doubt but that there still remain many things which I have omitted; for I am a mere mortal, and one that has many occupations. I have, therefore, been obliged to compose this work at interrupted intervals, indeed during the night, so that you will find that I have not been idle even during this period. The day I devote to you, exactly portioning out my sleep to the necessity of my health, and contenting myself with this reward, *that while we are musing on these subjects* (according to the remark of Varro) *we are adding to the length of our lives;* for life properly consists in being awake."

Page 180, note 1. Here follow, in the original, the words " Beauty is at home."

Page 181, note 1.

Blessed is he, who, playing deep, yet haply asks not why,
Too busied in the crowded hour to fear to live or die.

Quatrain, " Nature," Poems.

Page 182, note 1. A part of the song of the White Lady of Avenel in Sir Walter Scott's novel, *The Abbot.*

Page 184, note 1. In the essay " Aristocracy " (*Lectures and Biographical Sketches*), such is said to have been the practice of the Caliph Ali.

Page 185, note 1. When the lecture was first given, this

was Mr. Emerson's word for the hour to his countrymen: "This country has its proper glory, though now shrouded and unknown. We will let it shine. Let us set American free will against Asiatic fate; the American wilderness of capabilities and idealistic tendency, against the adamantine grooves of law and custom in which European thought travels.

"In my judgment the best use of Europe to our people is, its warnings to us, or we go to Europe to be Americanized."

BOOKS

That the value which Mr. Emerson set on books was a trait that had long characterized the family, the following extract from the will of his ancestor, the founder of Concord, will show: —

"I, Peter Bulkeley, . . . give to my son Edward certain books in my library; 1. Tarnovius on the Minor Prophets. 2. Piscator's Commentary. 3. Dr. Owen against the Arminians. 4. Dr. Willet on Exodus & Leviticus. 5. English Annotations. 6. Mr. Ainsworth's notes on 5 Books of Moses.

"To my son Eliazur, a hundred acres of land lying at the near end of the great meadow & 20 acres at the far end."

In 1835, when Mr. Emerson had just come back to the ancestral town to live there the life of a scholar, he wrote in his journal a sentence which he later turned for amusement into a rude rhyme: —

When shall I be tired of reading ?
When the moon is tired of waxing and waning,
When the cloud is tired of raining,
When the sea of ebbing and flowing,

When the grass is weary of growing,
When the planets tire of going,
And when Death is sick of feeding,
Then shall I be tired of reading.

It may be interesting to young people living in the twen-
tieth century to see a letter advising a course of reading which
Mr. Emerson wrote when he was twenty-eight years old to
Miss Elizabeth Tucker of Derry, New Hampshire, a young
girl " in her teens," who was a cousin of his first wife.

BOSTON, 1 FEB., 1832.

MY DEAR COUSIN, — If it were not true that it is never
too late to do right, I should be quite ashamed to send my list
of books at such a long distance behind my promise. When I
spent so pleasant a day at your house, I thought it would be
very easy, and I knew it would be very pleasant, for me to
make out a scheme of study for your vacation as soon as I got
home. But what to select out of so great a company of leather-
jackets and so deserving — and then a crowd of things to be
done — and withal a Quaker habit of never doing things till
their necessary time, in the hope of doing them better, has
postponed my letter from day to day and week to week. But
so you must never do, my dear Cousin. But for fear you
should quite forget your wise adviser, and should be a grown
lady and so I should lose the honor of having had any part in
your education, I hasten to send you my poor thoughts upon
what is good to be read. I make no pretensions to give you
a complete course, but only select a few good books of my
acquaintance — such as I think you will like, and such as will
serve you.

One more preliminary word. Never mind any silly people
that try to sneer you out of the love of reading. People are

fast outgrowing the old prejudice that a lady ought not to be acquainted with books. It is the display that disgusts; the knowledge that you get from them never disgusts anybody, but is all useful, and has comforted how many hours that would otherwise have been long, dull and lonely.

First then you must keep one or two books for the soul always by you, for monitors and angels, lest this world of trifles should run away with you. Such a book is Thomas à Kempis's *Imitation of Christ*, written by a German monk near four hundred years ago, and needs only a little allowance for a Roman Catholic's opinions, to make it express the religious sentiments of every good mind. Then there is a little book I value very much, Scougal's *Life of God in the Soul of Man*. Taylor's *Holy Dying* is a good book. Its author was called the "Shakspeare of divines." *Selections from Fénelon*, by Mrs. Follen. *Ware on the Formation of the Christian Character*. Sir Thomas Browne's *Religion of a Physician*. This is a beautiful work lately republished in this town. Young's *Night Thoughts*. A friend whom I value very much told Ellen always to keep Young upon her table. But I suppose you will think here are Sunday books enough. Now for History. The American Society for the Diffusion of Useful Knowledge are publishing Müller's *Universal History* in four duodecimo volumes. It is very much the best of all the General histories and is very easily read. They have yet only printed the first volume. The sketches of Rome and of Greece in it are excellent. Then the most important modern history to be read perhaps is Robertson's *Charles V.*, which is an account of Europe in the most interesting period. I would skip the first volume, which is a general view of Europe, and read the two last. Then you might take up Hume, say at the reign of Elizabeth, which would continue pretty

VII

well the line of events. The best history of Europe during
the French Revolution is Scott's *Life of Napoleon*. For the
American history, as you happen to live at Derry, N. H., I
would read Dr. Belknap's History of the State. It is not only
a very good book itself, but will give you a pretty good idea
of all the States, their story is so much alike. Morton's *New
England Memorial* is a little book and a pleasing account of
the Forefathers. . Milman's *History of the Jews* in the *Family
Library* is a very good book.

But what is far more soothing, and never painful, like the
history of man, is Natural History in its various parts. The
first volume of the *American Library of Useful Knowledge*
(and you must make the Social Library in Derry subscribe for
that book) contains *Mr. Brougham's Discourse* upon the advantage and prospects of Science, which is excellent, and Mr.
Herschel's, which is better. The same Mr. Herschel, son
of the famous astronomer, is about to publish a discourse on
astronomy which is expected with great interest. Then there
is a beautiful book on American birds by Mr. Nuttall (N.'s
Ornithology) that every one who lives in the country ought to
read. I suppose you have read at school *Conversations on
Chemistry*. The *Conversations on Vegetable Physiology* are
just as good. With this class of books I will put the *Account
of Polar Expeditions*, a volume of the *Family Library*.

I suppose to such a formidable list I must add a novel or
two, or you would think me very unkind. So I really hope
you will read *De Vere* by the author of *Tremaine*, and as
much Walter Scott and Miss Edgeworth as you please. For
Poetry read Milton; if the *Paradise Lost* tires you, it is so
stately, try the minor Poems. *Comus*, if the Mythology does
not make it sound strange, is a beautiful poem and makes one
holy to read it. Read Bryant's poems. I know you will love

them, and Cowper and Thomson, and perhaps (a very large perhaps) Wordsworth.

If you do not like poetry, which I suppose you do, the best way to learn is to write some.

Now I do not suppose that you will read all these books in a short time, or perhaps at any time, and some of them very probably you have read. I only wanted to fulfil your command, and speak a good word for some valued acquaintance of mine. The best of all ways to make one's reading valuable is to write about it, and so I hope my Cousin Elizabeth has a blank-book where she keeps some record of her thoughts. And if you think my letter very long, why you must bear in mind that once I was a schoolmaster, and I am so proud of my new scholar as to keep her long at my lecture.

Make my respectful remembrances to your mother and father and my compliments to your sister.

Your affectionate cousin,
R. W. EMERSON.

Of himself he wrote in 1859: "I am a natural reader and only a writer in the absence of natural writers. In a true time I should never have written."

In his Phi Beta Kappa Address (in *Nature, Addresses and Lectures*) Mr. Emerson pointed out to the American Scholar the right and the wrong use of books and said, "Man Thinking must not be subdued by his instruments. Books are for the scholar's idle times." Only in the intervals of direct illumination he may resort to their reflected light. And in "Nominalist and Realist" (*Essays, Second Series*) he admits that sometimes he reads even Plato "for the lustres," "for a mechanical help to the fancy and the imagination." He told a youthful writer "only to read to start his team." But in his journal of 1867, after saying that in proportion to your reality of life and perception will be your difficulty of finding yourself expressed in others' words or deeds, he interrupts himself, — "and yet — and yet — when the visions of my books come over me as I sit writing, when the remembrance of some poet comes, I accept it with pure joy, and quit my thinking as sad lumbering work; and hasten to my little heaven, if it is then accessible, as angels might."

Page 189, note 1. Mr. Emerson begins this estimate of books in the "low tone" which he often commends, avoiding superstition concerning them, and this gives opportunity for ascension in the treatment of the theme. In a note-book called *Literature*, under the heading "Skeptical," he wrote: "We must not inquire too curiously into the absolute value of literature. Enough that it amuses and exercises us. At least it leaves us where we were. It names things, but does not add things." But in a lecture "Some Good Books" he decides the matter more cheerfully, and after "value of literature" the passage goes on thus, — "yet books are to us angels of entertainment, sympathy and provocation. These silent wise, these tractable prophets and singers, who now and then cast their moonlight illumination over solitude, weariness and fallen fortunes."

Page 190, note 1. Cornelius Agrippa (1486–1535), a German scholar, alchemist and reputed magician, who wrote on *The Uncertainty and Vanity of the Sciences,* and on *Occult Philosophy.* His magic mirror, in which he showed to the Earl of Surrey his lady-love beyond the seas, is told of in song in Scott's *Lay of the Last Minstrel.* In the same poem the "book of spells," borrowed from the grave at Melrose Abbey of the wizard Michael Scott, plays an important part. Michael

Scott lived in the thirteenth century, and had great fame on the Continent as well as in Scotland. He is mentioned by Dante.

Page 190, note 2. The following account of the effect of a sentence from one of Emerson's books on a Virginian youth is best given in his own language: " Fresh from college, now from every career planned by parent or friend I had recoiled: some indefinable impediment barred each usual path. . . . Utterly miserable, self-accused amid sorrowful faces, with no outlook but to be the fettered master of slaves, I was wont to shun the world, with a gun for an apology. . . . So came I on a day [to the banks of the Rappahannock] and reclined on the grass reading in a magazine [*Blackwood's*] casually brought. . . . The church-bells across the river smote upon a heart discordant with them, at discord with itself. Nature had no meaning, life no promise and no aim. Listlessly turning to the printed page, one sentence caught my eye and held it; one sentence quoted from Emerson, which changed my world and me. A sentence only! I do not repeat it: it might not bear to others what it bore to me: its searching, subtle revelation defies any analysis I can make of its words. All I know is that it was the touch of flame I needed. That day my gun was laid aside to resume no more." [1]

The author, who under the new influence sacrificed his inheritance of slaves, and even his father's blessing, and later, place and influence as a clergyman because of his advocacy of human liberty, said to the editor, " But for the reading of that extract from Emerson in a critique in *Blackwood* on ' Six American Books,' I should be lying in a rebel's grave to-day."

An Austrian writer on Reading and Culture[2] in his preface

[1] *Emerson at Home and Abroad*, by Moncure Daniel Conway. Boston: J. R. Osgood & Co., 1882.
[2] *Ueber Lesen und Bildung*, von Anton E. Schönbach. Gratz, 1882.

says, "It will be noticed how strongly Ralph Waldo Emerson has influenced my entire conception of the matters treated."

Page 191, note 1. The following sentence seems to have been in this lecture as first delivered: "And Plutarch: if the world's library were burning, I should fly to save that, with our Bible and Shakspeare and Plato."

Page 192, note 1. When in Mr. Emerson's later years a book-agent was impertinently recommending to him some new work, he was moved to say, "Young man, it is not for you to tell me what to read. I read for other people." He wrote in his journal, "In college days Warren Burton used to come to my room, and said he did not like to read and did not remember what he read, but what I read or quoted to him he remembered, and never forgot."

Page 192, note 2. Johann Albert Fabricius, the German scholar (1668–1736), author of the *Bibliotheca Latina, Græca,* and *Ecclesiastica,* and *Bibliographia Antiquaria.* John Selden (1584–1654), called "the great dictator of learning of the English nation," though the author of many learned books, is best known by his *Table-Talk.* Giovanni Pico, Count of Mirandola (1463–1494), an Italian of very extraordinary acquirements in languages and philosophy. Joseph Justus Scaliger (1540–1609), son of a remarkable scholar, though Italian by birth, was educated in France. He became professor of Belles-lettres at Leyden, and surpassed his father in erudition. Antonio Magliabechi (1633–1714), a Florentine who, though a goldsmith's apprentice, became so eager a scholar that he was appointed by Cosmo III. his librarian. In this capacity he brought to notice many valuable but neglected manuscripts, and he bequeathed to Florence the important library which he had collected. Pierre Bayle (1647–1706), a French scholar remarkable for his courage and liberality, which virtues cost him in succession his professorships at Sedan and Rotterdam. His noted work is the *Dictionnaire historique et critique.*

Page 195, note 1. Professor Herman Grimm in his first letter to Mr. Emerson, whose writings, then newly read, had greatly stirred him, said, " Everywhere I seem to find my own thoughts, — even the words in which I would prefer to have expressed them; " and later, " You write so that every one reading your words must think you had thought of him alone."

Page 196, note 1. Journal, 1851. " One should dignify and entertain and signalize each journey or adventure by carry- ing to it a literary masterpiece, and making thorough acquaint- ance with that, on the way, as, the *Figaro* of Beaumarchais; the *Nuova Vita* of Dante; the *Bride of Corinth* of Goethe; the 47th Proposition of Euclid; ode of Horace or of Hafiz, and so on; *Clouds* of Aristophanes, a Trilogy of Æschylus."

Page 196, note 2. This suggests the advice to the Artist in the quatrain of that name.

> Quit the hut, frequent the palace,
> Reck not what the people say;
> For still, where'er the trees grow biggest,
> Huntsmen find the easiest way.

Page 196, note 3. Shakspeare, *Taming of the Shrew,* Act I., Sc. 1.

Page 197, note 1. Mr. Emerson wrote thus of his plea- sure in Greek mythology and poetry, in the journal of 1855: —

" A convertible proverb, *It is Greek to him.* These East- ern story-tellers whose oily tongues turn day into night and night into day, wh. lap their hearers in a sweet drunkness of fancy, so that they forget the taste of meat !"

Page 198, note 1. Mr. Emerson said to a young scholar, "I am glad you have so many of the Greek Tragedies. Read them largely and swiftly in translation to get their movement and flow; and then a little in the original every day. For the Greek is the fountain of language. The Latin has a definite shore-line, but the Greek is without bounds."

Page 199, note 1. "Read in Plato and you shall find Christian dogmas, and not only so, but stumble on our evangelical phrases." — "Quotation and Originality," *Letters and Social Aims.*

Page 199, note 2. Mr. Emerson's estimate of Plato may be read in full in *Representative Men* and of Plutarch in the essay of that name in *Lectures and Biographical Sketches.*

Page 201, note 1. Mr. Emerson himself never enjoyed Aristophanes, but read the comedies for such light as they gave on the age and country. Journal, 1865. "I am delighted to-day, in reading Schwegler's account of Socrates, to have justice done to Aristophanes. The rogue gets his dues."

Page 202, note 1. In a lecture given in Boston in 1861, called "Some Good Books," Mr. Emerson said: —

"What vitality has the Platonic Philosophy! I remember I expected a revival in the churches to be caused by reading Jamblichus. . . .

"When I read Proclus, I am astonished with the vigor and breadth of his performance. Here is an Atlantic strength which is everywhere equal to itself, and dares great attempts, because of the life with which it feels itself filled. Such a sense as dwells in these purple deeps of Proclus transforms every page into a slab of marble, and the book seems monumental. They suggest what magnificent dreams and projects! They show what literature should be. Rarely, rarely does the Imagination awake."

But in these authors, especially Proclus, he read rather for stimulation than continuously. "I think the Platonists may be read for sentences, though the reader fails to grasp the argument of the paragraph or chapter. He may yet obtain gleams and glimpses of a more excellent illumination from their genius, outvaluing the most distinct information he owes to other books. For I hold that the grandeur of the impression the stars and heavenly bodies make on us, is surely more valuable than our exact perception of a tub or a table on the ground."

Page 203, note 1. Thomas Taylor, the enthusiastic translator of the Neo-Platonists, was a remarkable character, a high-minded Greek Pagan in London. Mr. Emerson spoke of him as "a Greek born out of time and dropped on the ridicule of a blind and frivolous age." When he was in England in 1848 he was surprised to find how little was known of Taylor and his works by the cultivated men whom he met.

Mr. Charles J. Woodbury,[1] in his faithful and remarkable report of various conversations with Mr. Emerson at about the time this lecture was given, quotes him as saying of Plato, "He lifts man toward the divine, and I like it when I hear that a man reads Plato. I want to meet that man. For no man of self-conceit can go through Plato."

Page 203, note 2. Jamblichus of Chalcis, the pupil of Porphyry, succeeded him as the head of the Neo-Platonic school of Syria in the fourth century B. C. His writings combine the religious philosophies of the Greeks and Orientals.

Page 205, note 1. Journal, 1845. "Gibbon has a strength rare with such finish. He built a pyramid, and then enamelled it."

Mr. Emerson wrote in 1839 to his young cousin, David Greene Haskins (later an Episcopal clergyman and Doctor of

[1] *Talks with Ralph Waldo Emerson*, Baker and Taylor Co., 1890.

Divinity), a letter about Gibbon in which, after praising his devotion to his work, he expresses disgust at his "worst fault! the dirt he has defiled his notes with," but adds, "You must give this evil man his due and make it felt what condemnation his noble labor and perseverance cast upon scholars who have libraries which they never read, upon scholars who chide Gibbon, but are unable even to name his dignified studies, his original authorities, his great plan, and great execution of it." [1]

Page 205, note 2. Note-book on Literature: "Dante's *Vita Nuova* reads like the book of Genesis, as if written before literature, whilst truth yet existed. A few incidents are sufficient, and are displayed with Oriental amplitude and leisure. It is the Bible of love." And again of Dante: "He was free imagination, all wings, yet wrote like Euclid."

Page 206, note 1. In acknowledging Herman Grimm's gift of his *Life of Michelangelo* Mr. Emerson wrote in 1861: [2]

"MY DEAR FRIEND, —. . . The book is a treasure, — in the hero, the treatment, the frank criticism, the judicial opinions, and — what I value most — the interior convictions of the writer bravely imparted. . . . The book has research, method and daylight. . . . You step from stone to stone and advance ever. . . . Goethe and Michel Angelo deserve your fine speeches, and are not perilous for a long time. One may absorb great amounts of these with impunity; but we must watch the face of our proper Guardian, and if his eye dims a little, drop our trusted companions as profane."

Page 206, note 2. A passage in the oration delivered at Dartmouth College in 1838 seems to show that Mr. Emerson

[1] *Ralph Waldo Emerson; his Maternal Ancestors; with some Reminiscences of him.* By David Greene Haskins, D. D. Boston : Cupples, Upham & Co., 1887.

[2] *Correspondence between Ralph Waldo Emerson and Herman Grimm.* Boston : Houghton, Mifflin & Co., 1903.

in his youth had been much moved by Robertson's account of Charles V. (*Nature, Addresses and Lectures,* p. 162.)

Page 207, note 1. Note-book. "Spenser seems to delight in his art for his own skill's sake. In the *Muiopotmos* see the security and ostentation with which he draws out and refines his description of a butterfly's back and wings, of a spider's thread and spinning, of the butterfly's cruise among the flowers, —

" 'Bathing his tender feet in the dew which yet on them does lie.'

It is all like the working of an exquisite loom which unweariedly yields fine webs for exhibition and defiance of all spinners."

Page 207, note 2. Mr. Emerson quotes from Cowley: "He (Ben Jonson) esteemeth John Donne to be the first poet in the world in some things. His verses of the 'Lost Chaine' he hath by heart; and that passage 'The Calm'

" 'That dust and feathers do not stir,
All was so quiet.'

He affirmeth Donne to have written all his best pieces ere he was twenty-five years old."

Page 207, note 3. Journal. "Lord Bacon's method in his books is of the understanding, but his sentences are lighted by ideas."

In *English Traits* Mr. Emerson has much to say of Bacon (p. 238 ff.).

Page 208, note 1. Mr. Emerson was asked to write the Preface to the American edition of the *Gulistan* (Rose-garden) of Saadi, the translation of Francis Gladwin, with a preface by James Ross (Boston: Ticknor and Fields, 1865). In it he said: "Saadi, though he has not the lyric flights of Hafiz, has wit, practical sense, and just moral sentiment. . . . He is the poet of friendship, love, self-devotion and serenity. There is a uniform force in his page, and conspicuously a tone of cheerfulness which has almost made his name a synonyme for grace. . . . He inspires in the reader a good hope. What a contrast between the cynical tone of Byron and the benevolent wisdom of Saadi!''

Page 212, note 1. See the essay on Poetry and Imagination in *Letters and Social Aims.*

Page 213, note 1. For Mr. Emerson novels had little attraction. Mythology and epics, and heroic tradition and biography, took their place for him. He found no pleasure in Dickens or Thackeray. The Waverley Novels delighted him as a youth, and of ''Scott, the delight of generous boys,'' he had grateful remembrance. He read Disraeli's novels with some interest, but little real liking. George Sand's *Consuelo* gave him much pleasure, and he alludes to it several times in his writings, especially in the chapter on Goethe in *Representative Men.* He read little of Balzac or Dumas. Charles Reade's *Christie Johnstone* and *Peg Woffington* he read and praised. The *Jane Eyre* of Miss Brontë, mentioned farther on, he read with some interest.

Page 216, note 1. The poem ''The Park'' seems to be the expression of this mood.

Page 217, note 1. Firdusi, ''The Gardener'' (940–1020), under the encouragement and patronage of the Sultan Mahmoud, composed an epic poem of great length, but renowned for its beauty, the *Shah Nameh,* the mythology and history of Persia from the earliest times.

Page 218, note 1. The *Dial* magazine did much to introduce American readers to the ethical and religious writings of China, India, Persia and Arabia, in its selections called ''Ethnical Scriptures ''; also to the writings of the Neo-Platonists.

· *Page 221, note 1.* These notes on " Books " may properly end with two rules for reading given to scholars: I. *Read Proudly;* II. *As long as you feel the voracity of reading, read in God's name!*

CLUBS

Although Mr. Emerson bade the scholar go apart for oracles, and knew that his work must be done in solitude, he found that, as a corrective, he must seek company and be

" Kindly man moving among his kind "

to be helpful to them; also for material to show the working of the laws.

He was always more than willing to join in the formation of a club of men of varied gifts and powers. It is interesting to remember that his father had been one of the founders of a literary club in Boston, whose members were the contributors and supporters of the Anthology magazine, of which Rev. William Emerson was editor. The magazine did not survive him.

In 1836, Rev. William Ellery Channing, D. D., seems to have suggested to Mr. George Ripley the desirability of bringing together for help and counsel the persons of serious and advancing minds in Boston and its neighborhood in those days. Mr. Alcott, who was greatly interested, kept record in his journals of the meetings of this company, at first called the Symposium, later the Transcendental Club. Among the members were George Ripley, Convers Francis, Frederic H. Hedge, James Freeman Clarke, Cyrus A. Bartol, William Henry Channing, John S. Dwight, Theodore Parker, — all ministers, — Orestes A. Brownson, A. Bronson Alcott and

R. W. Emerson. Two ladies, Margaret Fuller and Elizabeth P. Peabody, and possibly others, were admitted.

Mr. Emerson in his chapter called " Historic Notes of Life and Letters in New England," in *Lectures and Biographical Sketches*, speaks of the *Dial* magazine as perhaps the most important result of these very informal meetings, which continued until about 1840. Perhaps eight years later a new attempt was made to supply the want of a literary club. Mrs. Ednah Cheney says,[1] " A certain almost forgotten institution, the Town and Country Club, where Concord and Boston were expected to meet and exchange the wisdom of the world and Nature, was established by Mr. Alcott about 1848, and Mr. Emerson and others heartily joined in the scheme." Mrs. Cheney tells elsewhere of the grievance that the club decided against the admission of women, influenced by Mr. Emerson's urgency on this subject, though it appears that they were admitted to its open meetings. Mr. George W. Cooke says in his book on Emerson: " The Town and Country Club was mainly organized by the efforts of Alcott. Emerson gave it its name, and he read before it the first essay to which it listened, on Books and Reading. This was May 2, 1849. Among its members were Garrison, Parker, W. H. Channing, W. E. Channing [of Concord], Alcott, Phillips, Hedge, Howe, King, Lowell, Weiss, Whipple, Higginson, Very, Pillsbury and Thoreau." It may well be doubted whether Thoreau joined, though Mr. Emerson would have been sure to have urged his doing so.

In his own village Mr. Emerson belonged to a club of a very different kind, the Social Circle, lineal descendant of the Committee of Safety during the Revolution, its avowed pur-

[1] " Emerson and Boston " in *The Genius and Character of Emerson.* Boston: J. R. Osgood & Co., 1885.

poses being, "to cultivate the social affections" and "for the diffusion of useful communications among its members." He was chosen a member in 1840 and continued one until his death. Of his appreciation of this club he wrote, in 1844, to a friend in Boston, a man of culture and of affairs: "Much the best society I have ever known is a club in Concord called the Social Circle, consisting always of twenty-five of our citizens, doctor, lawyer, farmer, trader, miller, mechanic, etc., solidest of men, who yield the solidest of gossip. Harvard University is a wafer compared to the solid land which my friends represent. I do not like to be absent from home on Tuesday evenings in winter." This club still exists, and organized the celebration of the Centenary of his birth.

As different from the Social Circle as well might be in membership and method, and in conversation, was the Saturday Club, from which he derived great pleasure for eighteen years, but his infirmity of memory prevented his attendance during the last years of his life.

I copy from his note book the membership before 1858; "Saturday Club, 1856–7. L. Agassiz, R. H. Dana, Jr., J. L. Motley, H. W. Longfellow, J. S. Dwight, E. R. Hoar, S. G. Ward, J. R. Lowell, B. Peirce, E. P. Whipple, H. Woodman, R. W. Emerson. 1857. O. W. Holmes, C. C. Felton, J. E. Cabot."[1]

To these were added during the first ten years of the Club's existence the names of Prescott, Whittier, Hawthorne, Thomas G. Appleton, John M. Forbes, Charles Eliot Norton, Dr. Howe, Rev. Frederic H. Hedge, Estes Howe, Charles Sumner, Henry James, Sr., Martin Brimmer, James T. Fields, S. W. Rowse, Governor Andrew and Dr. Jeffries Wyman.

[1] There appears to be a mistake here, for on the printed list of members the name of Mr. Cabot does not appear until 1861.

Dr. Holmes's account of this monthly gathering of friends, eminent in so many walks of life, is as follows: —

" At about the same time there grew up in Boston a literary association, which became at last well known as the ' Saturday Club,' the members dining together on the last Saturday of every month.

" The Magazine and the Club have existed and flourished to the present day. They have often been erroneously thought to have some organic connection, and the ' Atlantic Club' has been spoken of as if there was, or had been, such an institution, but it never existed.

" Emerson was a member of the Saturday Club from the first; in reality before it existed as an empirical fact, and when it was only a platonic idea. The Club seems to have shaped itself around him as a nucleus of crystallization, two or three friends of his having first formed the habit of meeting him at dinner at ' Parker's,' the ' Will's Coffee-House' of Boston. This little group gathered others to itself and grew into a club, as Rome grew into a city, almost without knowing how. During its first decade the Saturday Club brought together, as members or as visitors, many distinguished persons. At one end of the table sat Longfellow, florid, quiet, benignant, soft-voiced, a most agreeable rather than a brilliant talker, but a man upon whom it was always pleasant to look, — whose silence was better than many another man's conversation. At the other end of the table sat Agassiz, robust, sanguine, animated, full of talk, boy-like in his laughter. The stranger who should have asked who were the men ranged along the sides of the table would have heard in answer the names of Hawthorne, Motley, Dana, Lowell, Whipple, Peirce, the distinguished mathematician, Judge Hoar, eminent at the bar and in the cabinet, Dwight, the leading musical critic of Boston for a whole generation, Sumner, the academic champion of freedom, Andrew, 'the great War Governor' of Massachusetts, Dr. Howe, the philanthropist, William Hunt, the painter, with others not unworthy of such company. And with these, generally near the Longfellow end of the table, sat Emerson, talking in low tones and carefully measured utterances to his neighbor, or listening, and recording any stray word worth remembering on his mental phonograph. Emerson was a very regular attendant at the meetings of the Saturday Club, and continued to dine at its table, until within a year or two of his death.

"Unfortunately the Club had no Boswell, and its golden hours passed unrecorded."

Although there is no question of the profit in health and pleasure that Mr. Emerson found in the Club, proved by his regular attendance, and the happy report which he made of the meetings to his family, sometimes his belief of his unfitness for social gatherings weighed on him: —

Journal. "Most of my values are widely variable: My estimate of America, etc.; estimate of my mental means and resources is all or nothing, — in happy hours, life looking infinitely rich; and sterile at others. My value of my Club is as elastic as steam or gunpowder, — so great now, so little anon;" and it must have been when the pressure was low that he wrote in the journal of 1861: "I know the hollowness and superstition of a dinner, yet a certain health and good repair of social status comes of the habitude and well-informed chat there, which have great market value, though none to my solitude."

The quality of mind and the manners, friendly, simple yet reserved, of his friend James Elliot Cabot — I think Mr. Emerson said of him "Cabot is a Greek" — were very attractive to him. It is probably of Mr. Cabot that he wrote in the journal of 1869: —

VII

"At my club, I suppose I behave very ill in securing always, if I can, a place by a valued friend, and, though I suppose (though I have never heard it) that I offend by this selection, sometimes too visible, my reason is, that I, who see in ordinary, rarely, select society, must make the best use of this opportunity, having, at the same time, the feeling that

"'I could be happy with either,
    Were the other dear charmer away.'"

The mortification that Mr. Emerson felt, and the annoyance which he believed his increasing loss of memory for words occasioned his friends, led to infrequent attendance as he grew older. But the club celebrated his return from Europe and Egypt, to which countries his friends had sent him for his health after the burning of his house. Mr. Richard H. Dana wrote of this occasion: [1] —

"1873 [May 31, Saturday]. Our club dined to-day, — the largest number we ever sat down, partly as the last of the season to which many come, but chiefly to welcome Emerson, on his return from Europe and Egypt. . . . It was really rather a brilliant gathering. . . . Emerson looks years younger for his European tour, and is in good spirits. Even his hair has come back, which had nearly left his head last summer."

This lecture "Clubs" seems to have first been delivered in Boston as the third in a course at Freeman Place Chapel in the spring of 1859, but before its publication, like most of the later lectures, it underwent great modifications. A portion of the essay occurred in the lecture "Table-Talk," given in December, 1864, as one of the Parker Fraternity week-day course.

[1] *Richard Henry Dana, a Biography.* By Charles Francis Adams. Boston: Houghton, Mifflin & Co., 1890.

It is interesting to see how the last paragraph in the preceding essay leads to the subject of the present one. The mottoes are from the poems " Mithridates " and " Saadi," and, like the others in this volume, have been supplied by the editor.

Page 225, note 1. Mr. Emerson used to recommend as good treatment for a confirmed dyspeptic an occasional feast in good company, with wine.

Page 226, note 1.

Love wakes anew this throbbing heart,
And we are never old.
" The World-Soul," *Poems.*

Page 227, note 1. In " The Mind-Curer," in his charming little book *Prose Idylls*, Mr. John Albee gives, without naming him, an account of Mr. Emerson's healing and preventive counsels for the perplexities and troubles of youth.

Page 227, note 2. This, " the natural method " of acquiring knowledge, Mr. Emerson dwells upon very pleasantly in the essay on Education in *Lectures and Biographical Sketches.*

Page 228, note 1. It seems well to introduce here some passages from the lecture in early form: —

" There are two benefits, I said, in conversation; one, to detach our own thought, or find out what we know; the other, to find out what our companions know. There are great difficulties in both attempts.

" We have found insuperable obstacles in the attempt to obtain the knowledge which others possess, and were willing enough to impart. Barriers of society, barriers of language, inadequacy of the channels of communication, all choked up and disused.

" Each man has facts I am looking for, and, though I talk with him, I cannot get at them, for want of the clew. I do not know enough to ask the right question. It seems to me he does not know what to do with his facts. It seems to me that I know, if I could only have them. But I cannot have society on my own terms. If I want his facts, I must use his keys, — his keys, that is, his arrangements and ends. I want his facts for quite another use than he does. He uses them in his affairs, for profit, for power; I want them only to see how they fortify views and plans of mine. I have thoughts, which, wanting these examples, have no body. As the Indian said, ' I have no land to put my words on. Yet my words are true.' Here is all Boston, all railroads, all manufactures and commerce, in the head of this merchant. What would I not give for a peep at his rows and files and systems of facts ? Here is a philologist who knows all languages. Here is the king of chemists. Here is all anatomy, fossil and contemporary, in the mind of this zoölogist. All electro-magnetism in the next man; all geology in the third; all mechanism in the fourth; all American history in a fifth; and I cannot, with all my avarice of these facts, come at any fragment of all their experience. I would fain see their picture-books, as they see them. — This was the very promise which mesmerism made to the imagination of mankind. Now, said the adept, if I could cast a spell on this man, and see his pictures, by myself, without his intervention, — I see them, and not he report them ; — and having learned that lesson, turn the spell on another, lift the cover of another hive, see the cells, and suck the honey; — then another; and so without limit; — they were not the poorer, and I were rich indeed. This was the expedient of mesmerism, by way of suction-pump, to draw the most unwilling and valuable mass of experience from

every extraordinary individual at pleasure. With what joy
we began to put the experiment in practice. The eyes of the
man who saw through the earth the ingots of gold that were
lying a rod or two under the surface, or of the diver who
comes suddenly down full on a bed of pearl-oysters, all pearl,
were not to be compared to his, which put him in possession
of men. Here was a diving-bell, but it dived into *men*. (He
was the thought-vampire.) He became at once ten, twenty,
a hundred men, as he stood gorged with knowledges, and
turning his fierce eyes on the multitude of masters, in all
departments of human skill, and hesitating on which mass
of action and adventure to turn his all-commanding introspec-
tion.

" There lies the gold, and there it has slept, and will sleep,
unless you can manage the collisions of discourse, or the fires
of love, or the rasping of ambition, to overcome the strong
cohesion and detach the sparkling atom to the day.''

Page 228, note 2. In writing these sentences Mr. Emerson was recalling the memory of his relation to his brother
Charles. At the time of his death, in 1836, he wrote: " My
brother, my friend, my ornament, my joy and pride, has fallen
by the wayside, — or rather has risen out of this dust. . . .
I have felt in him the inestimable advantage, when God allows it, of finding a brother and a friend in one.'' In writing of the " valuable companion in a ship's cabin '' he had
in mind his happy but short companionship with Achille
Murat on his Southern journey in 1827.

Page 230, note 1. In his second poem " Merlin '' the
harmonious rhyme of things in Nature or the mind is celebrated, and in the chapter " Language '' in the essay " Nature '' in the first volume of the works, Mr. Emerson teaches
that Natural History, to be truly valuable, must be married to

human history, of which it is but a symbol. The relation seen, it becomes poetry.

Page 232, note 1.

> "Mark what another sayes; for many are
>   Full of themselves, and answer their own notion."
>   George Herbert, "The Church Porch."

Page 233, note 1.

> Amid the Muses, left thee deaf and dumb,
> Amid the gladiators, halt and numb.
>   "Terminus," *Poems.*

Page 233, note 2. This picture is perhaps a "composite" including Lowell, but an extract from the manuscript book called *Gulistan*, in which Mr. Emerson wrote about his friends, makes it probable that Dr. Holmes was in his mind.

"By his perfect finish, cabinet finish, gem finish, gem carved with a microscope on the carver's eye, and which perfection appears in every conversation, and in his part in a business debate, or at a college dinner-table as well as in his songs, — he resembles Fontenelle and Galiani, and Moore, though richer than either of them. Wonderful fertility and aptness of illustration. He is an illustrated magazine with twenty thousand accurate engravings. . . . His undersize might perhaps be suggested by his writings to one who had never seen him. It is compensated by the consummateness, as of a humming-bird, or of a flower, which defies the microscope to find a defect in Nature's favorite."

The tribute to another member may well be here given: "I call Longfellow the Perpetual Secretary of the Academy of American Poets, — remembering what Napoleon said of Cuvier: 'The Perpetual Secretary must be enabled to receive

at dinner all the learned foreigners who visit the Capital.'
Fate gave him the 6000 francs which Napoleon assigned to
the office of Cuvier. . . . March 29, 1869. Longfellow
said at the Saturday Club yesterday on the question of admit-
ting a new member not agreeable to some existing member, —
'I am sure there is no man living who could be admitted who
would drive me away.' "

Page 235, note 1. The following is from stray sheets of
the lecture " Clubs ": " Masters in any art like to meet masters. Mutual respect is a joyful tribute, honored and honoring;
conversation, — I have no book or pleasure in life comparable
to it. When that result is happily found, we can spare all
omens, prophecies, legends, for we see and know that which
these obscurely announce."

Page 235, note 2. " The Banquet of The Seven Wise
Men," Plutarch's *Morals.*

Page 236, note 1. Zertusht is another name for Zoroaster,
used in the *Desatir* or *Sacred Writings of the Persian Prophets.*

Page 238, note 1. Mr. Emerson's reading of this death-
word of the Jotun was startling to his hearers.

Page 239, note 1. This story was told of Dr. Samuel L.
Dana, the chemist noted for his studies and improvements in
chemistry as applied in the factories at Waltham and Lowell.

Page 240, note 1. Pierre Augustin Caron de Beaumarchais (1732–1799), whose address and ambition and eloquence succeeded in advancing him from a watchmaker's
apprentice to the nobility. His dramatic successes were *Le
Barbier de Séville* and *Le Mariage de Figaro.* It was the
latter that was frowned on by the Court. His eloquence in
persuading the King of France to send us aid during the
Revolution should be gratefully remembered by Americans.

Page 241, note 1. Mr. Emerson rejoiced in his friends, —

Carlyle, Sterling, Alcott, Thoreau, Channing, Hawthorne, Margaret Fuller, — and found them all better than their writings.

Page 244, note 1. He held in much honor his sturdy neighbors on the farms, and never ceased to

> Worship toil's wisdom that abides.

One of these helpful and kindly men — the same for whose marriage Mr. Emerson had performed the ceremony on first coming to Concord, Mr. Alcott being the witness, and who, as deputy-sheriff, had arrested and imprisoned Alcott and Thoreau for refusal to pay taxes, yet cared for them kindly, and had in vain offered to pay Thoreau's tax before seizing him — said of Mr. Emerson to a mutual friend: "Now it's remarkable how many persons go to see Mr. Emerson. Some of 'em come from Europe, I hear. Well, I suppose there's a good many things that he knows that I don't know anything about, and I *know* there's a lot o' things that I know a damn' sight more about than he does."

Page 246, note 1. Mr. Emerson himself always preferred the independence of a hotel or country tavern on his lecturing journeys to taxing private hospitality or taking its chances. He gave letters of introduction sparingly, but did not use them himself, writing his own from the inn, when in England, to the person he desired to meet, thus allowing him to judge from the letter whether he was willing to receive the visitor.

Page 247, note 1. From the lecture "Clubs": —

"What is material, is, to secure men of culture whose experience has large range, and who have seen low extremes in life, such as the ordinary routine of respectable society excludes from the knowledge of gentlemen, for there are heroes among beggars and jockeys."

Page 247, note 2. Mr. John T. Morse, Jr., gives an account of the Saturday Club, and quotes Dr. Holmes on this point: —

"Some outsiders furnished still another name for this much-entitled Club. They called it 'The Mutual Admiration Society,' and sometimes laughed a little, as though the designation were a trifle derogatory. Yet the brethren within the pale were nowise disturbed by this witticism. 'If there was not,' says Holmes, 'a certain amount of "mutual admiration" among some of those I have mentioned, it was a great pity, and implied a defect in the nature of men who were otherwise largely endowed.' Possibly one or two of these gentlemen might have been criticised for admiring *themselves,* but it did seem hard to blame them for being sufficiently intelligent and generous to admire each other. Would the scoffers have been better pleased to see them openly abusing or slyly depreciating each other ? There are enough such spectacles elsewhere in literature." [1]

Page 248, note 1. Robert Herrick's " Ode to Ben Jonson."

Page 250, note 1. Lecture sheets: "Homer said, 'When two men meet, one apprehends sooner than the other.' But it is because one man thinks well, that the other thinks better, for they mutually excite each other, each attempting to cap the other's thought."

Page 250, note 2. Mr. Emerson said that Nature's rule in conversing with man was " One to one, my dear."

Two sheets, the " salvage " of the lecture " Clubs," may be added in conclusion: —

" When I was in London, I fell in with the literary execu-

[1] *Life and Letters of Oliver Wendell Holmes,* by John T. Morse, Jr. Boston : Houghton, Mifflin & Co., 1896.

tor of Jeremy Bentham, who carried me to Bentham's house, and showed me, with much veneration, the apartments in which the philosopher lived. Especially his library, and the closet adjoining, in which Bentham was wont to receive his guests. He made me remark that there were but two chairs in the apartment as it was his invariable rule to receive but one person at a time. Every distinguished person in Europe, he said, had been here at some time, including Talleyrand. . . .

" But at all events it [conversation] must be sought and conducted as a religious rite. I think we all have owed some of the best hours and some of the grandest promises of our being to conversation, when all frivolous and disturbing accidents were removed, and the imagination was free to play, and, in happy hour, men emulated each other and provoked each other to read the deep secrets of Nature."

COURAGE

The lecture " Courage " was given in Boston at the Music Hall to Mr. Parker's Society in November, 1859. These were days of great excitement both in the North and South, for the brave but desperate attempt of John Brown to seize the United States Arsenal at Harper's Ferry, arm the slaves, who, he supposed, would flock to him, and lead them quickly along the Appalachian chain to Canada, had failed, and its leader, wounded, was on trial for his life in Virginia. This event had precipitated the issue between slavery and freedom, and begun to open the eyes of Northern people to the uselessness and unworthiness of their long submission to Southern dictation in hope of preserving the Union, and with it a

Southern market. However little the method of action of Brown in this raid commended itself to the best people of the North, their cheeks burned that such a condition of affairs existed as should drive men to treason simply for humanity's sake. John Brown's simple courage entrenched on the teaching of Jesus to " remember them that are in bonds as bound with them," contrasted with the shameful attitude of Government in half supporting Border Ruffianism in Kansas, stung tender consciences, and was working a sudden reaction in public opinion. Yet conservatism of what was then called the " Old Hunker " type was so strong among the aristocracy of Beacon Street, the business men of State Street, and the negro-hating and ruffianly element of the Democracy, that open speaking on behalf of Brown had its dangers. Mr. Cabot in his Memoir says: " It does not appear that Emerson was acquainted in advance with Brown's Virginia plot, but in this lecture, which was delivered while Brown was under sentence of death, he spoke of him as ' that new saint than whom none purer or more brave was ever led by love of men into conflict and death, — the new saint awaiting his martyrdom, and who, if he shall suffer, will make the gallows glorious like the cross.'" It is certain that Mr. Emerson did *not* know of the project. But the motive and the heroism made him think better of his countrymen in that sad time. John Brown had been his guest in the days of the Kansas struggle, and he knew the quality and the quiet force of the man.

In the eleven years between the delivery of the lecture and its publication as an essay it underwent many changes, passages written during the shame and anger of the dark days before the war disappearing when the essay took on its more classic form, and some proud memories of that great struggle taking their place.

Dr. Holmes says of his friend's right to speak on the theme: " All that Emerson has to say about Courage is worth listening to, for he was a truly brave man in that sphere of action where there are more cowards than are found on the battlefield. He spoke his convictions fearlessly; he carried the spear of Ithuriel, but he wore no breastplate save that which protects him

> " ' Whose armor is his honest thought,
>   And simple truth his utmost skill.' "

Margaret Fuller quoted Mr. Emerson as saying, " Careful of health, Careless of life, should be our motto."

Page 253, note 1. Journal, 1850. "The secret of Culture is to interest a man more in his public than in his private capacity."

Page 253, note 2. Speaking of the Persians, in his preface to Gladioni's translation of the *Gulistan* of Saadi, Mr. Emerson said, " Hatem Tai is their type of hospitality, who, when the Greek Emperor sent to pray him to bestow on him his incomparable horse, received the messenger with honor, and, having no meat in his tent, killed the horse for his banquet, before yet he knew the object of the visit."

Page 253, note 3. Another version of the paragraph was as follows: —

" Disinterestedness on the score of pelf, a purpose so sincere and generous that it cannot be tempted aside by any prospects of private advantage; like Aristides in the public treasury, poor when he entered it, poorer when he left it, like Chatham, to whom his scornful magnanimity," etc.

Page 255, note 1. "It is delightful to see that the one serious and formidable thing in nature is Will." — Miscellaneous sheets of " Courage."

It was this power in Wendell Phillips that Mr. Emerson chiefly admired, — "the steel hid under gauze and spangles;" that, with all the elegance and perfect finish of his speech and manner, he was not seen at his best until hostile dissent broke forth among his audience.

Page 259, note 1. These manly words for the hour in 1859 were omitted from the essay when the cloud was lifted:—

"The politics of Massachusetts are cowardly. We have a snappish criticism which watches and contradicts the opposite party, but we want will that advances and dictates. When we get an advantage, as in Congress the other day, it is because our adversary has made a fault, and not that we have made a thrust. Why do we not say, We are abolitionists of the most absolute abolition, as every man must be? Only the Hottentots, only the barbarous or semi-barbarous societies, are not. We do not try to alter your laws in Alabama, nor yours in Japan, or the Fee-jee Islands; but we do not admit them, or permit a trace of them here, nor shall we suffer you to carry your thuggism north, south, east or west, into a single rod of territory which we control. We intend to set and keep a *cordon sanitaire*, all around the infected district, and by no means suffer the pestilence to spread."

Page 260, note 1. This was the question asked in the Concord Town Hall by John Brown on one of his visits, seeking aid for the Free-State cause in Kansas.

Page 260, note 2. This was the good old George Minot, a man of the hoe and the shot-gun. It was he who, seeing Mr. Emerson pause, in thought, in the road before his house, said to his nephew, "Charley, that man ain't like other men. He's like Enoch; he walks with God and talks with his angels."

The end of the paragraph suggests the passage in "Heroism" (*Essays, First Series*, p. 249), in which is said, "Our culture must not omit the arming of the man."

Page 261, note 1. I give here more recent striking testimony which would have delighted Mr. Emerson.

An officer of the Army of the Potomac, after speaking of the ordinary duties of a campaign, for which "the merely staple quality of courage will usually suffice," said, "But when the exigencies of the service require a call for volunteers to attempt some desperate deed whose failure would smell like murder, and whose success would seem nearly as fatal, then comes an opportunity for the 'born' soldier. At this time there will arise, . . . even from the purlieus of the non-combatants, — the meek-eyed denizens of the commissariat, from hospital or wagon-trains, — men who will offer their lives so freely and so inexplicably that one is led to suspect they have waited for the occasion." He quotes also the words of one who had cared for the wounded, about "the woman's mouth so often found upon the face of the youth whose courage made sure martyrdom."[1]

Page 262, note 1. A similar story is told of Mr. Emerson's grandfather William Emerson, the patriotic young minister of Concord, who afterwards, a chaplain in the American army, died of fever near Ticonderoga.

A citizen of Rutland, Vermont, told the father of Professor Butler of Madison, Wisconsin (who told the editor), that, when a young man, he worked in Concord, and in the spring of 1775 enlisted in the Minute-Men. When on the morning of the 19th of April he stood in line among the village soldiers on the Common, and saw the British column advancing glittering in arms, he felt that if he did not run he should

---

[1] Colonel S. R. Elliott in "The Courage of a Soldier." *Atlantic Monthly*, February, 1893, p. 239.

die of fear. But at that moment the minister laid his hand on his shoulder and said, " Don't be afraid, Harry; God is on our side," and after that his mortal fear passed away.

Page 264, note 1. Mr. Emerson hurried with his neighbors to save the sacred woods, when afire, wielding his appropriate weapon, a pine bough.

Page 266, note 1. The following passage to the purpose is from a stray sheet of " Courage."

" People wrap themselves up in disguises, and the sincere man is hard to reach. A man is concealed in his nation, concealed in his party, concealed in his fortune, and estate, concealed in his office, in his profession, concealed in his body at last, and it is hard to find out his pure nature and will.

" They speak and act in each of these relations after the use and wont of those conditions. They talk as Americans, as Republicans, as men of position, men of business, and at last, as men of such appetite, decorum and habit are expected to talk, — each cunningly hiding under these wearisome commonplaces the character and flavor which is his peculiar gift from the author of his being, and which is all that can really make him interesting and valuable to us. Of course, he only half acts, — talks with his lips and not from his heart, — touches with fingers, and not with his strength. Bishop Latimer tells us, that his father taught him, when a boy, not to shoot with his arms but to lay his body to the bow."

Page 268, note 1. In the early years of his Concord life, Mr. Emerson made in his journal, on returning from church, the entry on which the sentence in the essay is founded: —

" I delight in our pretty church music and to hear that poor slip of a girl, without education, without thought, yet show this fine instinct in her singing, so that every note of her song sounds to me like an adventure and a victory in the ' *ton-welt* ';

and whilst all the choir beside stay fast by their leader and the bass-viol, this angel voice goes choosing, choosing on, and with the precision of genius keeps its faithful road and floods the house with melody.''

Page 270, note 1. This was Professor Andrews Norton of Harvard University.

Page 271, note 1. From Robert Herrick's poem `` Hesperides.''

Page 271, note 2. This passage from the original lecture has been omitted: —

`` A curious example is the recent history of the Southern States. The Southerners reckon the Yankees to be less brave than they. Yet the reign of terror is in the South. It is not to be believed that there was no minority in the South during the year 1856. Yet not a mutter or peep was heard with the exception of the explicit demonstration of Mr. Botts of Virginia and Mr. Davis of Maryland. Every gentleman in Carolina was mute as a fish. Is it to be believed that Cassius Clay is the only man in Kentucky of his opinion?

`` But I do not wish to make odious, least of all, unfounded distinctions. There are reigns of terror as well in the North as in the South, and we have no right to boast so long as our love of trade, or preference of peace to justice, or the frivolity which loves comfort at any cost withholds our vote and voice. It is perfectly certain that when a million or half a million of citizens in good earnest wish a thing done, they will fast enough find governors and judges and members of Congress to put it through all the forms; and if the laws of Massachusetts are not just and heroic, it is not the fault of the United States, but of ourselves.''

Page 271, note 3. Among the scattered sheets that remain of `` Courage '' as delivered at various times, is one headed

"The Aristocracy," in which this echo of 1859 remains: "Governor Wise and Mr. Mason no doubt have some right to their places. It is some superiority of working brain that put them there, and the aristocrats in every society. But when they come to deal with Brown they find that he speaks their own speech, — has whatever courage and directness they have and a great deal more of the same, so that they feel themselves timorous little fellows in his hand; he out-sees, out-thinks, out-acts them, and they are forced to shuffle and stammer in their turn. They painfully feel this, that he is their governor and superior, and the only alternative is to kneel to him, if they are truly noble, or else (if they wish to keep their places) to put this fact, which they know, out of sight of other people as fast as they can. Quick, drums and trumpets, strike up! Quick, judges and juries, silence him, by sentence and execution of sentence, and hide in the ground this alarming fact. For, if everything comes to its right place, he goes up and we down."

Page 272, note 1.

"And slow, as in a dream of bliss,
 The speechless sufferer turns to kiss
  Her shadow, as it falls
  Upon the darkening walls."
   Longfellow, "Santa Filomena."

After the quotation of Napoleon's words, the text runs as follows in one of the manuscript sheets: "So is it with the hero. No misgivings, no hesitations, but perfect continuity of nerve, so that what he thinks he enacts.

"The vulgar mind is embarrassed by petty considerations; does not penetrate to the end of the action, but stops short at an obstacle; sees the enmities it provokes; the loss of day-wages."

Page 274, note 1. Here followed in the lecture the allu-

VII

sion to John Brown, whose execution took place on the second day of December, a little more than three weeks later: —

"Look nearer at the ungathered relics of those who have gone to languish in prison or to die in rescuing others or rescuing themselves from chains in Slave States, or look at that new saint, than whom none purer or more brave ever was led by love of men into conflict and death, the new saint awaiting his martyrdom, and who, if he shall suffer, will make the gallows glorious like the cross."

Page 275, note 1. Sheet from lecture: "It is very certain that, of two men of whom each follows his own thought, he whose thought is deepest will be the strongest character. Always one man more than another represents the will of Divine Providence to the period, and the more serious the occasion, the more it tests and searches men. A holiday general may lead a holiday procession, but vanishes unaccountably into obscurity in the heroic times."

This tribute to the moral courage of the people of England may be here given: —

"The English nation have the common credit of being more individual, more outspoken, and downright, than we are. Each man of them is, very likely, narrow and committed to opinions of no great liberality or dignity, but, such as they are, he heartily stands for them; silent or loud, he is content to be known to all the world as their champion; they grow to him; he is enraged, he curses and swears for them. In the house of lords, the patrician states his opinion, very clumsily and drearily perhaps, but at least not looking for your ballot and approbation, rather with an air that says, Such is my opinion, and who the devil are you?"

Page 277, note 1. These passages from the lecture should be given in conclusion: —

"Whence does all power come? We are embosomed in the spiritual world. Yet none ever saw angel or spirit. Whence does our knowledge of it come? Only from men; the only Revealer of the divine mind is through the thoughts of a man.

"The statistics show you the whole world under the dominion of fate or circumstance or brute laws of chemistry. Life instantly contravenes or supervenes the low chemistry by higher. Thought resists and commands Nature by higher truth, and gives Nature a master. . . .

"Life is a medley, but the centre is great and eternal, and we must be real. We must know that it is as we are, and therefore the absurd accuses us. We must go for character, personal relations, poverty and honor.

"And wisdom is justified of her children. Valor pays rents as well as land. A little measure is always a great error. The noble course begets love and confidence, and has a late and sure reward. It suggests counsels proportionate to the end, broad measures, humane conduct.''

Page 277, note 2. The lady was Miss Elizabeth Hoar, who should have been, but for his untimely death, the wife of Charles Emerson. To Mr. Emerson she was a sister indeed, and her frequent presence illuminated the house for all of his family. The story of George Nidiver was told by her brother Edward, who had lived for several years in California. Mr. Emerson was so pleased with it that he obtained leave to print it with the essay in 1870. Before his death he learned that some one in California, reading the essay, found the poem, and knowing George Nidiver, took it to the old hunter, who was astonished and pleased to find that his act of generous impulse, when a youth, was known and celebrated on the other side of the continent a quarter of a century after its occurrence.

SUCCESS

In the autumn of 1833, when he had laid aside, with his gown, the profession for which he was bred, and at the age of thirty was facing an unknown future as a scholar and public speaker, Mr. Emerson wrote in his diary: —

"Were it not heroic venture in me to insist on being a popular speaker and run full tilt against the Fortune who, with such beautiful consistency, shows evermore her back?

"Charles's *naïf* censure last night provoked me to show him a fact apparently entirely new to him, that my entire success, such as it is, is composed wholly of particular failures, every public work of mine of the least importance having been, probably without exception, noted at the time as a failure. The only success (agreeably to common ideas) has been in the country, and there founded on the false notion that here was a Boston preacher. I will take Mrs. Barbauld's line for my motto [of a brook], —

"'And the more falls I get, move faster on.'"

In one of the earlier journals Mr. Emerson wrote of Osman, by which name he there called his ideal man: —

"I will add to the portrait of Osman that he was never interrupted by success. He had never to look after his fame and his compliments, his claps and editions."

In the middle of December, 1858, Mr. Emerson lectured on Success at Hartford, and in March, 1859, opened his course at the Freeman Place Chapel in Boston with "The Law of Success." These lectures were, without doubt, essentially the same as the present essay.

Page 284, note 1. It was known that Giotto had visited

a fellow artist by the circle that he drew, as a visiting-card. '
Strassburg Cathedral bears witness to the mastery of Erwin of
Steinbach. The feat of Olaf Trygvesson is told by Longfellow
in his version of the Saga of King Olaf, in the "Tales of a
Wayside Inn." Ojeda was a Spanish cavalier who sailed with
Columbus, and later with Vespucci. To Bernini St. Peter's
church in Rome owes its colonnade and the bronze canopy
over the tomb of the Saint.

Page 285, note 1. With Mr. Emerson's love for the
heavenly bodies, in their splendor, their majestic courses, and
more for what these signified, it is safe to believe that he attributes to the words of Columbus a higher and oracular sense.

Page 286, note 1. It is obvious that the writer of *Uncle
Tom's Cabin*, Mrs. Stowe, is referred to in this passage, and
Jenny Lind, whose beautiful singing had a few years earlier
delighted the people of two continents. Margaret Fuller had,
for her sympathy and zeal in the cause of the Italian patriots,
been put in charge of a hospital at Rome a few years before
this essay was written, and before its publication the Civil
War had called many devoted women to the military hospitals
and to the schools for the newly freed negroes.

Page 287, note 1. This verse, which Mr. Emerson liked
to repeat to his children, and which serves for the motto of
one of his journals, came from the rude but interesting Danish
ballad translated by George Borrow. It describes the Ber-
serker madness of the hero from whom it takes its name.

Page 289, note 1. This passage from the journal of 1859
gives the offset to the lower view: —

"Power even is not known to the pure. Power indicates
weakness and opposition. Health exists and unfolds in the
rose, in the sea, in the circular and endless astronomy. The
electricity is not less present in my body and my joy, for

twenty years, that I never saw or suspected it, than in the twenty-first, when I drew by art a spark from my knuckle."

Page 289, note 2. Of the monotones, both of the aggressive reform and mystic type, Mr. Emerson had all too much experience, yet was always good-natured to them. The remark of his friend ,Mr. Channing on the conversation of one of the latter type amused him, — "Biographie universelle de moi-même."

Page 292, note 1. Mr. Emerson had the strength and the skill to save himself for his own large mission in spite of the importunities that beset him to engage in causes, and yet kept the respect and good will of their advocates, and often helped bravely, but as a volunteer.

Page 292, note 2. Henry James, Jr., in one of his novels speaks of " the over-modelled American face."

Page 293, note 1.

> For thought, and not praise, —
> Thought is the wages
> For which I sell days.
>   " Fragments on The Poet," *Poems,* Appendix.

Page 293, note 2. "Commerce . . . is an apt illustration of the intellectual quality of the process of creating values, as much as is inventing, planting or manufacturing."— From a sheet of the lecture.

Page 295, note 1. The sentence about Alfred is followed in the lecture by this comment: "Good fortune is another name for perception and good will."

Page 296, note 1. Many an author, especially among Mr. Emerson's friends, was a gainer by " imputed righteousness," to borrow the phrase from the Church. His good will and his teeming mind sometimes read values into their work.

Lecture sheets: "Then for sensibility, I must add, that the great happiness of some of the best moments of life has been the enjoyment of books and works of art and science. And as Marcus Antoninus said, 'What matters it who found the truth, whether thyself or another, and where had been thy own intellect, if greater had not lived?' And, though I hate to be in any manner wanting to the claims of stern and manly Intellect, I must say, that the delight in the superior powers of others is one of the best gifts of God."

Page 296, note 2. Journal. "What's a book? Everything or nothing. The eye that sees it is all. What is the heaven's majestical roof fretted with golden fire to one man, but a foul and pestilent congregation of vapors? Well, a book is to a paddy a fair page smutted over with black marks; to a boy, a goodly collection of words he can read; to a half-wise man, it is a lesson which he wholly accepts or wholly rejects; but a sage shall see in it secrets yet unrevealed; shall weigh, as he reads, the author's mind; shall see the predominance of ideas which the writer could not extricate himself from, and oversee. *The Belfast Town and County Almanack* may be read by a sage; and wasteful as it would be in me to read Anti-Masonic or Jackson papers, yet whoso pierces through them to the deep Idea they embody, may well read them."

Page 297, note 1. The motto of "Culture," printed in the *Poems,* is on this theme.

Page 297, note 2. This sentence is a bit of autobiography.

Page 298, note 1.

> Wilt thou not ope thy heart to know
> What rainbows teach, and sunsets show?
>
> "Threnody," *Poems.*

> Still, still the secret presses;
> The nearing clouds draw down;

The crimson morning flames into
The fopperies of the town.
                              "The World-Soul."

Page 298, note 2. In the book in which Mr. Emerson wrote verses after 1850, this passage appears in poetic form : —

October woods wherein
The boy's dream comes to pass,
And Nature squanders on the boy her pomp,
And crowns him with a more than royal crown,
And unimagined splendor waits his steps.
The gazing urchin walks through tents of gold,
Through crimson chambers, porphyry and pearl,
Pavilion on pavilion garlanded,
Incensed, and starred with light and airs and shapes
Beyond the best conceit of pomp or power.

Page 299, note 1. Wordsworth's Ode, "Intimations of Immortality from Recollections of Early Childhood." The first line of the quotation should be

"Though nothing can bring back the hour."

Page 299, note 2. "Concord, 11 October, 1839. At Waltham, last Sunday, on the hill near the old meeting-house, I heard music so soft that I fancied it was a piano-forte in some neighboring farm-house; but on listening more attentively I found it was the church-bells in Boston, nine miles distant, which were playing for me this soft tune."

Page 300, note 1. This passage suggests his poem "Each and All."

Page 300, note 2. Of Nature's traits he wrote, —

She paints with white and red the moors
To draw the nations out of doors.

Page 300, note 3. In the autumn of 1834, immediately after his return from Europe, Mr. Emerson began his new life as a lecturer by giving two lectures before the Society of Natural History in Boston. In the Introductory Lecture he urged the fitness for men of the study of Nature, and the second lecture was " On the Relation of Man to the Globe," calling attention to the relation of use, but also to the relation of beauty.

Page 301, note 1.

> Tell men what they knew before;
> Paint the prospect from their door.
> " Fragments on Life," *Poems*, Appendix.

Page 302, note 1. Here followed in the lecture the words, —

" The deeper you bore, the farther you get away from the cause."

Page 303, note 1. Compare the quatrain called " Casella " in the *Poems*.

Page 304, note 1. These thoughts and images occur in " The Over-Soul " (*Essays, First Series*, p. 293), and in the *Poems* in " Manners " and the lines in " Saadi ": —

> Nor scour the seas, nor sift mankind,
> A poet or a friend to find:
> Behold, he watches at the door!
> Behold his shadow on the floor!

and in the " Fragments on Life " in the verses beginning

> Love asks nought his brother cannot give.

Page 305, note 1. Mr. Sanborn engaged a learned German, Dr. Solger, to give a course of lectures on History at his private school, and Mr. Emerson, with other residents of

Concord, attended them. This incident appears to have been the fruit that he carried away from the course.

Page 305, note 2. Mr. Charles Lane is here spoken of, one of the English gentlemen who returned with Mr. Alcott from England in 1844, bent upon trying in New England the experiment of a loftier and simpler method of living. The short-lived Fruitlands Community was the result.

Page 306, note 1. This paragraph in the lecture began, "The only Muse I know of is health, which is the timing, symmetry and coördination of all the faculties so that the nimble senses catch reports from things which in ordinary hours they do not render."

Page 306, note 2. Pons Capdueil, a Provençal gentleman in the twelfth century, skilled in all the accomplishments of a knight and minstrel.

Page 306, note 3. Couture, the eminent French painter, of the last generation, wrote, "You, painter, you are born to make men love and understand Earth's beauties, and not to startle us. . . . Dare to be yourself—there is light. . . . Soften your heart. Before all things be humble."

Page 307, note 1. This page on what is positive and abiding, from an old lecture, seems here appropriate:—

"We find stability central amidst all this dismaying whirl. Life looks so petty and frivolous around us, men so rude and incapable, victims of vanity, victims of appetite, scorners and corrupters of each other, and nothing so high and sacred but you shall find mobs of ferocious and ignorant men ready to tear and trample it down for some paltry bribe, were it only a bottle of brandy; and their leaders, for a bribe only a little less paltry, hounding them on. We see the historic culture of the most enlightened populations threatened by barbaric masses. We see empires subverted and the historic progress of civilization threatened. We see religious systems on which nations have been reared, pass away. The religion of one age is the literary entertainment of the next. Judaism, Stoicisim, Mahometism, Buddhism, all discredited and ending. Nay, the venerable and beautiful traditions of Christianity, in which we were educated, losing their hold on human belief, day by day; but central in the whirl a faith abides, which does not pass, a central doctrine which Judaism, Stoicism, Mahometism, Buddhism, Christianity, all teach."

Page 308, note 1. The test here mentioned, namely, the state of mind in which the new prophet or revelation leaves you, Mr. Emerson mentions in connection with so-called "Spiritualism" in the essay on Demonology in *Lectures and Biographical Sketches.*

In the lecture "Success" the following anecdote was at this point introduced: "When Campbell heard Joseph Gerald defend himself in the court in Edinburgh, he said to the stranger next him, ' By Heaven, sir, that is a great man !' ' Yes, sir,' he answered, ' he is not only a great man himself, but he makes every other man feel great who listens to him.' "

Page 308, note 2. Mr. Emerson notes, in his journal, of Socrates, that he was more afraid of himself than of the people of Athens. At the end of this paragraph in the lecture "Success" followed this sentence : "I value a man's trust in his fortune, when it is a hearing of voices that call him to his task. When he is conscious of a work laid on him to do, and that Nature cannot afford to lose him until it is done."

Page 308, note 3. In the lecture Mr. Emerson wrote " the picture of the crucifixion " instead of " some sacred subjects," and at the end of the sentence he added: " and so dead Romeos, and smothered princes; Nature does not so. Nature lays the ground-plan,'' etc.

Page 309, note 1. "Like Byron,'' which stood in the lecture, is here omitted.

Page 309, note 2. Wordsworth, "Poems dedicated to National Independence.''

Page 311, note 1. From the Manuscripts: "Be an opener of doors to those who come after you, and don't try to make the Universe a blind alley.''

Page 312, note 1. This passage is a fragment from the lost tragedy *Philoctetes* of Euripides.

OLD AGE

When boyhood and first youth had gone, and to the coming on of care and toil ill health was added, the young Emerson wrote, —

> I bear in youth the sad infirmities
> That use to undo the limb and strength of Age.

But a less impatient temper than that of his ardent brothers enabled him to pass through those critical years and emerge even from grief and disappointment to the cheerful courage of his new life. Thereafter he had nothing to do with Time, except to choose wisely the gift from each of the long procession of sacred Days. He used to tell that, when he was a growing boy, his uncle asked him how it was that the young people did not like him, while their elders did. "Now,'' he said, "the case is reversed: the old people distrust and dislike me, while the young come to me.''

And with courage and work, his eyes open to beauty, manifest or hidden, his ears open for the words of the Spirit, he did not seem to grow old, except in increasing mellowness of the affections and an afternoon serenity. The accidents of age befel him, but such mild complaint as he made of them was always humorous. Care and anxiety on pecuniary matters were there, but he kept them under. About the year 1870 his power of work, his memory and bodily strength began to fail, yet this was noticed by few until after the exposure and shock occasioned by the burning of his house two years later. The general muster of loving friends, near or far, to his aid, and their gift of restored house and freedom from anxiety, prolonged his life several years. His working power was gone, but he was happy. As he hints in the essay, the affections had their turn when the intellectual forces ebbed. He wrote his serene recognition of Age in his poem " Terminus," a portion of which serves for a motto of this chapter. In 1864, about the time that the poem was written, he wrote in his diary, " Within I do not find wrinkles and used heart, but unspent youth."

He wrote in his journal, of the increasing difficulty of composition and arrangement, —

1864. " I have heard that the engineers in the locomotives grow nervously vigilant with every year on the road until the employment is intolerable to them: and I think writing is more and more a terror to old scribes."

And again: —

1864. " The grief of old age is, that now, only in rare moments and by happiest combinations or consent of the elements, do I attain those enlargements which once were a daily gift."

Yet serene enjoyment of Nature, his friends and family remained: —

He had to the full, in the words of Shakspeare, —

> "That which should accompany old age,
>   As honour, love, obedience, troops of friends."

It does not appear exactly when and where the lecture on Old Age was first read, but the reference to the Phi Beta Kappa speech of the venerable ex-President of Harvard University, Josiah Quincy, in June, 1861, and the publication of "Old Age" in the January number of the *Atlantic Monthly* in 1862, fix the date sufficiently closely. The exordium of the lecture, evidently written during the anxious pause, after the defeat of Bull Run, of the war in Virginia, is as follows: —

"I hope I shall not shock the sentiment of the assembly when I say, that I have nothing to offer you this evening relating to war and its works; that, while I sympathize, as every good-hearted man must, with this concentrated curiosity on the public affairs, which listening with over-strained ear to every click of the telegraph, and hearing a cannon in every outdoor sound, makes every liberal study impertinent, I feel that our sanity requires some balance to this fever-heat; some diversion back to old studies and traditions which respect our permanent social welfare. The country which reads nothing but newspapers all day, can surely afford to leave the army bulletins out of its church and lyceum for an evening hour. I shall therefore risk to offer you a topic, the coldest and most remote from these heats, nay, perhaps more repulsive to the American than to any other national temperament."

Page 317, note 1. "The babe in arms is a channel through which the energies we call fate, love and reason visibly stream." — "Considerations by the Way," *Conduct of Life.*

On the day of the birth of his second daughter, Mr. Emerson wrote in his journal: —

Nov. 22, 1841. "There came into the house a young maiden, but she seemed to be more than a thousand years old. She came into the house naked and helpless, but she had for her defence more than the strength of millions. She brought into the day the manners of the Night."

Page 317, note 2. This is a version of lines quoted, but not credited, by Mr. Emerson in "The Over-Soul," of which I have in vain sought for the author. It is said that Spirit

> "Can crowd eternity into an hour
> Or stretch an hour into eternity."

Page 318, note 1. In his notes upon himself Mr. Emerson wrote, "My only secret was that all men were my masters. I thought each who talked with me older than I."

Page 319, note 1. "I find it a great and fatal difference whether I court the Muse, or the Muse courts me. That is the ugly disparity between age and youth."— Manuscript of "Old Age."

Page 320, note 1. In Tennyson's "Tithonus," the old and weary man says to Aurora, his divine mistress, —

> "I ask'd thee, 'Give me immortality.'
> Then didst thou grant mine asking with a smile,
> Like wealthy men who care not how they give.
> But thy strong Hours indignant work'd their wills,
> And beat me down and marr'd and wasted me,
> And tho' they could not end me, left me maimed
> To dwell in presence of immortal youth,
> Immortal age beside immortal youth,
> And all I was, in ashes."

Page 321, note 1. " Presque tous les bons ouvriers vivent longtemps: c'est qu'ils accomplissent une loi de la Providence." — Béranger.

Page 323, note 1. In connection with the mention of this great man, this quotation from a letter written in his old age is copied from Mr. Emerson's journal: —

"Humboldt in 1843 congratulates his friend Karl Ritter, on the appearance of Zimmermann's map of the Upper Nile. ' If,' he says, ' a life prolonged to an advanced period, brings with it several inconveniences to the individual, there is a compensation in the delight of being able to compare older states of knowledge with that which now exists, and to see great advances in knowledge develop themselves under our eyes in departments which had long slept in inactivity, with the exception perhaps of attempts by hypercriticism to render previous acquisitions doubtful. This enjoyment has fallen to our share in our geographical studies.' "

Page 324, note 1. In the journals written near Mr. Emerson's sixtieth year he good-naturedly treats the semi-comic aspects and compensations, as thus: —

" My humorous friend told me that old age was cheap: Time drew out his teeth gratis, and a suction-plate would last him as long as he lived; he does not go to the hair-dresser, for Time cut off his hair; and he had lived so long, and bought so many clothes, that he should not need to buy any more.

" N. said in the car to a chance companion — ' Yes, but I am an old man and can't do so or so.' Instead of the indignant denial he expected, the stranger replied, ' Yes, you are an old man and that makes a difference.' Vain was his use of the dodge of old men, giving themselves for ten years older than they are; the companion quietly accepted it as true."

In the journal of 1864 I find this entry: —

"The following page should have been printed in *Society and Solitude*, in the chapter called 'Old Age.'

"Old age brings along with its uglinesses the comfort that you will soon be out of it, — which ought to be a substantial relief to such discontented pendulums as we are. To be out of the war, out of debt, out of the drouth, out of the blues, out of the dentist's hands, out of the second thoughts, mortifications and remorses that inflict such twinges and shooting pains, — out of the next winter, and the high prices, and company below your ambition, — surely these are soothing hints. And harbinger of this, what an alleviator is sleep, which muzzles all these dogs for me every day? Old age —'T is proposed to call an indignation-meeting."

Page 324, note 2. A similar passage is in the first pages of the essay on Culture in *Conduct of Life*.

Page 325, note 1. "In his consciousness of deserving success, the caliph Ali constantly neglected the ordinary means of attaining it; and to the grand interests, a superficial success is of no account." — "Aristocracy," *Lectures and Biographical Sketches*.

Page 328, note 1.

> And, — fault of novel germs, —
> Mature the unfallen fruit.
>
> > "Terminus," *Poems*.

Page 329, note 1. The little white star-flower of our May woods, resembling an anemone.

Page 330, note 1. This must have been Dr. John Snelling Popkin, Eliot Professor of Greek Literature at Harvard College, a graduate of 1792.

Page 331, note 1. Virgil, *Æneid*, Book IV. 654.

VII

Page 331, note 2. Another view is taken in the Earth-Song in his poem " Hamatreya."

Page 334, note 1. George Whitefield (1714–1770), the English clergyman of humble origin, but devoted to religion from early youth. He studied at Oxford and formed a friendship with Wesley, and became, after his ordination, a preacher of extraordinary eloquence and power, addressing gatherings of thousands of people in the open air. He visited New England seven times, and preached with great effect, both in the North and the Southern States.

Page 336, note 1. Quisque amat, nulla est conditione senex.

Page 336, note 2. The following extracts show Mr. Emerson's calm philosophy.

Journal, 1864. " Let us not parade our rags; let us not, moved by vanity, tear our hair at the corners of streets, or in the sitting-room, but, as age and infirmity steal on us, contentedly resign the front seat and the games to these bright children, our better representatives; nor expect compliments or inquiries, much less gifts or love, any longer (which to expect is ridiculous), and not at all wondering why our friends do not come to us, much more wondering when they do, decently withdraw ourselves into modest and solitary resignation and rest."

Mr. Emerson's thought concerning old age in 1840 was borne out by his life to the end: —

" Old age . . . I see no need of it. Whilst we converse with what is above us we do not grow old, but grow young. Infancy, youth, receptive, aspiring, with religious eye looking upward, counts itself nothing and abandons itself to the instruction flowing in from all sides. But the man and woman of seventy assume to know all, throw up their hope, renounce aspiration, accept the actual for the necessary, and talk down to the young. . . . Is it possible a man should not grow old? I will not answer for this crazy body. It seems a ship which carries him through the waves of this world and whose timbers contract barnacles and dry-rot, and will not serve for a second course. But I refuse to admit this appeal to the old people we know as valid against a good hope. For do we know one who is an organ of the Holy Ghost?"

The Riverside Press
CAMBRIDGE . MASSACHUSETTS
U . S . A

www.ingramcontent.com/pod-product-compliance
Lightning Source LLC
LaVergne TN
LVHW012207040326
832903LV00003B/170